DELICIOUS
DESSERTS

Other Books by Family Circle

Recipes America Loves Best
Family Circle *Hints Book*
Family Circle *Great Meals on a Tight Budget*

DELICIOUS DESSERTS

More Than 300 Recipes for
Cookies, Cakes, Pies, Puddings, Ice Cream,
and Other Irresistible Sweets

•

THE EDITORS OF

FamilyCircle

NYT
Times
BOOKS

SPECIAL PROJECT STAFF

PROJECT EDITOR • *Lucy Wing*
FAMILY CIRCLE FOOD EDITOR • *Jean Hewitt*
FAMILY CIRCLE ASSOCIATE FOOD EDITOR • *David Ricketts*
FAMILY CIRCLE GREAT IDEAS EDITOR • *Marie Walsh*
TYPE SUPERVISOR • *Wendy Hylfelt*
TYPESETTING • *Vickie Almquist*
SPECIAL ASSISTANT • *Helen Russell*

PROJECT MANAGER • *Annabelle Arenz*

Published by TIMES BOOKS,
The New York Times Book Co., Inc.
130 Fifth Avenue, New York, N.Y. 10011

Published simultaneously in Canada by
Fitzhenry & Whiteside, Ltd., Toronto

Copyright © 1984 by The Family Circle, Inc.

Library of Congress Cataloging in Publication Data
Main entry under title:

Delicious desserts.

Includes index.
1. Desserts.   I. Family Circle.
TX773.D345 1984   641.8'6   84-40097
ISBN 0-8129-6341-5

Designed by Giorgetta Bell McRee/Early Birds

Manufactured in the United States of America

84 85 86 87 88 5 4 3 2 1

This book is dedicated to
all Family Circle *readers*
who trust our recipes to turn out
spectacular great-tasting desserts.

CONTENTS

FOREWORD

Family Circle magazine is published seventeen times a year, and each issue has an average of four food stories. That's a lot of recipes and a lot of planning.

In creating these recipes throughout the year, we try to anticipate your needs and address your grocery-shopping and meal-planning problems. We also think it's important to keep you up-to-date on new food trends and food products appearing on supermarket shelves. We know you are busy people; fifty percent of you work either full- or part-time and fix family dinners at least five times a week. Those family dinners include desserts on at least two or three of those occasions. And almost ninety percent of you serve dessert when you entertain friends.

According to the *Family Circle* research staff, issues that feature luscious desserts on the cover sell particularly well, and dessert stories inside get excellent readership. When we inserted dessert recipe cards into the magazine, you wrote and told us you enjoyed the convenience of easy clipping and filing.

Now, to make your dessert-making even easier, Special Editor Lucy Wing has sifted through our enormous dessert recipe collection and come up with the very best cakes, pies, cookies, puddings, fruit and frozen desserts, and holiday specialties to put into this special cookbook. There's even a separate section for chocolate desserts, because we know there are *many* chocoholics among you. Don't worry if you can't devote hours to making desserts or are lacking in sophisticated baking skills. Just turn to the Quick and Easy section and you'll have dessert ready in no time.

Happy Cooking!

Jean D. Hewitt
Family Circle Food Editor

DELICIOUS DESSERTS

INTRODUCTION:

Sweet Endings

To many people, a meal is incomplete without a sweet ending. Dessert is the part of the meal that everyone looks forward to. This book offers a treasury of over 300 recipes for all kinds of sweet endings to suit any occasion and preferance. Many of the recipes are from recent issues of *Family Circle*; others are classics. All are delicious. Some are simple while others are more elaborate.

There are favorites for family meals. There are desserts that kids will like. There are spectacular ones for special occasions. Each of these recipes has been triple-tested in *Family Circle*'s test kitchens. We have included tips and illustrations to assist you in special techniques or tricks to make a better dessert.

Start with Golden Butter Cake when you need a basic two-layer cake for a coffee break or afternoon tea. There are quick to mix one-bowl cakes, carrot cakes, pound cakes, and fruitcakes. There are luscious fresh fruit pies, cream pies, nut pies, berry tarts, turnovers, strudels, and tortes. Kids will surely love our cookie selection. They include some of their favorites from brownies to fancy cut-out shapes. Chocolate desserts deserve their own chapter of sensuous delights. Puddings are usually family favorites, but here you'll find some decorative steamed or baked puddings, ideal for holiday entertaining.

Ice cream and other frozen desserts will be everyone's favorites. Special-occasion desserts are spectacular for celebrations. For calorie watchers and the health conscious, there are light desserts which are low in calories but high in appeal. Quick and easy desserts get you out of the kitchen fast because they rely on packaged convenience foods, though they look like they have been days in the making. You can decorate cakes and cookies like a baker with our simple directions in our chapter on decorating.

The choice of a dessert is as important as the meal it will follow. We offer you quite a variety. Remember that desserts are an integral part of meal planning and as such should be given some consideration. Think of them not just as something sweet to be tacked on the end of a meal but as a way to round out the day's nutritional needs. Not enough fruit in the day's meals? Then include a fruit dessert. Insufficient milk or eggs for the day? Then plan to serve ice cream, custard, or a milk-rich pudding. The day's diet short on cereal? A cake or rice pudding will help fill in the gaps. Select desserts for a contrast of flavors, colors, and textures so that the meal, from start to finish, is delicately balanced. No matter which dessert you choose, you're bound to find it in these pages.

1

Cakes

Cakes are popular, easy to bake, and endless in their flavor combinations. They are also one of the very first things any cook learns to make. They offer a delicious ending to a family meal; they're great with coffee or tea when friends drop by; and they can be a fabulous company dinner dessert.

The double-layered, frosted butter or shortening cake is almost as American as apple pie. Although most Americans have succumbed to packaged cake mixes on the market, home-baked or "scratch" cakes still offer the best flavor.

Cake baking requires the proper ingredients in the proper proportions in order to transform a wet batter into a light, airy product. Once you understand the basic technique, variations in flavorings and presentations are unlimited. First, a word about the types of cakes. Cakes are classified according to the method of mixing based on the ingredients used. Butter or shortening cakes require creaming to incorporate air into the cake, in addition to baking powder or soda to leaven it. Foam cakes, the other kind, rely primarily on air beaten into eggs or egg whites as the leavening agent.

The butter cakes in this chapter include a basic yellow cake that you can ice with the frosting of your choice. Once you master this cake, you can go onto the unique Coconut Marmalade Cake that has three layers of which the center layer is made of vertical cake slices sandwiched with marmalade. Among the other butter cakes, you'll find several simple, single-layer cakes that are great for coffee or tea treats. Other cakes in this section include moist pound cakes, gingerbread, fruitcakes, tortes, and even cupcakes.

Angel food cakes, chiffon, and sponge cakes are all examples of foam cakes. Mimosa Cake is a golden yellow and white foam cake with a delicate lemony frosting. Angel Food Cake has had a resurgence in popularity recently because it is low in calories and has no cholesterol. Simple yet delicious, Strawberry Shortcake is rarely presented with a properly baked cake. You'll find a recipe for Imperial Strawberry Shortcake, which has tender sponge cake layers for its base.

One chapter of cake recipes is not enough to do justice to this broad category. That's why you'll find more cake recipes included in the Chocolate, Desserts for Special Occasions, and Cake Decorating chapters.

ABOUT THE INGREDIENTS

Our recipes call for sifted all-purpose or cake flour. Even though some flour packages say "presifted," you should still sift flour before you measure it. Use the measuring cups designated for measuring dry ingredients.

The sugar used is granulated unless 10X (confectioners') or brown sugar is specified. When you use brown sugar, pack it lightly into a cup to measure. Do not use granulated brown sugar or liquid brown sugar.

Eggs vary in size and thus in quantity of moisture they can add to a recipe. Large eggs were used in our recipes. In addition, double-acting baking powder was used to leaven our cakes.

GOLDEN BUTTER CAKE

Here's a basic double-layer cake to be filled or frosted with any filling or frosting you choose. The possibilities are limitless!

Bake at 350° for 30 minutes.
Makes one 9-inch cake or about 24 cupcakes.

3 cups *sifted* cake flour	1⅔ cups sugar
2½ teaspoons baking powder	2 eggs
½ teaspoon salt	2 teaspoons vanilla
¾ cup (1½ sticks) butter or margarine, softened	1⅓ cups milk

1. Grease two 9 x 1½-inch layer-cake pans or muffin tins for 24 cupcakes, lined with fluted paper cups if you wish. Dust lightly with flour; tap out excess. Preheat oven to 350°.
2. Sift flour, baking powder, and salt onto wax paper.
3. Beat butter, sugar, eggs, and vanilla in a large bowl with an electric mixer on high speed for 3 minutes.
4. Add flour mixture alternately with milk, beating after each addition until batter is smooth. Pour into prepared pans.
5. Bake in a preheated moderate oven (350°) for 30 minutes or until centers spring back when lightly pressed with fingertip.
6. Cool layers in pans on wire racks for 10 minutes. Loosen around edges with knife; turn out onto wire racks; cool completely.
7. Put layers together with Rich Butter Cream Frosting (page 278), White Mountain Frosting (page 280), or Chocolate Fudge Frosting (page 279).

WAYS TO AVOID CAKE FAILURE

Have you ever baked a cake only to realize it didn't rise one bit? Perhaps you forgot the baking powder. To assure success in cake baking, have all the ingredients measured out and placed on a tray; then remove the ingredients from the tray as you incorporate them into the batter.

FRESH ORANGE CAKE

Bake at 350° for 30 minutes.
Makes 12 servings.

2 cups *sifted* all-purpose flour
1 teaspoon baking powder
1 teaspoon baking soda
1 cup (2 sticks) butter or
  margarine, softened
1 cup sugar
3 eggs, separated
1 container (8 ounces) dairy
  sour cream

1 tablespoon grated orange
  rind
½ cup chopped walnuts
  Orange Butter Cream
  Frosting (page 276)
  Orange slices (optional)
  Walnut halves (optional)

1. Sift flour, baking powder, and baking soda onto wax paper. Grease and flour two 8 x 1½-inch layer-cake pans. Preheat oven to 350°.
2. Beat butter, ¾ cup of the sugar, and the egg yolks in a large bowl with electric mixer until light and fluffy.
3. Beat the egg whites in a small bowl until foamy. Beat in remaining ¼ cup sugar until meringue forms soft peaks.
4. Add flour mixture alternately with sour cream, beginning and ending with flour. Stir in orange rind and nuts. Fold in meringue until no streaks of white remain. Turn batter into prepared pans.
5. Bake in a preheated moderate oven (350°) for 30 minutes or until centers spring back when lightly pressed with fingertip.
6. Cool in pans on wire rack for 10 minutes. Remove from pans; cool completely. Fill and frost with Orange Butter Cream Frosting. Garnish with orange slices and walnut halves, if you wish.

TO GET FLAT-TOPPED ROUND CAKES

When spreading batter in a round cake pan, try to make the batter slightly higher around the edge than in the center so that after baking your cake, the cake layer will be as flat as possible rather than being rounded in the center.

SOUR CREAM CAKE
WITH COCONUT TOPPING

So quick to whip up when you're expecting a neighbor to stop by.

Bake at 350° for 35 minutes.
Makes 8 servings.

1 container (8 ounces) dairy
  sour cream
2 eggs
¾ cup sugar
1½ cups *sifted* all-purpose flour

2 teaspoons baking powder
½ teaspoon almond extract
  Coconut Topping (recipe
  below)

1. Let sour cream and eggs warm to room temperature for easy mixing. Remove 2 tablespoons sour cream to small bowl; reserve for Coconut Topping. Grease and flour an 8x8x2-inch baking pan. Preheat oven to 350°.
2. Combine remaining sour cream, eggs, sugar, flour, baking powder, and almond extract in a large bowl. Beat on medium speed with an electric mixer for 1 minute, scraping down side of bowl with plastic spatula. Pour into prepared pan.
3. Bake in a preheated moderate oven (350°) for 25 minutes or until center springs back when lightly pressed with fingertip.
4. Remove baked cake from oven. Spread Coconut Topping evenly over top. Return to oven. Bake 10 minutes longer. Cool in pan on wire rack.

Coconut Topping: Combine reserved sour cream, 2 tablespoons soft butter, ½ cup firmly packed brown sugar, and ½ cup flaked coconut until well mixed.

SCOOP BATTER FOR EVEN LAYERS

Do you have trouble making cake layers of the same height? Use an ice-cream scoop or measuring cup and fill pans by adding batter a scoop or cupful at a time to one pan then the other, back and forth.

COLONIAL SEED CAKE

Bake at 350° for 1 hour, 15 minutes.
Makes 12 servings.

½ cup (2 ounce jar) poppy seeds
¾ cup milk
¾ cup (1½ sticks) butter, softened
3 eggs

1¼ cups granulated sugar
1 teaspoon vanilla
2 teaspoons baking powder
2 cups *sifted* all-purpose flour
10X (confectioners') sugar

1. Combine poppy seeds and milk in a large bowl. Let stand at room temperature for 3 to 4 hours. Let butter and eggs warm to room temperature for easy mixing. (Butter should be *very* soft.) Grease and flour an 8½ x 4½ x 2½-inch loaf pan. Preheat oven to 350°.

2. Add butter, eggs, sugar, vanilla, baking powder, and flour to poppy seeds and milk. Beat on medium speed with an electric mixer for 1 minute, scraping side of bowl with plastic spatula. Pour into prepared pan.

3. Bake in a preheated moderate oven (350°) for 1 hour and 15 minutes or until center springs back when lightly pressed with fingertip. Cool in pan on wire rack for 5 minutes. Loosen around edges; turn out to cool. Sprinkle with 10X sugar. Serve plain or with Honey Whipped Cream (page 287), if you wish.

PREPARING CAKE PANS

To grease and flour pans, use solid vegetable shortening and a crumpled piece of wax paper or a pastry brush. Sprinkle pan with flour and shake out excess. Do not grease pans used for sponge, angel, or chiffon cakes unless the recipe calls for it.

APRICOT-GLAZED PEACH CAKE

Bake at 350° for 55 minutes.
Makes 8 servings.

2 cups *sifted* all-purpose flour	3 medium-size peaches
1 cup sugar	2 tablespoons sugar
1 tablespoon baking powder	½ teaspoon ground cinnamon
½ teaspoon salt	¼ teaspoon ground nutmeg
½ cup (1 stick) butter or margarine, softened	2 tablespoons butter or margarine, melted
1 egg	1 tablespoon slivered almonds
½ cup milk	¼ cup apricot preserves

1. Sift flour, the cup of sugar, baking powder, and salt into a large bowl; cut in the ½ cup butter until crumbly. Lightly grease a 6-cup baking dish. Dust lightly with flour; tap out excess. Preheat oven to 350°.
2. Beat egg in a small bowl until frothy; stir in milk. Pour milk mixture into flour, stirring until well mixed. Spread batter in prepared dish.
3. Drop peaches into boiling water for 15 seconds; lift out with a slotted spoon; peel and slice. Arrange peach slices on top of batter. Combine the 2 tablespoons sugar, cinnamon, and nutmeg; sprinkle over peaches; drizzle melted butter over all.
4. Bake in a preheated moderate oven (350°) for 55 minutes or until center springs back when lightly pressed with fingertip. Sprinkle almonds over top of cake. Heat apricot preserves until melted; brush over top of cake. Cool in pan on wire rack.

MAKE A GREASE MITT

If you bake a lot, keep a small can of shortening in the refrigerator with a plastic sandwich bag inside. Slip your hand into the bag and use it as a mitt to grease pans. Return bag to can for use the next time.

QUICK BANANA CAKE

Bake at 350° for 45 minutes.
Makes 8 servings.

3 fully ripe bananas
1 cup vegetable oil
2 eggs
1½ cups *sifted* all-purpose flour
1 cup sugar

1 teaspoon baking soda
½ teaspoon salt
Honey Whipped Cream
(page 287)

1. Grease a 9 x 9 x 2-inch baking pan. Preheat oven to 350°.
2. Whirl bananas in the container of an electric blender to make 1 cup puree. Add oil and eggs; whirl until well blended.
3. Sift together flour, sugar, baking soda, and salt into a medium-size bowl. Pour banana mixture all at once into dry ingredients. Mix just until blended.
4. Pour into prepared pan. Bake in a preheated moderate oven (350°) for 45 minutes or until center springs back when lightly pressed with fingertip. Cool on wire rack. Serve with Honey Whipped Cream.

FREEZE BANANA SURPLUS

If you have overripe bananas on hand, peel and mash them with a little lemon juice and freeze for use in cakes or cookies.

THE PROPER TEMPERATURE FOR CAKE INGREDIENTS

For better cake volume, have ingredients at room temperature. However, if your recipe requires separated eggs, separate egg yolks from egg whites while the eggs are cold; then let them warm to room temperature.

CARROT-PINEAPPLE CAKE

Recipes for carrot cakes are popping up all over. Their popularity is well deserved, as they are moist, flavorful, and very good keepers.

Bake at 350° for 1 hour, 15 minutes.
Makes 12 servings.

4 eggs	1 teaspoon ground cinnamon
1½ cups sugar	1 can (8 ounces) crushed
1½ cups vegetable oil	pineapple in pineapple juice,
3¼ cups whole wheat flour	drained
2 teaspoons baking powder	2 cups shredded carrots
2 teaspoons baking soda	1 cup chopped pecans
½ teaspoon salt	1 cup chopped dates

1. Grease a 10 x 4-inch tube pan; line bottom with wax paper. Preheat oven to 350°.

2. Beat eggs in a large mixing bowl. Gradually beat in sugar. Stir in oil.

3. Combine 3 cups of the whole wheat flour with the baking powder, baking soda, salt, and cinnamon. Stir into egg mixture. Add drained pineapple and carrots; mix well.

4. Toss pecans and dates with remaining ¼ cup whole wheat flour; stir into batter. Turn into prepared pan.

5. Bake in a preheated moderate oven (350°) for 1 hour and 15 minutes or until center of cake springs back when lightly pressed with fingertip. Cool cake in pan on wire rack about 15 minutes. Remove cake from pan; peel off wax paper. Cool completely before cutting. Wrap tightly in foil or plastic wrap to store.

A PLACE FOR SKEWERS

To keep small metal cake testers or skewers orderly in your kitchen drawer, stick the pointed tip into a wine bottle cork.

STRAWBERRY-MERINGUE TORTE

Bake at 350° for 30 minutes.
Makes 12 servings.

1⅓ cups *sifted* cake flour	½ cup sliced blanched almonds
1¼ teaspoons baking powder	2 tablespoons sugar
¼ teaspoon salt	3 pints strawberries, washed
½ cup vegetable shortening	and hulled
1¼ cups sugar	¼ cup sugar
4 eggs, separated	1 tablespoon cornstarch
1 teaspoon almond extract	½ cup currant jelly
⅓ cup milk	1 tablespoon water

1. Sift flour, baking powder, and salt onto wax paper. Beat shortening, ½ cup of the sugar, egg yolks, and almond extract in a large mixing bowl until fluffy. Grease and flour two 9 x 1½-inch layer-cake pans. Preheat oven to 350°.

2. Stir in flour mixture alternately with milk; spread batter into prepared pans.

3. Beat egg whites until foamy. Gradually beat in remaining ¾ cup sugar until meringue is stiff; spread over batter. Sprinkle with almonds and 2 tablespoons sugar.

4. Bake in a preheated moderate oven (350°) for 30 minutes. Cool on wire racks.

5. Prepare strawberry filling: Crush 1 pint of the berries; let stand with ¼ cup sugar for 1 hour. Add cornstarch; transfer to a medium-size saucepan. Cook, stirring until thick. Cool.

6. Spread strawberry filling on one layer; top with second layer. Melt jelly with water; cool. Dip remaining strawberries in jelly; arrange on cake. Refrigerate.

GOLDEN HONEY GINGERBREAD

Bake at 350° for 35 minutes.
Makes 12 servings.

2½ cups *sifted* all-purpose flour	½ cup sugar
1½ teaspoons baking soda	¾ cup honey
¼ teaspoon salt	1 egg
¾ teaspoon ground cinnamon	1 cup hot water
½ teaspoon ground nutmeg	Honey Whipped Cream
¼ teaspoon ground allspice	(page 287)
½ cup vegetable shortening	Orange slices (optional)

1. Sift flour, baking soda, salt, cinnamon, nutmeg, and allspice onto wax paper.
2. Preheat oven to 350°. Beat shortening with sugar in a large bowl until fluffy; beat in honey and egg.
3. Stir in flour mixture, half at a time, just until blended; beat in hot water until smooth. Pour into a greased 13 x 9 x 2-inch baking pan.
4. Bake in a preheated moderate oven (350°) for 35 minutes or until center springs back when lightly pressed with fingertip. Cut into rectangles. Top with Honey Whipped Cream and orange slices, if you wish.

ORANGE-GLAZED GINGERBREAD

Bake at 325° for 45 minutes.
Makes 8 servings.

2¼ cups *sifted* all-purpose flour	½ cup sugar
1 teaspoon baking soda	1 egg
½ teaspoon salt	¾ cup molasses
1 teaspoon ground cinnamon	1 cup soured milk*
1 teaspoon ground ginger	⅓ cup orange marmalade
½ cup vegetable shortening	Lemon Sauce (page 292)

1. Grease and flour a 9-inch six-cup ring mold. Preheat oven to 325°.
2. Sift flour, baking soda, salt, cinnamon, and ginger onto wax paper.
3. Beat shortening, sugar, and egg in a medium-sized bowl with an electric mixer until fluffy and light. Beat in molasses and soured milk until blended. Beat in dry ingredients on medium speed just until smooth and blended. Turn batter into prepared pan.
4. Bake in a preheated slow oven (325°) for 45 minutes or until center springs back when lightly pressed with fingertip. Cool in pan on wire rack for 10 minutes. Loosen around edge; unmold onto serving plate.
5. Melt marmalade in a small saucepan over low heat. Brush over gingerbread while still warm. Serve gingerbread in thick slices topped with Lemon Sauce.

*To sour milk: Put 1 tablespoon lemon juice in a 1-cup measure. Add sweet milk to the 1-cup mark and stir; let stand 2 minutes.

COCONUT-MARMALADE CAKE

Bake at 375° for 25 minutes.
Makes 12 servings.

1½ cups *sifted* cake flour
1 teaspoon baking powder
½ teaspoon salt
6 eggs, separated
½ teaspoon cream of tartar
1½ cups granulated sugar
⅓ cup water
1 teaspoon vanilla

10X (confectioners') sugar
1 jar (18 ounces) orange marmalade or peach jam
White Mountain Frosting (page 280)
1 can (3½ or 4 ounces) shredded coconut

1. Grease bottoms of a 15½ x 10½ x 1-inch jelly roll pan and two 8 x 1½-inch layer-cake pans; line with wax paper; grease again. Flour pans lightly, tapping out excess. Preheat oven to 375°.

2. Sift the flour, baking powder, and salt onto wax paper.

3. Beat egg whites and cream of tartar in a large bowl with an electric mixer on high speed until foamy-white and double in volume. Slowly beat in ½ cup of the sugar until meringue stands in soft peaks.

4. Beat egg yolks in a medium-size bowl with mixer on high speed until thick and lemon-colored. Gradually beat in the remaining cup of sugar until mixture is very thick and fluffy. Beat in the water and vanilla on low speed.

5. Fold flour mixture into egg yolk mixture until completely blended.

6. Fold yolk mixture into meringue until no white streaks remain.

7. Measure 4 cups batter into prepared jelly roll pan, spreading evenly into corners; divide remaining batter evenly into layer-cake pans. Place jelly roll pan on lower shelf in oven, cake pans on middle shelf.

8. Bake in a preheated moderate oven (375°) for 15 minutes. Reverse pans in oven and continue baking for 10 minutes or until centers spring back when lightly pressed with fingertip.

9. As soon as cakes are done, loosen around sides of pans with knife; invert oblong cake onto a clean towel dusted with 10X sugar; peel off wax paper. Gently roll up with towel; let cool 10 minutes. Invert cake layers onto racks. Peel off wax paper; cool layers.

10. Unroll oblong cake; spread with 1 cup of the jam. Divide remaining jam between the tops of the round cakes.

11. Place one cake, jam side up, on serving plate. Cut oblong cake lengthwise into 8 strips, each 1¼ inches wide. (Measure with ruler so strips will be even.) Roll up one strip, jelly roll fashion; place in center of cake layer, pressing gently. Wind remaining strips clockwise, one at

a time, around roll, making 1 large pinwheel. Invert second cake layer, jam-side down, on top of the pinwheel; press gently once more.
12. Prepare frosting. Frost sides, then top of cake. Press coconut onto sides and top of cake while frosting is moist. Chill several hours. Cut with sharp knife dipped in hot water.

SPICY OATMEAL CUPCAKES

Bake at 375° for 20 minutes.
Makes 24 to 26 cupcakes.

1½ cups *sifted* cake flour	¼ teaspoon ground cloves
1 cup quick oats	¼ teaspoon ground allspice
¾ cup firmly packed light brown sugar	½ cup vegetable shortening
	1 cup milk
½ cup granulated sugar	2 eggs
1 teaspoon baking soda	Honey-Cream Cheese
½ teaspoon salt	Frosting (page 277)
½ teaspoon ground cinnamon	

1. Combine flour, oats, sugars, baking soda, salt, cinnamon, cloves, and allspice in a large bowl. Add shortening and ¾ cup of the milk. Beat on low speed with an electric mixer for ½ minute to combine ingredients, then at high speed for 2 minutes. Preheat oven to 375°.
2. Add remaining ¼ cup milk and eggs and continue to beat an additional 2 minutes. Fill paper-lined muffin cups half full.
3. Bake in a preheated moderate oven (375°) for 20 minutes or until centers spring back when lightly pressed with fingertip. Remove from pans; cool on wire racks. Frost with Honey Cream Cheese Frosting.

MAKING CUPCAKES

Most butter cake recipes will make between 24 and 36 medium-size cupcakes. To make cupcakes, place pleated paper baking cups in muffin-pan cups. Fill each ⅔ full with batter. Bake in a preheated moderate oven (375°) for 20 minutes or until centers spring back when lightly pressed with fingertip.

GREEK WALNUT CAKES

Bake at 350° for 30 minutes.
Makes about 2 dozen squares.

Honey Syrup (recipe below)
1½ cups *sifted* all-purpose flour
2 teaspoons baking powder
1 teaspoon ground cinnamon
¼ teaspoon salt
1 cup (2 sticks) butter or margarine, softened

1 cup sugar
4 eggs
1 tablespoon grated orange rind
⅓ cup orange juice
2 cups finely chopped walnuts
Walnut halves (optional)

1. Prepare and cool Honey Syrup.
2. Sift flour, baking powder, cinnamon, and salt onto wax paper. Butter a 13 x 9 x 2-inch pan. Preheat oven to 350°.
3. Beat butter with sugar in a large bowl with an electric mixer until well blended. Beat in eggs, 1 at a time, until mixture is light and fluffy. Stir in orange rind.
4. Stir in flour mixture alternately with orange juice, beating after each addition, until batter is smooth. Stir in walnuts. Pour into prepared pan.
5. Bake in a preheated moderate oven (350°) for 30 minutes or until center springs back when lightly pressed with fingertip.
6. Cool cake in pan on wire rack 10 minutes; gradually pour cooled syrup over cake, letting syrup soak into cake before adding more. Or, cool cake completely, then pour *hot* syrup over cake.
7. To serve: Cut cake into small squares (about 2 inches each) or into 2-inch diamond shapes. Put each cake into a fluted paper baking cup. Garnish each square or diamond shape with walnut halves, if you wish.

Honey Syrup: Combine one 2-inch piece orange rind (no white), ½ cup sugar, ½ cup water, and one 1-inch piece stick cinnamon in a small saucepan. Bring to boiling; lower heat; simmer 25 minutes or to 230° on a candy thermometer. Stir in ½ cup honey. Remove rind and cinnamon stick; cool.

CAKE FLOUR ALTERNATIVE

Out of cake flour? Use ⅞ cup (1 cup minus 2 tablespoons) all-purpose flour for each cup of cake flour.

CARROT-PINEAPPLE UPSIDE-DOWN CAKES

These can be baked ahead, frozen, and then thawed at room temperature.

Bake at 350° for 30 minutes.
Makes 10 cakes.

¼ cup (½ stick) butter or margarine, melted
½ cup firmly packed light brown sugar
1 can (20 ounces) pineapple slices in pineapple juice, drained, and juice reserved
20 pecan halves
2 cups finely shredded carrots (about 4 medium-size carrots)

2 cups *sifted* all-purpose flour
1¼ cups granulated sugar
1¼ teaspoons baking soda
1 teaspoon salt
1 teaspoon ground cinnamon
1 teaspoon ground nutmeg
½ teaspoon ground cloves
½ cup vegetable oil
3 eggs
1 teaspoon vanilla

1. Preheat oven to 350°.
2. Pour melted butter into ten 4-inch tart pans, dividing evenly. Sprinkle brown sugar evenly over butter in each pan. Place 1 whole pineapple slice in each pan. Place 2 pecan halves in center of each slice. Set aside.
3. Heat ⅓ cup reserved pineapple juice in small saucepan to boiling. Pour over carrots in a large mixing bowl; let stand 5 minutes. Add flour, sugar, baking soda, salt, cinnamon, nutmeg, and cloves; beat with an electric mixer until well blended.
4. Add oil, eggs, and vanilla; beat 2 minutes longer. Pour batter evenly over pineapple slice in each pan.
5. Bake in a preheated moderate oven (350°) for 30 minutes or until center springs back when lightly pressed with fingertip.
6. Invert pans onto wire rack; leave pans in place 2 minutes. Carefully lift off pans; cool cakes completely. Serve. To freeze, wrap each tightly in aluminum foil; freeze. When ready to serve, unwrap cakes; thaw at room temperature 30 to 45 minutes.

TESTING FOR DONENESS

The easiest way to tell if a cake is done is to touch it lightly in the center. If it springs back, it's done. Another test is to insert a wooden pick in the center of the cake. If batter or crumbs cling to the pick, bake the cake for an additional 5 minutes; then test it again.

SHERRIED POUND CAKE

Bake at 350° for 1 hour, 20 minutes.
Makes 12 servings.

3½ cups *sifted* all-purpose flour	5 eggs
1½ teaspoons baking powder	2 teaspoons vanilla
½ teaspoon ground nutmeg	½ cup milk
1½ cups (3 sticks) butter, softened	½ cup cream sherry
	Vanilla Sugar Glaze
3 cups firmly packed light brown sugar	(page 287)
	Sliced almonds (optional)

1. Grease and flour a heavy 12-cup Bundt® pan.
2. Sift flour, baking powder, and nutmeg onto wax paper. Preheat oven to 350°.
3. Beat butter in a large bowl with an electric mixer until creamy. Beat in sugar gradually until well mixed. Add eggs, 1 at a time, beating well after each addition. Beat in vanilla.
4. Combine milk and sherry in a 1-cup measure. Stir dry ingredients alternately with milk and sherry into butter mixture just until smooth. Pour into prepared pan.
5. Bake in a preheated moderate oven (350°) for 1 hour and 20 minutes or until center springs back when lightly pressed with fingertip. Cool in pan on wire rack 10 minutes. Loosen around edge with spatula; turn out onto wire rack; cool completely. Wrap in foil and keep at room temperature overnight. Store in refrigerator.
6. Just before serving, drizzle with Vanilla Sugar Glaze. Garnish with sliced almonds, if you wish.

LEMON POUND CAKE

Lemony and refreshing.

Bake at 350° for 1 hour, 5 minutes.
Makes 12 servings.

2⅓ cups *sifted* cake flour	3 eggs
1 teaspoon baking powder	¾ cup milk
½ teaspoon salt	1 teaspoon grated lemon rind
⅔ cup vegetable shortening	1 tablespoon lemon juice
1⅓ cups granulated sugar	10X (confectioners') sugar

1. Grease and flour a 9 x 5 x 3-inch loaf pan.
2. Sift flour, baking powder, and salt onto wax paper. Preheat oven to 350°.
3. Beat shortening, sugar, and eggs in a large bowl with an electric mixer on high speed for 3 minutes or until light and fluffy.
4. Add flour mixture alternately with milk on low speed. Stir in lemon rind and juice. Turn into prepared pan.
5. Bake in a preheated moderate oven (350°) for 1 hour and 5 minutes or until center springs back when lightly pressed with fingertip.
6. Cool in pan on wire rack 10 minutes. Loosen edge with spatula; turn out onto a wire rack; cool completely. Dust lightly with 10X sugar.

GINGER POUND CAKE

Bake at 350° for 1 hour.
Makes 12 servings.

3	cups *sifted* all-purpose flour	8	eggs, separated
1	teaspoon baking powder	1	tablespoon grated orange
½	teaspoon salt		rind
2	cups (4 sticks) butter, softened	1	tablepoon vanilla
		¼	cup shredded preserved or
1¾	cups sugar		crystallized ginger

1. Grease and flour a 10-inch tube pan.
2. Sift flour, baking powder, and salt onto wax paper, Preheat oven to 350°.
3. Beat butter in a large bowl with an electric mixer until creamy. Beat in ¾ cup of the sugar. Add egg yolks, 1 at a time, beating well after each addition. Stir in orange rind, vanilla, and flour mixture until smooth and well blended.
4. Beat egg whites in a large bowl with an electric mixer until foamy. Slowly beat in remaining 1 cup sugar until meringue holds soft peaks. Fold into batter until no white streaks remain.
5. Spoon half the batter into prepared pan. Sprinkle 2 tablespoons of the ginger over batter; spoon in remaining batter; top with remaining ginger.
6. Bake in a preheated moderate oven (350°) for 1 hour or until center springs back when lightly pressed with fingertip. Let cool in pan on wire rack 10 minutes. Loosen around edges with spatula; lift out onto wire rack; cool completely. Wrap in foil and keep at room temperature overnight. Store in refrigerator.

APPLE POUND CAKE

Bake at 350° for 1 hour, 15 minutes.
Makes 9 servings.

4	medium-size tart apples	1	cup sugar
2	tablespoons sugar	3	eggs
1	teaspoon ground cinnamon	1	teaspoon vanilla
2	cups *sifted* all-purpose flour	½	cup dairy sour cream
1½	teaspoons baking powder	¼	cup currant jelly, melted
¼	teaspoon salt	2	tablespoons toasted slivered
¾	cup (1½ sticks) butter or		almonds
	margarine, softened		

1. Pare, quarter, and core apples; slice thinly into a large bowl; toss with the 2 tablespoons sugar and the cinnamon.
2. Preheat oven to 350°. Grease a 9 x 9 x 2-inch baking pan. Sift flour, baking powder, and salt onto wax paper.
3. Beat butter, sugar, eggs, and vanilla in a large bowl with an electric mixer on high speed for 3 minutes or until very light and fluffy.
4. Stir in dry ingredients alternately with sour cream. Beat until batter is smooth. Turn into prepared pan. Arrange apple slices on top.
5. Bake in a preheated moderate oven (350°) for 1 hour and 15 minutes or until center springs back when lightly pressed with fingertip. Cool in pan on wire rack. Brush with melted jelly; sprinkle with nuts.

PROPER FRUITCAKE STORAGE

Fruitcakes must be stored properly so that they will mellow in flavor and stay moist. For best results, wrap them in brandy- or orange-juice-soaked cheesecloth, then in foil, and place in a cool, dark place.

KEEPING DRIED FRUIT SUSPENDED

When making cakes with dried fruit or nuts, toss them in about ¼ cup of the flour from the recipe, depending on the quantity of fruit or nuts used, to coat them so that they won't sink to the bottom of the batter.

GOLDEN LIGHT FRUITCAKE

*Bake at 300°: 1½ hours for a small cake, 2 hours for a loaf cake,
or 30 minutes for miniature cakes.
Makes 2 small fruitcakes or 1 loaf fruitcake,
or 8 dozen miniature fruitcakes.*

1 container (8 ounces) candied red cherries, chopped	1 cup (2 sticks) butter or margarine, softened
1 package (15 ounces) golden raisins	1 cup sugar
	5 eggs
1 can (3½ ounces) sliced almonds	1 teaspoon vanilla
	½ cup apricot preserves
½ cup light rum	2 tablespoons light rum or orange juice
2 cups *sifted* all-purpose flour	
½ teaspoon salt	

1. Combine cherries, raisins, nuts, and the ½ cup rum in a large bowl. Allow to stand 1 hour.
2. Grease two 4-cup molds or one 9 x 5 x 3-inch loaf pan. Dust lightly with flour; tap out excess. For miniature cakes you will need 8 dozen small paper baking cups (petits fours or baking cases—1 tablespoon capacity) set in miniature muffin tins.
3. Preheat oven to 300°. Sift flour and salt onto wax paper. Sprinkle ¼ cup of flour over fruits and nuts; toss to coat well.
4. Beat butter, sugar, eggs, and vanilla in a large bowl of an electric mixer on high speed for 3 minutes or until fluffy.
5. Stir in remaining flour mixture until batter is smooth. Pour over prepared fruit and nuts and fold just until well blended. Spoon batter into prepared pans. For miniatures, drop batter by heaping tablespoonfuls into paper baking cups.
6. Bake in a preheated slow oven (300°). Bake large loaf for 2 hours, small cakes for 1½ hours or until centers spring back when lightly pressed with fingertip. Cool in pans on wire racks 15 minutes. Loosen around edges of pans with a knife; turn out. Cool completely. Bake miniatures for 30 minutes. Remove from tins; cool on wire racks.
7. To glaze: Heat apricot preserves with 2 tablespoons light rum or orange juice until bubbly in a small saucepan. Press through a sieve. Brush hot mixture on fruitcakes.

Note: Cakes may be kept at room temperature for 1 week, in the refrigerator for 1 month, and in the freezer for 3 months.

WHISKEY CAKE

Bake at 325° for 1 hour.
Makes 12 servings.

3 eggs, separated
¾ cup granulated sugar
½ cup (1 stick) butter
¼ cup firmly packed dark
  brown sugar
1½ cups *sifted* unbleached
  all-purpose flour

1 can (8 ounces) pecans,
  chopped (2 cups)
1 cup raisins
1 teaspoon baking powder
2 teaspoons ground nutmeg
  Dash salt
½ cup bourbon
  Pecan halves for decoration

1. Grease and flour a 10 x 4-inch tube pan.

2. Beat egg whites in a small bowl with an electric mixer until foamy-white. Slowly beat in ¼ cup of the granulated sugar until meringue forms stiff peaks; reserve.

3. Beat butter, brown sugar, remaining granulated sugar, and egg yolks in a large bowl with an electric mixer until light and fluffy.

4. Mix ¼ cup of the flour with pecans and raisins in a small bowl, stirring until nuts and fruit are coated. Preheat oven to 325°.

5. Sift remaining 1¼ cups flour with baking powder, nutmeg, and salt onto wax paper. Beat into batter alternately with bourbon until well blended. Stir in pecans and raisins. Fold in reserved meringue until no streaks of white remain.

6. Spoon batter into prepared pan, pressing down with spoon to settle batter. Decorate top with pecan halves.

7. Bake in a preheated slow oven (325°) for 1 hour or until center springs back when lightly pressed with fingertip. Cool in pan on wire rack for 1 hour. Remove from pan; cool completely. Wrap cake with cheesecloth soaked with bourbon. Store in tightly covered container several days.

EMERGENCY BROWN SUGAR

Out of brown sugar? Try making some by mixing ½ cup granulated sugar with 2 tablespoons molasses. The yield is about ½ cup.

RECYCLE COFFEE CANS

Save your empty 1-pound coffee cans. They make good small-size baking pans for gift fruitcakes or for storing cookies.

MACADAMIA NUT FRUITCAKE

Bake at 300° for 2 hours.
Makes 2 medium-size loaves (about 16 servings).

1	cup golden raisins	1	can (5 ounces) macadamia
1	container (4 ounces) candied		nuts, chopped
	red cherries, quartered	1	cup *sifted* all-purpose flour
1	container (4 ounces) candied	1½	teaspoons baking powder
	green cherries, quartered	½	teaspoon ground mace
2	containers (4 ounces each)	4	eggs
	candied citron	1	cup sugar
2	containers (4 ounces each)	¼	cup light corn syrup
	candied pineapple, chopped		Candied red and green
1	package (6 ounces) dried		cherries, halved (for garnish)
	apricots, chopped		Macadamia nuts (optional)

1. Combine fruit and nuts in bowl.
2. Sift flour, baking powder, and mace over fruit mixture. Toss. Grease two 7⅜ x 3⅜ x 2¼-inch loaf pans. Preheat oven to 300°.
3. Beat eggs and sugar together in a small bowl with an electric mixer. Pour over fruit, stirring to coat well.
4. Pour into prepared pans.
5. Bake in a preheated slow oven (300°) for 2 hours or until centers spring back when lightly pressed with fingertip.
6. Cool cakes in pans on wire racks 10 minutes; loosen around edges with a spatula. Turn out onto wire racks; cool completely.
7. To decorate: Heat corn syrup in small saucepan until bubbly; brush over cakes. Garnish cakes with halved candied cherries and nuts, if desired.
8. To store: This cake keeps well. Wrap in foil; refrigerate for up to 3 weeks.

TO MOISTEN DRIED-OUT FRUIT

If your raisins, dried apricots, or prunes have hardened, steam them over water to plump them quickly.

CLEAN CUT STICKY FRUIT

To snip or cut sticky dried fruit, such as prunes, dates, or apricots, spray the blade of your scissors or knife with nonstick vegetable cooking spray before cutting.

BAKING AT HIGH ALTITUDES

Most cake recipes are developed for altitudes from sea level up to 3,000 feet. Above that, it is often necessary to adjust the proportions of certain ingredients, usually a decrease in leavening or sugar or both and an increase in the amount of liquid. Make the following adjustments for high altitudes:

Altitude	3,000-4,000'	4,000-6,000'	6,000-7,500'
Reduce Baking Powder For each teaspoon, decrease	⅛ tsp.	⅛ to ¼ tsp.	¼ tsp.
Reduce Sugar For each cup, decrease	1 tb.	1-2 tbs.	3-4 tbs.
Increase Liquid For each cup, add	1-2 tbs.	2-4 tbs.	3-4 tbs.
Increase Baking Temperature	25°	25°	25°

• For particularly rich butter or shortening cakes, try reducing the shortening by 1 or 2 tablespoons.
• If you live at an extremely high altitude, you may wish to increase the amount of egg in angel food, chiffon, or sponge cakes.
• Only by experimenting will you find the right modifications for your needs. Try the smaller adjustments on any recipe the first time you make it; then, next time, if necessary, make a larger adjustment.

SUBSTITUTING PANS

If your recipe calls for three 8 x 1½-inch round pans, you may also use two 9 x 9 x 2-inch square pans. If your recipe calls for two 9 x 1½-inch round pans, you may also use two 8 x 8 x 2-inch square pans, or one 13 x 9 x 2-inch oblong pan. If your recipe calls for one 9 x 5 x 3-inch loaf pan, you may also use one 9 x 9 x 2-inch square pan.

COCONUT CREAM CAKE

Bake at 350° for 30 minutes.
Makes 12 servings.

1	package (18¾ ounces) yellow cake with pudding mix	1½	cups heavy cream
3	eggs	3	tablespoons 10X (confectioners') sugar
1	cup water		Coconut Cream Filling
⅓	cup vegetable oil		(page 282)
2	tablespoons grated orange rind		Flaked coconut

1. Grease and flour two 9 x 1½-inch layer-cake pans. Preheat oven to 350°. Prepare cake mix according to package directions with eggs, water, and oil, adding orange rind. Divide batter into prepared pans.
2. Bake in a preheated moderate oven (350°) for 30 minutes or until centers spring back when lightly pressed with fingertip.
3. Cool in pans on wire racks 10 minutes; turn out onto racks and cool completely. Split each layer in half to make 4 thin layers.
4. Beat cream with 10X sugar in a small bowl until stiff. Prepare Coconut Cream Filling.
5. Put layers together with Coconut Cream Filling. Frost side and top with whipped cream. Sprinkle generously with flaked coconut.

WHIPPING CREAM

Ultra-pasturized heavy cream or whipping cream is terrific for long-term storage, but it can be difficult to whip. The best way to whip this cream is to chill the bowl and beaters. Use an electric mixer on medium speed. When the cream starts to hold its shape, finish the whipping on low speed or whip by hand using a wire whisk. Properly whipped cream should hold its shape when a spatula is drawn through it and it forms soft peaks.

FOLLOW RECIPES EXACTLY

When making a cake, *never* use vegetable oil or melted shortening unless the recipe specifically calls for it; otherwise, your cake will turn out heavy and tough, and may sink in the middle.

WALNUT-SPICE CAKE

Bake at 350° for 25 minutes.
Makes 12 servings.

1	package (18¾ ounces) yellow cake with pudding mix	⅓	cup vegetable oil Cinnamon-Whipped Cream Filling (page 282)
1	cup finely chopped walnuts		Orange-Butter Glaze
¾	teaspoon ground cloves		(page 286)
3	eggs		
1	cup water	¾	cup coarsely chopped walnuts

1. Combine cake mix, finely chopped nuts, cloves, eggs, water, and oil in a large bowl. Grease and flour two 9 x 1½-inch layer-cake pans. Preheat oven to 350°.

2. Beat on low speed with an electric mixer to blend; increase speed to high; beat 2 minutes. Pour into prepared layer-cake pans, dividing evenly.

3. Bake in a preheated moderate oven (350°) for 25 minutes or until centers spring back when lightly touched with fingertip. Cool in pans on wire racks 10 minutes; loosen around edges with a small spatula. Turn out onto wire racks; cool completely. Chill layers several hours or overnight. Split each layer in two.

4. Put layers together with ½ to ¾ cup Cinnamon-Whipped Cream Filling for each layer; spread Orange-Butter Glaze over top. Frost sides with remaining Cinnamon Whipped Cream Filling, reserving about ½ cup to pipe on top, if you wish. Press coarsely chopped nuts on side of cake. Chill until serving time.

ANGEL FOOD CAKE

A real American favorite.

Bake at 375° for 35 minutes.
Makes 12 servings.

1	cup *sifted* cake flour	1½	teaspoons cream of tartar
1½	cups granulated sugar Or:	¼	teaspoon salt
	1¼ cups *sifted* 10X (confectioners') sugar	1	teaspoon vanilla
1½	cups egg whites (12 to 14 eggs), at room temperature	½	teaspoon almond extract

1. Combine sifted flour with ¾ cup of the granulated sugar; sift three more times. Set aside.

2. Beat egg whites in a large bowl until foamy. Add cream of tartar and salt; beat until soft peaks form. Gradually beat in remaining granulated sugar, 2 tablespoons at a time, until stiff peaks form. Add vanilla and almond extract.

3. Preheat oven to 375°. Place oven rack in lower third of oven.

4. Sift ¼ cup of the flour mixture at a time over the meringue; gently fold in after each addition. Turn into an ungreased 10 x 4-inch tube pan. Gently cut through batter with knife to prevent air pockets from forming.

5. Bake in lower third of a preheated moderate oven (375°) for 30 to 35 minutes or until center springs back when lightly pressed with fingertip. Remove cake from oven; immediately invert pan, placing tube on a bottle. Let cake cool in pan about 2 hours.

6. To remove cake from pan, run sharp thin knife around sides of pan; remove outside rim. Run knife under cake and around inside rim to separate from bottom of pan.

COOLING FOAM CAKES

Cool foam cakes upside down, over a funnel or bottle, to keep the cake high and light, until the walls are cool and strong enough to support the weight of the cake once it is turned right side up.

FOR MOST EGG VOLUME

With all foam cakes, it's particularly important to have eggs at room temperature. That way, you'll get the maximum volume when you beat them.

FILLED ORANGE CHIFFON CAKE

Bake at 325° for 55 minutes, then at 350° for 10 minutes.
Makes 16 servings.

2¼	cups *sifted* cake flour	7	egg whites
1½	cups sugar	½	teaspoon cream of tartar
1	tablespoon baking powder		Orange Butter Cream
1	teaspoon salt		Frosting (page 276)
½	cup vegetable oil		Orange Date Filling
5	egg yolks		(page 284)
¾	cup cold water		Orange slices (optional)
3	tablespoons grated orange		Grated orange rind
	rind		(optional)

1. Preheat oven to 325°.

2. Sift cake flour, sugar, baking powder, and salt into a large bowl. Make a well in the center; add oil, egg yolks, cold water, and orange rind. Stir until smooth and well blended.

3. Beat egg whites and cream of tartar in a large bowl with an electric mixer until soft peaks form. Fold egg yolk mixture into beaten whites until well blended and no streaks of white remain.

4. Pour batter into an ungreased 10 x 4-inch tube pan with a removable bottom.

5. Bake in a preheated slow oven (325°) for 55 minutes; increase oven temperature to moderate (350°). Bake for 10 minutes longer or until center springs back when lightly pressed with fingertip. Invert onto a funnel or tall bottle. Leave until cool. Remove from pan.

6. Prepare Orange Butter Cream Frosting and Orange Date Filling while cake cools.

7. Cut cooled cake into 3 equal crosswise layers, using a serrated knife. Add ½ cup of frosting to date filling, blending well. Spread on cake layers. Assemble cake. Frost with remaining Orange Butter Cream Frosting. Decorate with fresh orange slices and grated orange rind, if you wish.

MIMOSA CAKE

The traditional tube cake with an old-fashioned butter cream frosting. Decorate with butter cream mimosa, or fresh mimosa, if available.

Bake at 375° for 35 minutes.
Makes 12 servings.

1¼ cups *sifted* cake flour	4 egg yolks
1½ cups sugar	1 teaspoon grated lemon rind
10 egg whites	1 teaspoon vanilla
1½ teaspoons cream of tartar	Lemon Butter Cream Frosting
¼ teaspoon salt	(page 276)

1. Preheat oven to 375°.
2. Sift flour and ½ cup of the sugar onto wax paper; set aside.
3. Beat egg whites, cream of tartar, and salt in a large bowl with an electric mixer on high speed until foamy. Beat in remaining 1 cup sugar, 1 tablespoon at a time, until meringue forms soft peaks.
4. Fold flour mixture into meringue, ⅓ at a time, until completely blended.
5. Beat egg yolks in a small bowl with electric mixer on high speed until thick and lemon-colored. Beat in lemon rind and vanilla.
6. Fold half of the meringue batter into the beaten egg yolks until no streaks of white remain.
7. Alternately spoon batters by tablespoonfuls into an ungreased 10 x 4-inch tube pan. (Do not stir batters in pan.)
8. Bake in a preheated moderate oven (375°) for 35 minutes, or until center springs back when lightly pressed with fingertip.
9. Invert pan, placing tube over a funnel or tall bottle; let cake cool completely. Loosen cake around the edge and the tube with a spatula. Cover pan with serving plate; turn upside down. Shake gently; remove pan.
10. Prepare Lemon Butter Cream Frosting, reserving ⅓ cup. Tint ½ the reserved butter cream yellow for mimosa flowers and other ½ green for stems and leaves.
11. Frost top and side of cake with frosting. Decorate as desired with reserved tinted butter cream.

HOW TO COOL CAKES

Always leave cakes in pans on wire racks for at least 10 minutes to cool. Then loosen sides with a knife or spatula, invert each cake on wire rack or plate, and *immediately* turn cake right side up on wire rack to complete cooling.

WHERE TO PUT CAKE PANS IN THE OVEN

• When baking an oblong, or one-layer cake, place pan on center of rack, in center of oven.
• When baking two layers, use two racks in center third of oven, layers in opposite corners.
• When baking three or four layers, use two racks in center third of oven. Stagger pans in opposite corners of both racks so they do not block heat circulation.
• For a tube cake, place pan on center rack, in lower third of oven.

IMPERIAL STRAWBERRY SHORTCAKE

The All-American dessert favorite is certainly strawberry shortcake.
This mouth-watering version is made with soft spongecake and
whipped cream.

Bake at 350° for 25 minutes.
Makes 8 servings.

1	cup *sifted* all-purpose flour	1	teaspoon vanilla
1	teaspoon baking powder	2	pints fresh strawberries Or:
¼	teaspoon salt		1 package (1 pound) frozen
⅓	cup milk		unsweetened strawberries,
2	tablespoons butter or		thawed
	margarine	½	to ¾ cup sugar
3	eggs	1	cup heavy cream
1	cup sugar		

1. Sift flour, baking powder, and salt onto wax paper. Grease and flour two 8 x 1½-inch layer-cake pans or one 8-inch springform pan. Preheat oven to 350°.

2. Heat milk with butter just to scalding; cool slightly.

3. Beat eggs until foamy in a small bowl with an electric mixer. Add the 1 cup sugar gradually until mixture is very thick and fluffy. Add vanilla.

4. Sprinkle flour mixture ⅓ at a time over eggs, alternating with warmed milk and beginning and ending with flour mixture. Pour into prepared pans.

5. Bake in a preheated moderate oven (350°) for 25 minutes (35 minutes for springform pan) or until centers spring back when lightly pressed with fingertip. Cool layers on wire rack 10 minutes. Loosen around edges with knife; turn out. Cool completely.

6. Wash and hull strawberries; reserve 1 cup whole berries for garnish. Slice remaining strawberries into a large bowl. (For frozen berries, sprinkle with sugar and let stand while defrosting.) Add sugar; stir lightly, crushing a few of the berries. Let stand 30 minutes or until juices run freely.

7. Whip cream in a small bowl until soft peaks form.

8. Place one cake layer on serving plate (split cake in half if using a springform pan). Top with half of the cream and strawberries. Top with remaining cake layer and cream. Place 1 whole strawberry in center of cake; cut remaining reserved strawberries in half. Arrange halved strawberries cut side up in rosette pattern over the cream.

LEMONY SPONGE CAKE

Bake at 350° for 25 minutes.
Makes 12 servings.

¾ cup *sifted* cake flour
½ teaspoon baking powder
¼ teaspoon salt
4 eggs, separated
¾ cup granulated sugar

2 tablespoons lemon juice
2 tablespoons water
1 teaspoon vanilla
   10X (confectioners') sugar

1. Sift flour, baking powder, and salt onto wax paper. Preheat oven to 350°.

2. Beat egg whites in a large bowl with an electric mixer on high speed until foamy-white and double in volume. Gradually beat in half of the sugar until meringue stands in firm peaks when beaters are slowly raised.

3. With same beaters, beat egg yolks with remaining sugar in a small bowl for 5 minutes or until light and fluffy; beat in lemon juice, water, and vanilla.

4. Add flour mixture on low speed until completely blended. Fold into meringue until no streaks of white remain. Pour into an ungreased 9- or 10-inch springform pan; smooth top.

5. Bake in a preheated moderate oven (350°) for 25 minutes or until center springs back when lightly pressed with fingertip. Invert pan over a wire rack to cool completely, upside down. If cake top is higher than top rim of pan, balance inverted edge of pan on custard cups so it hangs free. Loosen around edge with small spatula; release and remove side; loosen and remove from bottom. Sprinkle top with 10X sugar or serve cake with Brandied Fruit Sauce (page 293) or Strawberry Sauce (page 290), if you wish.

STALE CAKE MAKEOVER

Don't throw out stale sponge cake. You can make a super dessert with it. Soak pieces in rum, them mix into a thick vanilla pudding. Cover with whipped cream or decorate with slivered almonds, or garnish with canned fruit and syrup.

BLUEBERRRY/STRAWBERRY-TOPPED SPONGE FLAN

Bake at 350° for 25 minutes.
Makes 12 servings.

1	cup *sifted* all-purpose flour	1	teaspoon vanilla
1	teaspoon baking powder	½	cup strawberry jelly
¼	teaspoon salt	1	tablespoon water
⅓	cup milk		Pastry Cream (page 288)
2	tablespoons butter	1	pint fresh blueberries
3	eggs	7	to 8 large strawberries,
1	cup sugar		hulled

1. Sift flour, baking powder, and salt onto wax paper. Grease and flour one 10-inch sponge flan pan. Preheat oven to 350°.
2. Heat milk with butter just to scalding; cool slightly.
3. Beat eggs with sugar and vanilla until thick and creamy in a medium-size bowl with an electric mixer. Add flour mixture alternately with milk mixture, beating after each addition. Pour into prepared pan. Bake in preheated moderate oven (350°) for 25 minutes or until center springs back when lightly pressed with fingertip.
4. Cool layer in pan on wire rack 10 minutes. Loosen around edges with a knife; turn out onto wire rack. Cool completely.
5. Heat strawberry jelly and water in a small saucepan until melted and bubbly. Brush over interior of shell and sides of cake; allow to set for 5 minutes.
6. To assemble: Fill center of sponge flan with pastry cream. Arrange 7 or 8 strawberries in center, stem ends down; arrange blueberries around top. Glaze berries with additional melted strawberry jelly, if you wish.

BAKING POWDER FRESHNESS CHECK

You remembered to add the baking powder but your cake still didn't rise? Perhaps the baking powder has lost its pizzazz. To see if the baking powder is still active, add a teaspoon of baking powder to ⅓ cup warm water. If it fizzes, it's still active. If not, throw it out and buy a fresh can.

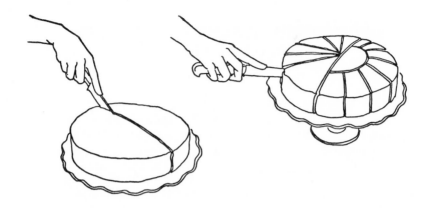

CUTTING CAKES

The best way to cut a layer or loaf cake is to use a long, thin sharp knife with a sawing motion. For angel, chiffon, or sponge cakes, use a cake breaker or serrated knife with a sawing motion. Chill fruitcakes for easier slicing.

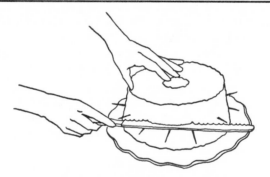

SPLITTING LAYERS

To split any cake (butter or foam) into layers, measure vertically with a ruler; mark cake all around with wooden picks. Slice across tops of picks, using a long, serrated knife, cutting with a sawing motion. Make a shallow vertical cut into side of cake before separating the layers so that you reassemble the cake layers in their original position when you begin to fill or frost the cake. Just align the marks when putting the layers together again.

APRICOT CAKE ROLL

Bake at 375° for 12 to 15 minutes.
Makes 8 servings.

1 cup *sifted* cake flour	⅓ cup water
1 teaspoon baking powder	1 teaspoon vanilla
¼ teaspoon salt	10X (confectioners') sugar
3 eggs	¾ cup apricot preserves
¾ cup granulated sugar	

1. Grease a 15½ x 10½ x 1-inch jelly roll pan. Line bottom with wax paper; grease paper.
2. Sift flour, baking powder, and salt onto wax paper. Preheat oven to 375°.
3. Beat eggs in a medium-size bowl with an electric mixer until thick and creamy. Gradually add sugar, beating constantly until mixture is very thick. (This will take at least 5 minutes.) Blend in water and vanilla on low speed. Add flour mixture, beating on low speed, just until batter is smooth. Pour into prepared pan, spreading evenly into corners.
4. Bake in a preheated moderate oven (375°) for 12 to 15 minutes or until center of cake springs back when lightly pressed with fingertip.
5. Loosen cake around edges with a small knife; invert onto a clean towel dusted with 10X sugar; peel off wax paper. Starting at short end, roll up cake and towel together. Cool on wire rack. When cool, unroll carefully; spread evenly with preserves. Reroll cake. Place seam side down on platter or small cookie sheet until ready to slice and serve.

A BETTER CAKE ROLL

With "jelly" roll cakes, try using the nonstick vegetable cooking sprays on the pan and wax paper instead of shortening.

A DUSTING OF SUGAR

To sprinkle 10X (confectioners') sugar evenly on top of a cake, place sugar in a small strainer or shaker and shake over the cake top.

MOCHA VELVET CAKE

So impressive looking, yet amazingly easy to make.

Makes 12 servings.

1	baker's 8- or 9 x 3-inch angel food cake, about 1 pound	¼	cup water
		¼	cup sugar
8	squares semisweet chocolate	1	cup heavy cream, whipped
3	tablespoons butter or margarine	½	cup apricot preserves
		1	tablespoon dark rum or orange juice
3	eggs, separated		
1	tablespoon instant coffee		Whipped cream (optional)

1. With a sharp knife, cut down into cake about ½-inch from outer edge, cutting not quite through to bottom. With the help of a spoon or small knife, remove cake part in center, leaving a shell about ½ inch thick; fill hole in bottom with a round slice cut from removed cake. (Freeze remaining crumbled cake to use with packaged pudding for a quick dessert for another meal.)
2. Melt chocolate and butter in top of double boiler over hot, not boiling, water; stir to blend. Remove from water.
3. Beat egg yolks into chocolate, 1 at a time, beating well after each addition. Dissolve coffee in ¼ cup water and add to chocolate mixture. Set aside to cool.
4. Beat egg whites until foamy-white and double in volume. Add sugar, 1 tablespoon at a time, beating until meringue stands in firm peaks.
5. Fold meringue into cooled chocolate mixture until no streaks of white remain; fold in whipped cream. Spoon into prepared cake shell. Chill at least 6 hours or overnight.
6. Heat apricot preserves in small saucepan until bubbly; press through a strainer; stir in rum or orange juice. Brush over side of cake. Pipe small rosettes of whipped cream around top edge and base of cake, if you wish. Cut into wedges to serve.

ITALIAN RUM CAKE

Makes 12 servings.

1	baker's 8- or 9 x 3-inch sponge cake	½	cup pineapple juice
2	cups ricotta cheese	½	cup light or dark rum
1	package (3 ounces) cream cheese	½	cup (1 stick) butter
3	tablespoons granulated sugar	2	teaspoons instant espresso coffee
8	squares semisweet chocolate	½	cup hot water
½	cup mixed candied fruits, chopped	3	cups 10X (confectioners') sugar

1. Split cake into 4 thin layers. Beat ricotta, cream cheese, and sugar until smooth. Finely chop 2 squares chocolate; stir into cheese along with the candied fruits. Combine pineapple juice and rum in a cup.
2. Drizzle each of 3 layers with ¼ cup of the rum syrup. Spread each with ⅓ of the cheese filling. Assemble cake with plain layer on top. Brush top and side with remaining rum syrup.
3. Melt remaining 6 squares chocolate with butter in a medium-size bowl over hot, not boiling, water; remove from heat. Dissolve coffee in hot water; add to chocolate. Stir in 10X sugar until smooth. Chill until thick enough to spread. Frost top and side of cake. Decorate with candied fruits and nuts, if you wish.

2

Pies and Pastries

What can be more American than pie? Throughout the year, pies are dished out and served more than any other dessert—from cherry pies around Washington's birthday to pumpkin and mince pies for the holidays. Light chiffon pies, berry pies, and tarts are typically summer pies. Pies may be made with a conventional pastry, a crumb, or cookie crust. A vast assortment are included here—double-crusted fruit pies, open-faced tarts, tartlets, custard and cream pies.

Cream puff pastry (or *pâte à choux*), is a basic dough you can use to make not only cream puffs and eclairs but also fancy shapes and deep-fried fritters or doughnuts. Eggs stirred into a cooked flour mixture give cream puff pastry the power to expand or puff. For the best results, use unbleached or bread flour. A hard-wheat flour will give the dough greater elasticity or higher puffs. Regular all-purpose flour may be used, but the puffs will not be quite so high.

Puff pastry is a multilayered French pastry used for Napoleons, cookies, and turnovers. The beginner can learn to make the basic version or use packaged puff pastry dough to make crisp, golden desserts.

Paper-thin phyllo (pronounced fee-low) is traditionally used for Greek or Middle Eastern pastries such as baklava. Phyllo leaves are available frozen in supermarket freezer cases or fresh from specialty food stores. Strudel pastry, a Hungarian specialty, is a dough that is stretched and pulled into a large sheet until it is paper-thin. It is then filled with apples, dried fruits, nuts, or cream cheese, and rolled and baked. Though phyllo and strudel dough are similar, the difference lies in the final shape of the dessert. Strudel dough is usually home-made, but it may also be purchased or phyllo can be used in its place.

Cream puffs, éclairs, Napoleans, baklavas, and strudels are pastry contributions from abroad which are easily made at home. Recipes for all of these and more are to be found in the following pages.

Here are a few pointers to help make your pastry flaky, light, and easy to make:

• Handle pastry dough *as little as possible;* unlike bread dough, pastry dough that's overhandled will become tough. As soon as the dough holds together, form a ball; flatten the ball; then roll the dough out to the size specified.

• Always roll pastry dough from the center to the edge. That way, your crust will be even in size and thickness.

• Turn the dough gently as you roll it, to prevent it from sticking.

• For a good size marker, use your pie plate! Turn it upside down on the rolled dough. Then, you can judge how much more rolling to do.

• To help center the pastry dough in your pie plate, fold the rolled pastry in half over your rolling pin; lay one half over the pie plate. When the rolling pin is across the center, flip the other half over the rest of the pie plate.

• Be sure to fit the dough *loosely* in your pie plate. If the dough is streched taut, it will shrink during baking.

• Trimmings from pastry can be re-rolled, cut, and sprinkled with sugar and cinnamon for extra treats.

FLAKY PASTRY I

Makes enough for one 9-inch double-crust pie or lattice-top pie.

2	cups *sifted* all-purpose flour	⅔	cup vegetable shortening
1	teaspoon salt	4	or 5 tablespoons cold water

1. Sift flour and salt into a medium-size bowl; cut in shortening with a fork or pastry blender until mixture is crumbly.
2. Sprinkle water over mixture, 1 tablespoon at a time; mix lightly with a fork just until pastry holds together and leaves sides of bowl clean. Divide dough in half.
3. To make bottom crust, roll out half to a 12-inch round on a lightly floured surface. Fit into a 9-inch pie plate. Trim overhang to ½ inch.
4. To make top crust, roll out remaining pastry to an 11-inch round. Cut several slits or decorator cutouts near the center to let steam escape.
5. Once pie is filled, place top crust over filling. Trim overhang to ½ inch, even with bottom pastry. Pinch to seal. Turn edge up and in, to seal in juices. Pinch again to make stand-up edge; flute.
6. Bake pie, and cool, following directions in individual recipes.

FLAKY PASTRY II

Makes enough for one 9-inch pastry shell, for a single-crust pie.

1½	cups *sifted* all-purpose flour	4	tablespoons cold water
½	teaspoon salt		(about)
½	cup vegetable shortening		

1. Sift flour and salt in a medium-size bowl; cut in shortening with a fork or pastry blender, until mixture is crumbly.
2. Sprinkle water over mixture, 1 tablespoon at a time; mix lightly with a fork just until pastry holds together and leaves sides of bowl clean. Make a ball; flatten it.
3. Roll out to a 12-inch round on a lightly floured surface; fit into a 9-inch pie plate. Trim overhang to ½ inch. Turn edge under. Pinch to make a stand-up edge; flute.

For baked pastry shell: Prick shell well all over with a fork. Bake in a preheated very hot oven (450°) for 5 minutes. Look at shell; if bubbles have formed, prick again. (After about 5 minutes of baking, pastry will have set and any bubbles formed will be permanent.) Continue to bake another 10 minutes or until pastry is golden brown. Cool completely in pie plate on a wire rack.

OIL PIE PASTRY

Makes enough for one 9-inch double-crust pie.

2 cups *sifted* all-purpose flour	⅓ cup corn or other vegetable
1¼ teaspoons salt (can be	oil
reduced or eliminated)	3 tablespoons cold skim milk

1. Sift flour and salt together in a medium-size mixing bowl. Make a well in the center.
2. Mix oil and cold milk in a small bowl. Pour all at once into the well. Stir lightly with fork until blended; add more liquid if necessary to make dough hold together in a ball. Divide in half. Refrigerate a few minutes to rest dough.
3. Use as you would any pie pastry, rolling out between pieces of wax paper.

Note: You can use this crust with your favorite fruit filling.

BUBBLE-FREE PASTRY SHELLS

There's another way to bake your unfilled pastry shell smooth and bubble-free besides pricking it all over with a fork. Fit a piece of foil or wax paper in bottom of plate over pastry; fill the shell with rice or beans (which can be reused) or aluminum pellets; then bake 5 minutes, or until pastry is set. Remove rice, beans, or pellets and foil or wax paper. Continue to bake until crust is golden brown.

CRUMB CRUST

Makes one unbaked 9-inch crust.

1⅓ cups graham cracker crumbs   ¼   cup butter margarine,
    (about 18 squares)   softened
¼   cup sugar

1. Mix graham cracker crumbs and sugar in a small bowl; blend in butter or margarine.
2. Press firmly over bottom and side of a buttered 9-inch pie plate; chill while making pie filling.

Vanilla Wafer-Pecan Crumb Crust: Combine 1 cup vanilla wafer crumbs with ½ cup ground pecans and ¼ cup softened butter or margarine in a small bowl. Press firmly over bottom and side of a lightly buttered 9-inch pie plate.

For baked crumb crusts: Bake in a preheated moderate oven (350°) for 8 minutes or until set. Cool completely on a wire rack.

MANAGING CRUMB CRUSTS

Ever have problems with broken or stuck-on crumb crusts? When baking a crumb crust, line pie plate with foil first, press in crumb crust mixture and bake. Cool and freeze crust for at least 1 hour. Lift foil and frozen crust from plate and peel off foil carefully. Return crust to plate and fill.

Rolling Out Piecrust: Roll out dough into a circle that is about 2 inches larger than the pie pan. Always work from the center to the edges—in one direction, never rolling back and forth.

Method 1: Roll up dough onto rolling pin. Position rolling pin over pie pan and unroll.

Method 2: Fold dough carefully in half. Then fold in half again. Scoop up with a large flat spatula and position dough over pan. Carefully unfold into pan.

Gently press dough against sides and into corners without stretching.

Edging Piecrusts: For pastry shells and many lattice pies, turn edges of dough *under* and pinch to form a stand-up edge. Reason: There's no need to seal in juices, as there is with most two-crust pies, so the edge can be turned under for a neater appearance.

DECORATIVE PIECRUSTS

The real beauty of any pie lies in its tasty filling and light, flaky crust. But appearance is important, too, and here we show you numerous ways to heighten the eye appeal of your favorite pies— without a great deal of effort.

Make a Fluted Edge: Press right forefinger along inside rim between thumb and forefinger on outside. Repeat about every inch.

Ruffled Edge: With right forefinger and thumb on the outside of the rim, press pastry into ridges with a slight twist.

Rope Edge: Twisting slightly, press a slim pencil (or wooden skewer) diagonally into pastry all around edge to make even, widely spaced ridges.

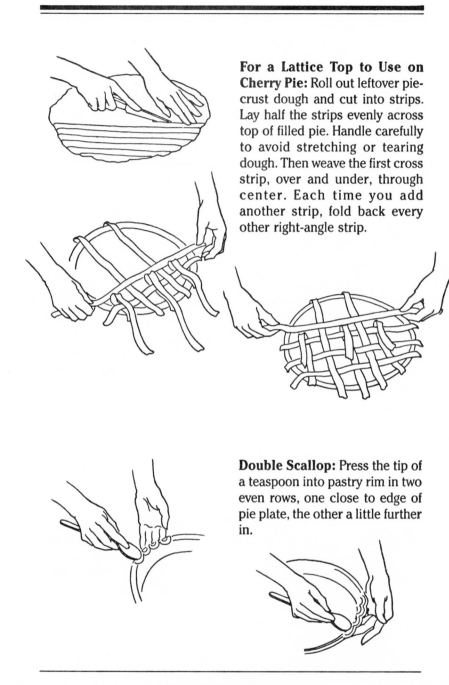

For a Lattice Top to Use on Cherry Pie: Roll out leftover pie-crust dough and cut into strips. Lay half the strips evenly across top of filled pie. Handle carefully to avoid stretching or tearing dough. Then weave the first cross strip, over and under, through center. Each time you add another strip, fold back every other right-angle strip.

Double Scallop: Press the tip of a teaspoon into pastry rim in two even rows, one close to edge of pie plate, the other a little further in.

Braided Edge: Trim overhang from bottom crust. Cut thin pastry strips from leftover pie-crust dough. Braid three, piecing enough together to go around pie plate. Brush pastry rim with water; press braid on top.

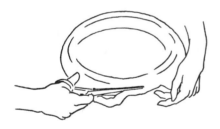

For a Fancy One-Crust Pie Edging: Fit the bottom crust into pie plate, leaving an overhang of 1½ inches. With scissors to speed up the job, snip even saw-tooth cuts all around and fold edge over filling toward center.

THE PERFECT APPLE PIE

Bake at 425° for 40 minutes.
Makes 6 servings.

2½ pounds cooking apples, pared, quartered, cored, and thinly sliced (8 cups)
⅓ cup firmly packed light brown sugar
⅓ cup granulated sugar
1 tablespoon cornstarch
   Or: 2½ tablespoons all-purpose flour
1 teaspoon ground cinnamon
¼ teaspoon ground nutmeg
¼ teaspoon salt
1 package piecrust mix
   Or: Flaky Pastry I (page 43)
2 tablespoons butter or margarine
   Water or milk
   Sugar
   Vanilla ice cream (optional)
   Cheese curls (optional)

1. Place apples in a large bowl; let stand until a little juice forms, about 10 minutes. Meanwhile, mix sugars, cornstarch, cinnamon, nutmeg, and salt in a small bowl; sprinkle over apples; toss gently to mix.
2. Prepare piecrust mix, following label directions or recipe. Roll out ½ of dough to 12-inch round on a lightly floured surface; fit into a 9-inch pie plate. Trim overhang to ½ inch.
3. Roll out remaining pastry for top to a 12-inch round; fold into quarters; make 3 slits near center in each of folded edges for steam to escape. Pile apple mixture into pastry shell; dot with butter. Moisten edge of bottom pastry with water. Place folded pastry on apples so point is on center; unfold. Trim overhang to 1 inch; turn edges under and press together to seal. Pinch to make stand-up edge; flute or make your favorite edging. Preheat oven to 425°.
4. For a crispy-sugary top, brush top of pastry with a little water or milk and sprinkle lightly with sugar.
5. Bake pie in a preheated hot oven (425°) for 40 minutes or until juices bubble through slits and apples are tender. If edge is browning too fast, cover with a narrow strip of foil. If you wish, serve warm with scoops of vanilla ice cream or garnish with Cheese curls.

APPLE PIE GARNISH

Cheese curls: Shave thin strips from a small block of Cheddar cheese using a vegetable parer or cheese plane. Roll the strips around your finger; slide off gently and chill. Pile onto an apple pie.

FRESH CHERRY PIE

Bake at 425° for 45 minutes.
Makes 6 servings.

1   package piecrust mix
½   cup ground blanched
    almonds
4   cups pitted fresh
    sour cherries
    Or: 2 cans (16 ounces each)
    pitted sour red cherries,
    drained

1¼ cups sugar
2   tablespoons quick-cooking
    tapioca
¼   teaspoon salt
    Vanilla ice cream (optional)

1. Combine piecrust mix with almonds in a medium-size bowl; prepare piecrust mix following label directions.
2. Mix cherries, sugar, tapioca, and salt in a medium-size bowl. Toss lightly to coat fruit; let stand 20 minutes.
3. Roll out half of pastry to a 12-inch round on a lightly floured surface; fit into a 9-inch pie plate; trim overhang to ½ inch. Spoon cherry mixture into prepared pastry shell. Preheat oven to 425°.
4. Roll out remaining pastry to an 11-inch round. Cut in ½-inch strips with a pastry wheel or knife. Weave strips into lattice over filling. Turn ends under; flute. Tear off 2-inch piece of aluminum foil; crumple lightly over fluted edge to keep edge from over-browning.
5. Bake in a preheated hot oven (425°) for 30 minutes; remove foil; continue baking 15 minutes or until pastry is brown and filling bubbly. Serve warm with vanilla ice cream, if you wish.

SPRINKLING FLOUR

Keep flour in a shaker to have on hand whenever you need to dust a baking pan or flour a pastry board to roll crusts or doughs.

PIE SERVICE

How many servings do you get from one pie? It all depends upon the richness. For fruit pies, figure 6 generous servings. For custard, cream, and other rich pies, count on 8 servings.

PEAR CRUMB PIE

A gem of a pie from the Northwest, where pear and apple orchards criss-cross the land. Crunchy crumbs top the lightly spiced juicy pears.

Bake at 400° for 40 minutes.
Makes 6 servings.

1 package piecrust mix	1 tablespoon lemon juice
1 cup *sifted* all-purpose flour	⅔ cup granulated sugar
⅓ cup firmly packed light brown sugar	1 teaspoon ground cinnamon
⅓ cup butter or margarine	¼ teaspoon ground mace
2½ pounds firm-ripe Anjou or Bosc pears	1 tablespoon all-purpose flour
	10X (confectioners') sugar

1. Prepare piecrust mix, following label directions for a 9-inch pastry shell with a high fluted edge; chill while preparing filling.
2. Combine the 1 cup flour and the ⅓ cup brown sugar in a small bowl. Cut in the butter with a pastry blender until coarse crumbs form; reserve.
3. Preheat oven to 400°.
4. Pare, quarter, and core pears. Slice into a large bowl; sprinkle with lemon juice.
5. Combine the granulated sugar, cinnamon, mace, and flour in a small bowl; sprinkle over pears. Toss gently to mix well; spoon into prepared pastry shell. Sprinkle with reserved brown sugar topping.
6. Bake in a preheated hot oven (400°) for 40 minutes or until juices bubble and top browns. If pie is browning too rapidly after 20 minutes of baking, cover top loosely with foil; remove foil 5 minutes before end of baking time. Cool on wire rack. Sprinkle cooled pie with 10X sugar, and serve with wedges of Cheddar, or with ice cream, if you wish.

CRISP CUSTARD PIECRUST

To keep unbaked piecrusts from getting soggy when making custard pies, brush them with beaten egg white before filling.

OLD-FASHIONED TWO-CRUST LEMON PIE

Bake at 375° for 30 minutes, then at 425° for 10 minutes.
Makes 8 servings.

¼	cup cornstarch	2	eggs, slightly beaten
¼	cup water	2	tablespoons grated lemon
1½	cups boiling water		rind
1½	cups sugar	¼	cup lemon juice
1	tablespoon butter	1	tablespoon milk
1	package piecrust mix	1	tablespoon sugar

1. Blend cornstarch and the ¼ cup water in a saucepan. Stir in boiling water. Cook, stirring constantly, over medium heat until mixture thickens and bubbles. Cook 1 minute. Remove from heat; stir in the 1½ cups sugar and the butter; cool.
2. Preheat oven to 375°.
3. Prepare piecrust mix following label directions for a 9-inch double-crust pie. Roll out half the pastry to a 13-inch round; line a 9-inch pie plate.
4. Stir eggs, lemon rind, and juice into cooled cornstarch mixture until blended. Pour into pastry-lined pie plate. Roll out remaining pastry to a 12-inch round; cut slits to let steam escape. Top pie; pinch to make a stand-up edge; flute. Brush pastry with milk; sprinkle with sugar.
5. Bake in a preheated moderate oven (375°) for 30 minutes. Increase oven temperature to hot (425°). Bake 10 minutes longer or until pastry is brown. Cool on a wire rack.

REMOVING RIND

To remove grated lemon ro orange rind from a grater, use a clean stiff pastry brush.

MERINGUE SECRET

The secret to good meringue is having as much sugar dissolve as possible. For best results, add sugar *only* after egg whites are foamy-white.

SPICY RHUBARB STREUSEL PIE

Bake at 425° for 25 minutes.
Makes 8 servings.

2   cups quick oats
⅓   cup firmly packed light
    brown sugar
⅛   teaspoon salt
½   cup (1 stick) butter or
    margarine, melted
1½ pounds rhubarb, washed,
    trimmed, and cut into 1-inch
    pieces (about 4 cups)

¾   cup water
1   cup granulated sugar
⅓   cup cornstarch
¼   teaspoon salt
½   teaspoon ground cinnamon
¼   teaspoon ground nutmeg
⅛   teaspoon ground cloves

1. Combine oats, brown sugar, salt, and butter in a medium-size bowl, blending well. Press ⅔ of the mixture firmly and evenly onto the bottom and side of a 9-inch pie plate; reserve remaining mixture. Preheat oven to 425°.
2. Combine rhubarb, water, granulated sugar, cornstarch, salt, cinnamon, nutmeg, and cloves in a medium-size saucepan. Cook over medium heat, stirring often, until thickened, about 10 minutes. Spoon into prepared crust. Sprinkle with the remaining oat-crumb mixture.
3. Bake in a preheated hot oven (425°) for 25 minutes or until golden brown. Cool to room temperature on a wire rack.

APRICOT-PRUNE LATTICE PIE

Chopped whole lemon and port wine provide exciting flavor accents in this luscious dried fruit mixture that goes into a flaky sour cream pastry.

Bake at 425° for 35 minutes.
Makes 6 servings.

½   cup (1 stick) butter or
    margarine
2   cups *sifted* all-purpose flour
2   tablespoons sugar
½   cup dairy sour cream
1   package (8 ounces) dried
    apricots, diced
    (about 1½ cups)
1   cup diced pitted prunes
1½ cups water

½   cup sugar
2   teaspoons cornstarch
½   whole lemon, coarsely
    chopped (about ¼ cup)
2   tablespoons tawny port wine
    or sweet sherry
1   tablespoon sugar
1   tablespoon chopped walnuts
    or pecans

1. Cut butter into flour with a pastry blender until mixture is crumbly. Add sugar and sour cream; mix lightly with a fork until dough holds together and starts to leave side of bowl clean. Gather dough together with your hands and knead a few times. Wrap in wax paper; chill at least 1 hour.
2. Combine apricots, prunes, and water in a medium-size saucepan; bring to a boil. Simmer, covered, 5 minutes. Mix sugar and cornstarch, and stir into boiling mixture. Cook, stirring often, for 5 minutes. Remove from heat; stir in lemon and port wine.
3. Roll out 2/3 of pastry on lightly floured surface to a 12-inch round; fit into a 9-inch pie plate; trim overhang to ½ inch. Pour in the apricot-prune filling.
4. Preheat oven to 425°. Roll out remaining pastry to a 10-inch round. Cut into 10 strips; weave strips over filling. Turn edge under flush with rim; flute edge. Brush top with water; mix sugar and nuts; sprinkle over pie.
5. Bake in preheated hot oven (425°) for 35 minutes or until pastry is golden and filling is bubbling hot. Cool on a wire rack. Serve slightly warm.

CARAMEL-NUT SWEET POTATO PIE

Bake at 425°, then 350° for 40 minutes.
Makes 8 servings.

1	9-inch unbaked pastry shell with high fluted edge	2	eggs
1	can (17 ounces) sweet potatoes, drained	1⅔	cups light cream or half and half
¾	cup firmly packed light brown sugar	¼	cup finely chopped preserved ginger
1	teaspoon ground cinnamon		Caramel-Nut Topping (recipe below)
¼	teaspoon ground cloves Dash salt		Whipped cream

1. Prepare pastry shell; chill. Preheat oven to 425°.
2. Combine sweet potatoes, sugar, cinnamon, cloves, salt, eggs, and cream in container of an electric blender. Cover; whirl until smooth. Stir in ginger. Pour mixture into pastry shell.
3. Place in a preheated hot oven (425°) ; lower oven temperature to 350°. Bake 40 minutes or until center is almost set but still soft.

(Do not overbake; custard will set as it cools.) Cool pie on a wire rack. *Note*: Surface of pie may crack, but topping will cover it.
4. Spread Caramel-Nut Topping over the cooled pie. Garnish with whipped cream just before serving.

Caramel-Nut Topping: Combine 3 tablespoons light brown sugar, 2 tablespoons butter or margarine, and 1 tablespoon cream in small skillet; heat, stirring constantly, until melted and mixture bubbles for 1 minute. Stir in ½ cup coarsely chopped peanuts or cashews; heat and stir over low heat for 1 minute.

SOUR CREAM-WALNUT PIE

Originally made with native black walnuts, this kissin' cousin of the famed pecan pie stirs in a lip-smacking variation—cool sour cream.

Bake at 350° for 40 minutes.
Makes 8 servings.

½	package piecrust mix		½	cup light or dark corn syrup
⅓	cup butter or margarine		¾	cup dairy sour cream
½	cup firmly packed light brown sugar		1	cup broken walnuts
			1	teaspoon vanilla
4	eggs		½	cup heavy cream, whipped
¾	cup granulated sugar			Walnut halves (optional)
¼	teaspoon salt			

1. Prepare piecrust mix following label directions for a 9-inch pastry crust with a high fluted edge. Chill while preparing filling.
2. Preheat oven to 350°.
3. Combine butter and brown sugar in the top of a double boiler over *simmering* water. Heat just until butter is melted.
4. Beat eggs slightly in a medium-size bowl. Beat in granulated sugar, salt, corn syrup, and sour cream just until smooth. Pour into butter mixture, stirring until well blended. Cook over hot, not boiling water, stirring constantly, for 5 minutes. Remove from heat; stir in walnuts and vanilla. Pour mixture into prepared pastry shell.
5. Bake in a preheated moderate oven (350°) for 40 minutes. Filling will be a little soft in center, but do not overbake. Cool on a wire rack. Garnish with whipped cream and walnut halves, if you wish. Keep any leftovers refrigerated.

BANANA CREAM PIE

Creamy-smooth, and oh, so delicious!

Makes 6 servings.

½ package piecrust mix
⅔ cup sugar
3 tablespoons all-purpose
   flour
2 tablespoons cornstarch
¼ teaspoon salt

3 cups milk
3 eggs
2 teaspoons vanilla
3 medium-size ripe bananas
1 cup heavy cream

1. Prepare piecrust mix following label directions for a baked pastry shell.
2. Combine sugar, flour, cornstarch, and salt in a large saucepan. Stir in milk slowly.
3. Cook, stirring constantly, over moderate heat, until mixture thickens and bubbles. Continue cooking and stirring until mixture is very thick, about 6 minutes longer.
4. Beat eggs in a medium-size bowl until frothy. Stir in half of the cooked mixture until blended. Return to saucepan, blending in thoroughly. Cook 2 minutes more over low heat, stirring constantly.
5. Remove from heat; stir in vanilla. Place a piece of wax paper directly on surface; cool.
6. Peel and slice bananas into pie shell. Pour cooled cream filling over bananas; chill several hours. Whip cream in a medium-size bowl until stiff. Spoon over top of pie.

CUSTARD PIE TEST

To tell if a custard pie is set, hold edge and jiggle slightly. If pie still has large ripples, it's not ready. It should just "shiver" a bit.

STORING EGG YOLKS

Leftover egg yolks can be covered with water in a small jar and refrigerated up to 4 days. Drain off water before using.

DEEP-DISH APPLE PIE

A deep layer of juicy, lightly spiced apples topped with a golden-crisp pastry crust.

Bake at 425° for 45 minutes.
Makes 8 servings.

10	medium-size apples (McIntosh, Granny Smith), pared, quartered, cored, and sliced (about 10 cups)	1	teaspoon ground cinnamon
		¼	teaspoon ground cloves
		¼	teaspoon ground allspice
		1	package piecrust mix
⅓	cup firmly packed light brown sugar	2	tablespoons butter or margarine
⅓	cup granulated sugar		Water
3	tablespoons all-purpose flour	1	tablespoon granulated sugar

1. Combine apples, brown sugar, the ⅓ cup granulated sugar, flour, cinnamon, cloves, and allspice in a large bowl; toss lightly to mix. Let stand while making pastry.

2. Prepare piecrust mix following label directions. Roll out on a lightly floured surface to a 12-inch round. Cut several slits near center to let steam escape.

3. Preheat oven to 425°. Spoon apple mixture into a 10-inch deep pie plate; dot with butter. Cover with pastry; fold edges under, flush with sides of dish. (Pastry should be inside dish.) Pinch to make a stand-up edge; flute. Brush lightly with water; sprinkle with remaining tablespoon of sugar.

4. Bake in a preheated hot oven (425°)for 45 minutes or until pastry is golden and juices bubble. (Place a piece of aluminum foil on a rack under pie to catch any juices that may run over.) Cool at least 1 hour. Serve in individual bowls; pass sour cream, or serve with softened vanilla ice cream, if you wish.

DOUBLE YOUR APPLE PLEASURE

When making fresh apple pies, try substituting apple cider for water in the crust. For added variety, try cutting apples into cubes instead of slices.

COUNTRY DEEP-DISH CHERRY PIE

Plump sweet cherries mingle with juicy tart ones for a fantastic, delicious dessert.

Bake at 375° for 35 minutes.
Makes 8 servings.

1	can (17 ounces) pitted dark sweet cherries	2	tablespoon butter or margarine
2	cans (16 ounces each) pitted tart red cherries	2	cups buttermilk baking mix
¾	cup sugar	5	tablespoons sugar
¼	cup cornstarch	¼	cup dairy sour cream
½	teaspoon ground cinnamon	3	tablespoons water
¼	teaspoon ground mace or nutmeg		

1. Lightly grease an 8-cup shallow baking dish. Drain syrup from dark cherries into 2-cup measure. Drain tart red cherries adding enough of their juice to the dark cherry syrup to make 2 cups. Combine the ¾ cup sugar, cornstarch, cinnamon, and mace in a large saucepan; gradually stir in reserved juice. Cook over medium heat, stirring constantly, until mixture thickens and bubbles 1 minute. Add cherries. Spoon filling into prepared dish. Preheat oven to 375°.

2. Combine baking mix, 3 tablespoons sugar, sour cream, and water in a medium-size bowl. Mix lightly with a fork, just until dough holds together. Turn out onto a floured surface; knead 10 times. Roll to a 12 x 10-inch rectangle; cut crosswise into about ¾-inch wide strips. Weave strips over filling; turn ends under to fit dish. Sprinkle with remaining sugar.

3. Bake in a preheated moderate oven (375°) for 35 minutes or until pastry is golden and juices bubble. (Place a piece of aluminum foil on a rack under pie to catch any juices that may run over.) Cool. Serve warm with cream, if you wish.

TO CATCH A DRIP

To catch any syrup that may boil over during baking, slide a piece of aluminum foil on the rack below the pie.

ORANGE-RUM PIE

Bake at 425° for 12 minutes.
Makes 6 servings.

½	package piecrust mix	1	cup sugar
2	envelopes unflavored gelatin	¼	cup light or golden rum
⅔	cup orange juice	1	cup heavy cream, whipped
2	eggs		Whipped cream
4	egg yolks		Preserved kumquats, halved

1. Preheat oven to 425°. Prepare piecrust mix following label directions. Roll out to a 12-inch round on a lightly floured board; fit into a 9-inch pie plate. Trim overhang to ½-inch; turn edge under, flush with rim. Make a scalloped or fluted edge. Prick shell well with a fork.

2. Bake in a preheated hot oven (425°) for 12 minutes or until golden; cool completely on a wire rack.

3. Sprinkle gelatin over orange juice in a small saucepan; let stand 5 minutes to soften. Place saucepan over low heat until gelatin dissolves. Remove from heat; cool.

4. Combine whole eggs, egg yolks, and sugar in a large bowl. Beat with an electric mixer on high speed until very thick and light.

5. Combine cooled gelatin mixture with rum. Pour into egg mixture while beating slowly.

6. Remove bowl from mixer. Chill briefly either in refrigerator or by placing bowl in ice and cold water. Stir often, just until mixture mounds.

7. Fold in whipped cream. Spoon into cooled pastry shell. Chill several hours or until firm. Garnish with additional whipped cream and kumquats.

HANDLING EGGS

To beat egg whites to the greatest volume, have them at room temperature. The bowl and beaters must be absolutely clean. (A bit of fat or even egg yolk will reduce its volume). Use glass or aluminum bowls, not plastic. Do not overbeat egg whites; they will become dry.

STRAWBERRY-CREAM CHEESE CHIFFON PIE

Bake at 400° for 15 minutes.
Makes 8 servings.

1 cup *sifted* all-purpose flour	⅔ cup sugar
1 teaspoon sugar	1 envelope unflavored gelatin
½ teaspoon salt	¼ cup water
½ cup macaroon crumbs (amaretti)	1 package (8 ounces) cream cheese, softened
⅓ cup butter, melted	2 egg whites
1 egg yolk	½ cup sugar
2 to 3 tablespoons cold water	1 cup heavy cream
2 pints strawberries, washed and hulled	¼ cup currant jelly, melted

1. Preheat oven to 400°. Combine flour, the 1 teaspoon sugar, salt, and macaroon crumbs in a medium-size bowl. Add butter, egg yolk, and enough water to make a dough. Blend until dough sticks together and forms a ball.

2. Roll pastry out on a lightly floured surface or between two sheets of wax paper to a 12-inch round. Fit into a 9-inch pie plate. Trim overhang; flute edge.

3. Bake in a preheated hot oven (400°) for 15 minutes or until golden brown. Cool.

4. Reserve 10 strawberries for garnish. Halve remaining berries into a medium-size bowl; add the ⅔ cup sugar. Let stand for 15 minutes or until sugar dissolves and juice has formed. Sprinkle gelatin over water; let stand 5 minutes to soften.

5. Drain strawberry juice from berries into a saucepan; add softened gelatin. Heat until gelatin is dissolved.

6. Beat cream cheese until soft and fluffy; gradually beat in strawberry juice.

7. Beat egg whites until foamy. Gradually beat in the ½ cup sugar, 1 tablespoon at a time, until meringue forms soft peaks. Fold into strawberry-cheese mixture. Fold in berries.

8. Beat ½ cup heavy cream in a small bowl until stiff. Fold into strawberry mixture. Spoon into cooled crust. Chill several hours or until firm.

9. To serve: Halve reserved berries; arrange around outer edge of pie. Brush berries with melted jelly. Whip remaining ½ cup heavy cream until stiff. Pipe rosettes of cream onto pie.

ESPRESSO PARFAIT PIE

Makes 8 servings.

12 to 14 chocolate chip cookies
2 tablespoons butter or margarine
1 pint vanilla or coffee ice cream
1 envelope plus 1 teaspoon unflavored gelatin
3 tablespoons sugar

3 eggs, separated
2 tablespoons instant espresso coffee
¾ cup cold water
2 teaspoons grated lemon rind
2 tablespoons sugar
Lemon rind strips (optional)

1. Crush enough cookies in a plastic bag with a rolling pin to make about 1¼ cups. Melt butter in a medium-size heavy skillet. Add cookie crumbs; stir over medium heat 1 minute. Press crumb mixture against side and bottom of a 9-inch pie plate. Chill while preparing filling.
2. Remove ice cream from freezer to soften.
3. Mix gelatin and the 3 tablespoons of sugar in a medium-size heavy saucepan; beat in egg yolks until well blended. Dissolve coffee in water; gradually stir into yolk mixture. Cook, stirring constantly, over low heat, 8 to 10 minutes or until gelatin is completely dissolved and mixture is slightly thickened and coats a spoon. Remove from heat; stir in lemon rind.
4. Beat egg whites in a medium-size bowl until foamy-white; gradually beat in the 2 tablespoons of sugar until meringue stands in soft peaks.
5. Beat ice cream into hot gelatin mixture a few tablespoons at a time. (Ice cream should set gelatin just enough to fold in meringue.) Fold in meringue quickly until no streaks of white remain. Spoon into prepared piecrust. Chill 4 hours or until firm. Garnish with thin strips of lemon rind, if you wish.

MARGARITA PIE

Makes 8 servings.

1½ cups finely crushed pretzels
½ cup (1 stick) butter, softened
3 tablespoons sugar
1 envelope unflavored gelatin
½ cup lemon juice
4 eggs, separated
1 cup sugar

1 teaspoon grated lemon rind
¼ teaspoon salt
3 tablespoons Tequilla
1 tablespoon Triple Sec
Lemon and lime slices
Pretzel sticks

1. Grease a 9-inch plate. Combine pretzel crumbs, butter, and the 3 tablespoons of sugar in a large bowl until well blended. Press mixture evenly against side and bottom of prepared pie plate. Chill.
2. Sprinkle gelatin over lemon juice in a small cup; let stand 5 minutes to soften.
3. Beat yolks in top of double boiler until foamy. Beat in ½ cup of the sugar; stir in lemon rind, salt, and gelatin. Cook over simmering water, stirring constantly, until gelatin is completely dissolved and mixture is slightly thickened, about 8 minutes. Remove from heat; stir in Tequilla and Triple Sec. Place pan in bowl of ice and cold water; Chill, stirring often, until mixture mounds when spooned.
4. Beat egg whites in medium-size bowl until foamy. Gradually beat in the remaining ½ cup sugar until meringue forms soft peaks. Fold meringue into gelatin mixture until no streaks of white remain.
5. Spoon into crust; chill. Garnish with lemon and lime slices and pretzels.

PEACHES AND CREAM TART

Peach slices baked in a rich custardy cream make a luscious company dessert. This tart is best made early in the day.

Bake at 400° for 40 minutes.
Makes 10 servings.

Rich Tart Pastry:
1½ cups *unsifted* all-purpose
  flour
2 tablespoons sugar
1 teaspoon baking powder
⅛ teaspoon salt
½ cup (1 stick) butter or
  margarine
1 egg
½ teaspoon grated lemon rind

Filling:
4 to 6 large peaches
½ cup sugar
1 tablespoon cornstarch
1 tablespoon lemon juice
2 eggs
1 cup heavy cream
¼ teaspoon ground nutmeg

1. Prepare Pastry: Combine flour, sugar, baking powder, and salt in medium-size bowl. Cut in butter with a pastry blender until mixture is crumbly. Beat egg with lemon rind in cup; sprinkle over flour mixture. Toss with fork just until pastry is moist. Work with fingers until pastry holds together.
2. Press dough evenly over bottom and 2 inches up side of a 9-inch springform or removable-bottom fluted tart pan. Preheat oven to 400°.

3. Prepare Filling: Dip peaches into boiling water for 30 seconds, then into ice water for 1 minute. Peel, halve, pit, and slice (you should have about 5 cups.) Combine peaches, sugar, cornstarch, and lemon juice in a medium-size bowl; toss to mix. Arrange peach slices, overlapping, in bottom of pastry-lined pan.

4. Bake in a preheated hot oven (400°) for 20 minutes.

5. Meanwhile, beat eggs, cream, and nutmeg in a small bowl. Pour over baked peaches. Return tart to oven.

6. Bake 20 minutes more or until cream is firm around the edge but soft-set in the center and top is golden. Cool tart on a wire rack at least 2 hours. Remove side of pan. Serve cool but not chilled.

BLUEBERRY-LEMON CURD TART

Bake at 450° for 8 minutes.
Makes 12 servings.

1	package piecrust mix	⅓	cup lemon juice
2	tablespoons sugar	1	pint fresh blueberries
7	eggs	⅓	cup sugar
1	cup sugar	1	tablespoon cornstarch
½	cup (1 stick) butter	¼	cup orange juice
2	teaspoons grated lemon rind		

1. Preheat oven to 450°.

2. Combine piecrust mix, the 2 tablespoons sugar, and 1 egg in a medium-size bowl, blending well. Press mixture onto bottom and side of fluted 10-inch tart pan with a removable bottom or a 10-inch pie plate.

3. Bake in a preheated very hot oven (450°) for 8 minutes or until golden brown; cool on a wire rack.

4. Beat remaining eggs in top of a double boiler; stir in the 1 cup sugar, butter, lemon rind, and juice. Cook over hot, not boiling, water, stirring constantly until thickened, about 15 minutes. Remove top of double boiler from hot water; cool 20 minutes, stirring 2 or 3 times. Turn into cooled pastry shell; chill.

5. Combine blueberries and sugar in a medium-size saucepan. Dissolve cornstarch in orange juice; stir into blueberries. Cook over medium heat, stirring constantly until mixture thickens and clears, about 5 minutes. Cool thoroughly. Spoon around outer edge of filled tart. Refrigerate until ready to serve.

MACADAMIA NUT TARTS

Bake at 400° for 15 minutes.
Makes 16 tarts.

1   package piecrust mix
½   cup (1 stick) butter, softened
¾   cup firmly packed light brown sugar
¾   cup light corn syrup
¼   cup honey

4   eggs, beaten
1   teaspoon vanilla
1   can (5 ounces) macadamia nuts, coarsely chopped
    Whipped cream (optional)

1. Prepare piecrust following label directions; roll out; cut into sixteen 4½-inch rounds. Fit into 3½-inch tart pans. Preheat oven to 400°.
2. Beat butter and sugar in a large bowl with an electric mixer until creamy. Beat in corn syrup and honey, then eggs and vanilla. Stir in nuts.
3. Place about ¼ cup filling in each tart shell. Place on cookie sheet.
4. Bake in a preheated hot oven (400°) for 15 minutes or until golden brown. Cool before serving. Decorate with whipped cream, if you wish.

For 9-inch pie: Use ½ package piecrust mix to prepare one 9-inch crust. Proceed as directed with remaining ingredients; pour into pie shell. Bake on bottom rack in a hot oven (425°) for 10 minutes. Lower oven temperature to slow (325°) and continue baking for 25 minutes or until golden.

Note: Tarts or pie may be made ahead and frozen; cool thoroughly and wrap well with aluminum foil before freezing.

STRAWBERRY-KIWI TART

Bake at 400° for 10 minutes, then at 350° for 5 minutes.
Makes 10 servings.

1⅓ cups *sifted* all-purpose flour
¼ cup sugar
½ cup (1 stick) butter or margarine, softened
2 egg yolks
1 cup half and half or light cream
⅓ cup sugar
3 tablespoons cornstarch
⅓ cup milk

4 egg yolks, lightly beaten
1½ teaspoons vanilla
3 tablespoons plus ⅓ cup bottled strawberry ice cream topping
1 pint strawberries, washed, hulled, and halved
2 kiwi fruit, peeled and sliced crosswise

1. Preheat oven to 400°. Mix flour and sugar in a medium-size bowl. Add butter and the 2 egg yolks; stir with a fork until mixture clings together in a ball. Press dough into an 11-inch tart pan with removable bottom; chill 15 minutes.

2. Bake shell in a preheated hot oven (400°) for 10 minutes (no need to prick bottom); lower heat to moderate (350°) and bake 5 minutes longer or until shell is lightly browned. Transfer to a wire rack to cool completely.

3. Heat cream and sugar in a small saucepan until mixture comes to a boil. Combine cornstarch and milk in a cup; stir into cream mixture and cook a few seconds longer, stirring until thick.

4. Beat a small amount of the cream mixture into the 4 egg yolks; return mixture to pan and cook over low heat for about 10 minutes longer or until thick. *Do not overcook* or mixture will curdle. Remove from heat; stir in vanilla.

5. Pour filling into a small bowl; press a piece of wax paper directly on the surface of the filling to keep film from forming. Chill until very cold.

6. Spread 3 tablespoons strawberry topping over the bottom of the tart shell. Spread chilled custard filling on top. Brush strawberries with remaining strawberry topping and arrange over filling with kiwi slices. Chill until ready to serve, up to 2 hours later.

COCONUT CREAM CHIFFON TARTS

These individual tarts, perfect for a dessert buffet, are filled with a luscious, fresh-tasting coconut chiffon cream.

Bake shells at 450° for 10 minutes.
Makes 36 tarts.

Pastry Shells:
2   packages piecrust mix
¼   cup sugar
2   eggs

Filling:
½   cup sugar
1   envelope unflavored gelatin
1   cup milk
4   eggs, separated
1½   teaspoons vanilla

½   teaspoon almond extract
¼   cup sugar
⅔   cup heavy cream
½   cup flaked coconut
1   can (8 ounces) crushed pineapple in pineapple juice, drained
     Toasted flaked coconut (optional)
     Maraschino cherries (optional)

1. Make Shells: Preheat oven to 450°.

2. Combine piecrust mix and the ¼ cup sugar in a medium-size bowl. Lightly beat eggs in a small bowl; blend into piecrust mix with a fork until pastry is moistened and leaves side of bowl clean. Press 1 tablespoon of the dough into tiny (2- to 3-inch) fluted tart pans. Prick shells all over with a fork. Place on cookie sheets; chill 15 minutes.

3. Bake in a preheated very hot oven (450°) for 10 minutes or until golden brown. Cool on wire racks. Remove shells from pans and set aside.

4. Make Filling: Combine the ½ cup sugar and gelatin in top of a double boiler; gradually stir in milk. Cook over simmering water until gelatin is dissolved. Beat a little of the hot milk mixture into the egg yolks; return to pan. Cook over hot, not boiling, water for 3 to 5 minutes or until mixture thickens. Stir in vanilla and almond extracts. Remove from heat; turn into a medium-size bowl. Cool mixture, stirring often, until mixture mounds when spooned.

5. Beat egg whites until foamy in a small bowl; gradually beat in remaining ¼ cup sugar until meringue forms soft peaks. Gently fold into cooled custard.

6. Beat ⅓ cup of the heavy cream until stiff; fold into custard mixture with the flaked coconut and the drained pineapple. Spoon into cooled pastry shells.

7. Refrigerate for 2 hours. Beat remaining ⅓ cup heavy cream until stiff. Spoon into a pastry bag with small star tip. Pipe a small rosette on top of each tart. Garnish with toasted coconut and a cherry, if you wish.

Note: If you don't have enough tart pans, fill those you have, bake, and refill.

AMBROSIA TARTS

Easy-to-make crunchy coconut tart shells hold a heavenly fruit and cheese filling.

Makes 8 tarts.

2	eggs	2	packages (3 ounces each) cream cheese
½	cup sugar		
1	tablespoon grated lemon rind	1	to 2 bananas
¼	cup lemon juice	3	kiwi fruit
¼	cup (½ stick) butter or margarine	¼	cup orange marmalade
	Toasted Coconut Tart Shells (recipe below)		

1. Combine eggs, sugar, lemon rind, lemon juice, and butter in top of a double boiler. Cook over simmering water, stirring constantly, until mixture thickens, about 8 minutes. Remove from heat; cool completely.

2. Prepare Toasted Coconut Tart Shells.

3. Soften cream cheese in a small bowl; gradually blend in cooled lemon mixture. Spoon filling into prepared tart shells. Peel and slice banana and kiwi; arrange slices on top of tarts.

4. Melt orange marmalade in a small saucepan over low heat; brush over fruits. Refrigerate until ready to serve.

Toasted Coconut Tart Shells: Crush 20 vanilla wafer cookies in a plastic bag with a rolling pin. Heat ½ cup flaked coconut in a heavy skillet over medium heat, stirring often until golden. Stir in 3 tablespoons butter until melted. Remove from heat; stir in cookie crumbs. Press mixture into 8 individual aluminum foil tart pans, dividing evenly. Chill until firm.

APPLE DUMPLINGS IN CHEESE-WALNUT PASTRY

Whole apples spiced and sugared and enclosed
in a Cheddar cheese pastry.

Bake at 425° for 45 minutes.
Makes 6 apple dumplings.

3 cups *sifted* **all-purpose flour**	**¼** cup (½ stick) butter or
1½ teaspoons salt	margarine, softened
¾ cup vegetable shortening	**⅓** cup sugar
2 ounces Cheddar cheese,	**½** teaspoon apple pie spice
shredded (1½ cup)	Or: A combination of
¼ cup ground or finely chopped	ground cinnamon, nutmeg,
walnuts	and cloves
10 to 12 tablespoons ice water	**1** egg yolk, slightly beaten
6 medium-size baking apples	Custard Sauce (page 291)
(Rome Beauty, Granny Smith)	

1. Sift flour and salt into a medium-size bowl; cut in shortening with a fork or pastry blender until mixture is crumbly; stir in cheese and walnuts.

2. Sprinkle water over mixture; mix lightly with a fork just until pastry holds together and leaves side of bowl clean.

3. Pare apples and core ⅔ way down. Remove any remaining seeds. Combine butter, sugar, and apple pie spice in a small bowl until smooth and paste-like. Spoon into centers of apples, dividing evenly. Preheat oven to 425°. Lightly grease a 13 x 9 x 2-inch baking pan.

4. Roll out pastry on a lightly floured surface to a 21 x 14-inch rectangle; trim excess and reserve. Cut into six 7-inch squares; place apple in center of each square. Press pastry firmly around apple. Brush with part of the beaten yolk. Place in prepared pan.

5. Roll out pastry trimmings; cut out leaf shapes with hors d'ouevre cutter or knife. Cut out six 1 x ¼-inch wide strips. Press 1 strip on center top of dumpling and arrange leaves around "stem". Brush with remaining beaten egg yolk.

6. Bake in a preheated hot oven (425°) for 45 minutes or until apples are tender and pastry is golden. Serve warm with Custard Sauce.

CRANBERRY-PECAN TURNOVERS

Bake at 375° for 18 minutes.
Makes 18 turnovers.

½ cup sugar
½ cup water
1½ cups fresh or frozen cranberries (½ package)
¼ cup golden raisins, chopped
¼ cup chopped pecans
1½ cups unbleached all-purpose flour
2 tablespoons sugar

½ teaspoon baking powder
⅛ teaspoon salt
½ cup vegetable shortening
¼ cup milk
1 egg
1½ teaspoons water
Confectioners' Frosting (recipe below), optional

1. Heat sugar and water in a large saucepan, stirring until sugar is dissolved. Bring to a boil; add cranberries. Boil for 10 minutes, stirring frequently until sauce thickens.

2. Add raisins. Cook for 2 to 3 minutes at medium heat, stirring. Remove from heat. Stir in pecans. Cool completely.

3. Preheat oven to 375°. Combine flour, sugar, baking powder, and salt in a large bowl. Cut in shortening with a pastry blender or fork until mixture is crumbly. Add milk. Stir with fork just until pastry holds together and forms a ball. Turn out onto a lightly floured surface and knead 4 or 5 times until smooth.

4. Roll to a ¹⁄₁₆- to ⅛-inch thick sheet on a lightly floured surface. Cut into eighteen 3-inch circles. Place on ungreased cookie sheets. Top circles with a level teaspoon of filling.

5. Mix egg and water in a cup; brush edges of pastry circles. Fold circle in half and press edges together with tines of fork to seal. Brush tops with egg-water mixture.

6. Bake in a preheated moderate oven (375°) for 18 minutes or until crust is a light golden brown. Drizzle with Confectioners' Frosting, if you wish. Serve warm or at room temperature.

Confectioners' Frosting: Blend 1 cup 10X (confectioners') sugar with 2 tablespoons milk or cream in a small bowl.

PINEAPPLE-CREAM CHEESE PUFFS

Easy-to-make puffs hold a tempting filling.

Bake at 400° for 40 minutes.
Makes 8 puffs.

¾ **cup water**
6 **tablespoons butter or margarine**
1 **teaspoon granulated sugar**
¼ **teaspoon salt**
¾ **cup unbleached or bread flour**
3 **eggs**
2 **cans (8 ounces each) crushed pineapple in pineapple juice**
1 **package (8 ounces) cream cheese**
½ **cup heavy cream**
3 **tablespoons 10X (confectioners') sugar**
⅓ **cup flaked coconut**
½ **recipe Chocolate Glaze (page 287)**

1. Heat water, butter, sugar, and salt in a medium-size saucepan to a full boil.

2. Add flour all at once. Stir vigorously with a wooden spoon until mixture forms a thick smooth paste that leaves side of pan clean, about 1 minute. Remove from heat; cool slightly.

3. Preheat oven to 400°. Add eggs, 1 at a time, beating well after each addition, until paste is smooth.

4. Drop paste by rounded tablespoonsful into 8 even mounds, 2 inches apart, on an ungreased large cookie sheet.

5. Bake in a preheated hot oven (400°) for 40 minutes or until puffed and golden brown. Remove to wire rack; cool completely.

6. Make filling: Drain juice from pineapple, reserving ¼ cup. Soften cream cheese in a medium-size bowl. Beat in reserved pineapple juice until smooth; stir in pineapple. Beat cream with 10X sugar in a small bowl until stiff. Fold whipped cream and coconut into cream cheese.

7. Cut a slice from top of each puff; remove any filaments of soft dough. Spoon filling into puffs, dividing evenly; replace tops. Just before serving, spoon Chocolate Glaze over each puff or simply sieve 10X sugar over top.

PUMPKIN-ORANGE-CHEESE PIE

Bake at 350° for 35 minutes.
Makes 8 servings.

½ package piecrust mix
4 packages (3 ounces each) cream cheese, softened
¾ cup firmly packed brown sugar
2 eggs
1 teaspoon ground cinnamon
¼ teaspoon ground nutmeg

1 teaspoon grated orange rind
1 can (16 ounces) solid pack cooked pumpkin
Dairy sour cream
Glacéed Orange Slices (recipe below)
Chopped pistachio nuts

1. Prepare piecrust mix following label directions for a 9-inch pastry shell with a high fluted edge.

2. Preheat oven to 425°. Beat cream cheese and sugar in a large bowl with an electric mixer, until light and fluffy. Beat in eggs, 1 at a time. Stir in cinnamon, nutmeg, orange rind, and pumpkin until smooth. Pour mixture into prepared pastry shell.

3. Place in a preheated hot oven (425°); lower temperature to moderate (350°). Bake for 35 minutes or until center is almost set. Cool completely on a wire rack. Just before serving, top with sour cream and halved Glacéed Orange Slices; sprinkle with pistachio nuts.

Glacéed Orange Slices: Combine ½ cup sugar and 2 tablespoons water in a small skillet; boil 1 minute. Add 4 thin orange slices; cook over low heat, turning slices several times, until they are almost translucent, about 5 minutes. Cool on wire rack.

FRENCH CRULLERS

Makes about 1 dozen crullers.

1 cup water
¼ cup (½ stick) butter or margarine
¼ cup sugar
½ teaspoon salt

1 cup *sifted* all-purpose flour
3 eggs
Vegetable oil for frying
Honey Glaze (page 286)

1. Combine water, butter, sugar, and salt in a large saucepan; bring to a boil.

2. Add flour all at once. Stir vigorously just until mixture leaves side of pan. Remove from heat. Add eggs, 1 at a time, beating well after each addition. Refrigerate mixture 15 minutes.
3. Cut twelve 3-inch squares of aluminum foil; oil each. Fit pastry bag with a ½-inch star tube; fill with dough. Press a 3-inch ring of dough onto each square.
4. Fill a large saucepan or a high-sided large skillet ½ full with vegetable oil. Heat to 370° on a deep-fat thermometer. Hold ring of dough close to surface of oil; carefully slip from foil into oil. Or, drop dough and foil into hot oil. Crullers will slip off foil as they cook; remove foil with tongs. Fry 3 at a time, turning once, about 3 to 5 minutes or until golden and puffed. Remove with tongs. Drain on paper toweling; cool.
5. Dip top half of crullers into Honey Glaze, letting excess drip back into bowl. Place, glazed side up, on a wire rack over wax paper. Let crullers stand until dry.

CREAM PUFF PASTE (Pâte à Choux)

*Makes 12 large cream puffs or 12 large éclairs or
2 Viennese Mocha-Nut Crowns.*

1 **cup water**	¼ **teaspoon salt**
½ **cup (1 stick) butter or margarine**	1 **cup** *sifted* **all-purpose flour**
	4 **eggs**

1. Heat water, butter, and salt to a rolling boil in a large saucepan.
2. Add flour all at once. Stir vigorously with a wooden spoon until mixture forms a thick, smooth ball that leaves the side of pan clean (about 1 minute). Remove from heat; cool slightly.
3. Add eggs, 1 at a time, beating well after each addition, until paste is shiny and smooth. (Paste will separate as you add each egg, but with continued beating, it will smooth out.)
4. Shape, following recipe instructions.

VIENNESE MOCHA-NUT CROWN

A regal dessert that would have pleased the Emperor Franz Joseph himself; truly a royal treat.

Bake at 400° for 40 minutes.
Makes one ring, 6 servings.

½ recipe Cream Puff Paste
(page 73)

Chocolate Praline Filling:
½ cup hazelnuts or almonds,
unblanched
⅓ cup granulated sugar
⅓ cup water
2 cups heavy cream

⅓ cup unsweetened cocoa
powder
½ cup 10X (confectioners')
sugar
½ recipe Chocolate Glaze
(page 287)
Coffee Butter Cream
(page 288)
Whole nuts (optional)

1. Preheat oven to 400°. Make Cream Puff Paste. Make a 7-inch ring with vegetable shortening on an ungreased cookie sheet. Spoon paste in 6 mounds, just inside circle. Or, press paste through a pastry bag. Puffs should almost touch.

2. Bake in a preheated hot oven (400°) for 40 minutes or until puffed and golden brown. With a small knife, make slits in ring to let steam escape. Turn off heat; leave ring in oven 5 minutes longer. Remove to wire rack; cool completely.

3. Make Chocolate Praline Filling: Combine nuts, sugar, and water in a small heavy skillet. Bring to a boil, stirring constantly. Boil rapidly, uncovered, until nuts make a popping sound, about 10 minutes. Remove from heat; stir with a wooden spoon until sugar crystallizes and becomes dry. Return pan to heat; cook over low heat until sugar starts to melt and form a glaze on nuts. Turn out onto a cookie sheet; separate with a fork; cool completely. Crush with a rolling pin or whirl in a blender until almost powdery. Beat cream with cocoa and 10X sugar in a large bowl until stiff; fold in crushed nuts; chill.

4. To assemble: Split ring in half horizontally. Scoop out any filaments of soft dough.

5. Place bottom half of ring on serving plate. Spread with Chocolate Praline Filling. Place top of ring in place. Spoon Chocolate Glaze over each puff. Decorate top with small rosettes of Coffee Butter Cream. Garnish with whole nuts, if you wish. Refrigerate 1 hour or until ready to serve.

NAPOLEONS

This golden pastry is layered with a creamy vanilla filling.

Bake at 450° for 15 minutes, then 350° for 45 minutes.
Makes 12 pastries.

Basic French Pastry
(page 76)
Royal Cream Filling
(page 284)
Vanilla Sugar Glaze
(page 287)

⅓ **cup semisweet chocolate**
pieces
1 **teaspoon vegetable**
shortening

1. Roll out Basic French Pastry evenly to a 16 x 10-inch rectangle, on a floured pastry cloth or board. Pastry should be ⅜ inch thick. Trim to make a 15 x 9-inch rectangle. Divide in half lengthwise.; cut each half into 6 even-size blocks. Place on cookie sheets; prick with fork; chill 30 minutes.

2. Preheat oven to 450°.

3. Bake pastries in a preheated very hot oven (450°) for 15 minutes; reduce heat to moderate (350°); bake 45 minutes longer or until puffed and a rich brown. Cool completely on racks.

4. While pastry bakes, make Royal Cream Filling.

5. When ready to fill, split each rectangle lengthwise into layers; put 2 layers together with Royal Cream Filling, leaving top plain.

6. Make Vanilla Sugar Glaze. Melt chocolate pieces with shortening in a small saucepan. Spread glaze on top of each pastry.

7. Spoon chocolate into a small wax paper cone; cut off tip to make a ⅛-inch opening. While glaze is still soft, pipe 3 thin lines of cholcolate crosswise over glaze then draw a knife tip in 2 even lines lengthwise through to make a feathered pattern. Place top pastry over filled layers. (Layers may be filled and frosted about 1 hour before serving; keep chilled.)

BASIC FRENCH PASTRY

The foundation of wispy-flaky patty shells, Napoleons, and pastry horns.

Makes 1 dozen 3-inch shells, 2 dozen pastry horns,
or 1 dozen Napoleons.

1   pound (4 sticks) butter, well
    chilled
4¼ cups *sifted* all-purpose flour

1   cup ice water
2   tablespoons lemon juice

1. Cut ½ pound (2 sticks) of the butter into the flour with a fork or pastry blender in a large bowl until mixture is crumbly and pale yellow. (Chill remaining 2 sticks butter for step 4.)

2. Stir ice water and lemon juice all at once into crumbly mixture. Continue stirring with fork until mixture is completely moistened and pastry is very stiff. Wrap in wax paper, foil, or plastic wrap; chill 30 minutes.

3. Unwrap the pastry and roll out to an 18 x 12-inch rectangle, on a well-floured pastry cloth or board. Pastry should be ¼ inch thick. Roll straight, lifting the rolling pin each time as you reach the edge, so pastry will be evenly thick.

4. Slice reserved ½ pound chilled butter into thin even pats over ⅔ of pastry to form a 12-inch square.

5. Fold uncovered ⅓ side of pastry over middle ⅓, as though folding an envelope. Fold opposite side over middle. Then fold pastry in thirds crosswise to make a block. Now you have 9 layers of pastry with pats of butter between each. Roll out again to an even, 18 x 12-inch rectangle; repeat folding as above; chill 30 minutes.

6. Repeat rolling, folding, and chilling 3 more times. Pastry is stiff and cold, so first pound firmly with your rolling pin to flatten, watching carefully to keep thickness even. After rolling and folding the last time, wrap and chill pastry overnight, or several days, then shape.

FOLLOW THESE SIMPLE STEPS
TO PUFF-PERFECT FRENCH PASTRY

• Take butter from the refrigerator *just* before using. It must be well chilled. Be sure to use only regular butter, *not* whipped butter or margarine, vegetable shortening, or the soft or diet margarines.

• Use ice water. Measure just before you add it.

• Roll pastry just to edges—not over them—to keep it evenly thick so it will puff evenly in baking.

• Use a ruler to measure rectangles; be sure to cut lines straight. Use your sharpest long-blade knife for cutting.

• Chill pastry well before each rolling; then chill 30 minutes after shaping and before baking it—this is one secret to its puffy, flaky, shattery, crispness.

• Cut off just the amount of pastry you'll need for each shaping. Keep the rest chilled. Avoid rerolling as pastry will not puff as high or as evenly. Don't waste the cuttings. Instead, shape with your hands into twists or rounds for canapé bases, or crispy treats with ice cream, cut-up fruit, pudding, or coffee.

• Follow baking directions carefully: A high temperature at first, then a lower temperature, is the secret to making pastry puff several times its height. Bake the pastries crisply all the way through—they should be rich, golden brown when they come from the oven.

• Bake pastries ahead, if you like, then store in a single layer in a tightly covered container. About 1 hour before filling or serving, recrisp for 10 minutes in a moderate oven (350°).

• Store any unbaked pastry in the freezer or refrigerator. To freeze: Wrap tightly in plastic wrap or foil, then thaw for 1 hour before shaping. Plan to use pastry within a month. To store in refrigerator: Wrap in waxed paper, aluminum foil, or plastic wrap. Plan to bake pastry within a week.

LEMONY CHEESE PIES

Bake at 450° then at 400° for 30 minutes.
Makes 8 pies.

1   container (15 ounces) ricotta   ½   teaspoon vanilla
     cheese, drained if necessary   ⅓   cup raisins
½   cup 10X (confectioners')   1   package (17¼ ounces)
     sugar   pre-rolled frozen puff pastry
1   egg yolk   1   egg white, lightly beaten
1   teaspoon grated lemon rind

1. Beat ricotta, 10X sugar, egg yolk, lemon rind, and vanilla in a small bowl until well blended; stir in raisins.

2. Thaw frozen pastry sheets 20 minutes at room temperature or until pliable, but still very cold. Roll out each sheet on a lightly floured surface to a 13-inch square; divide into 4 equal quarters; repeat with second sheet.

3. Divide filling equally among the 8 pastry squares, leaving a 1-inch border of uncovered pastry on all sides. Brush borders generously with some of the beaten egg white. Fold squares diagonally in half to form triangles. Press edges firmly together; then press with tines of fork to seal securely. Brush tops with egg white. Pierce each top in center with small paring knife to allow steam to escape. Arrange pies 1 inch apart on cookie sheets. Place in freezer while oven heats.

4. Preheat oven to 450°. Place pies in very hot (450°) oven. Immediately lower temperature to 400°. Bake pies for 30 minutes. Serve warm or at room temperature.

STRAWBERRY STRIPS

Tart, juicy strawberries top this ready-to-bake airy pastry.

Bake at 350° for 20 minutes.
Makes 16 strips.

½ of a 17¼ ounce package of pre-rolled frozen puff pastry (1 sheet)
Water
3 teaspoons sugar
½ recipe Instant Pastry Cream (page 289)

1 pint medium-size straw-berries, washed and hulled
¼ cup strawberry jelly
2 tablespoons chopped pistachio nuts

1. Thaw pastry sheet 20 minutes; place on a large cookie sheet; unfold.
2. Preheat oven to 350°. Cut pastry in half lengthwise. Cut a ½-inch lengthwise strip from the 2 long sides of each pastry rectangle; prick pastry sheet well with fork. Brush all 4 narrow strips with water. Press a strip, moistened-side down, along each of the 4 long sides of the 2 pastry rectangles to form "sides" to hold in the filling. Press strips down with tines of fork to make a decorative pattern; brush again with water; sprinkle with 2 teaspoons of the sugar.
3. Bake in a preheated moderate oven (350°) for 20 minutes or until light golden brown. Cool completely on a wire rack.
4. Spread ½ cup Instant Pastry Cream down length of each strip. Top with strawberries, pointed ends up, 2 to a row, to make 8 rows.
5. Melt strawberry jelly with the remaining 1 teaspoon sugar in a small skillet over low heat; let bubble ½ minute; cool slightly. Brush over strawberries to glaze, sprinkle nuts down sides of strawberry strips. Chill until serving time. Cut in serving pieces across rows of strawberries.

LINZER TORTE

A lovely, spicy almond pastry that holds a generous filling of
tart raspberry preserves.

Bake at 350° for 50 minutes.
Makes 12 servings.

1¾ cups *sifted* all-purpose flour
1 teaspoon ground cinnamon
¼ teaspoon ground cloves
¾ cup granulated sugar
1 can (4½ ounces) whole
  almonds, ground (1 cup)
¾ cup (1½ sticks) butter or
  margarine

1½ teaspoons grated lemon rind
2 egg yolks
1 teaspoon vanilla
1 jar (10 ounces) red raspberry
  jam
  Whole blanched almonds
  (optional)
  10X (confectioners') sugar

1. Sift flour, cinnamon, and cloves into a large bowl; add sugar and almonds. Cut in butter with a pastry blender or a fork until crumbly. Blend in lemon rind, egg yolks, and vanilla; knead a few times until smooth. Chill dough about 1 hour.

2. Press ⅔ of dough evenly on bottom and up 1 inch of the side of a 9-inch tart pan with a removable bottom. Spread ¾ of the jam over dough.

3. Preheat oven to 350°. Roll remaining pastry between 2 sheets of wax paper to 9 x 6-inch rectangle; cut lengthwise into 6 strips. Arrange strips over jam to form a lattice top. Press down all around to form rim. Arrange whole almonds on rim, if you wish.

4. Bake in a preheated moderate oven (350°) for 50 minutes or until browned. Cool 10 minutes on a wire rack. Remove outer rim of pan; cool completely. Fill lattices with remaining jam; sprinkle with 10X sugar before serving.

HONEY BUBBLES

Makes about 4 cups.

3 cups *sifted* all-purpose flour
1 tablespoon sugar
½ teaspoon salt
4 eggs
¼ cup (½ stick) butter or margarine, softened
Vegetable oil for frying

Honey Syrup (recipe below)
½ cup diced citron
¼ cup toasted pine nuts (optional)
1 to 2 tablespoons multicolored sprinkles

1. Sift flour, sugar, and salt into a large bowl; make a well in center of flour; add eggs and butter. Stir with a fork to mix flour gradually into eggs. When dough is stiff enough to handle, turn out onto a lightly floured surface and knead with your hands until very smooth and no longer sticky, about 5 minutes. Cover dough; refrigerate at least 1 hour.
2. Divide dough into 10 pieces; roll each piece into a rope about 18 inches long; cut each into about 36 small pieces.
3. Pour oil in a deep-fat fryer or heavy kettle to 3-inch depth. Heat to 375° on a deep-fat frying thermometer. Drop enough dough pieces into hot oil from a broad spatula to just cover the surface. Stir with a slotted spoon to separate. Cook until evenly golden, 2 to 3 minutes. Lift out with slotted spoon; drain on paper toweling.
4. Make Honey Syrup. Add the "bubbles" to Honey Syrup and stir with a rubber spatula or wooden spoon until syrup is absorbed and "bubbles" stick together. Add citron and pine nuts, if using. Pile onto a serving plate into a cone or ring or dome shape. Sprinkle with multicolored sprinkles.

Honey Syrup: Combine ¾ cup honey, ⅓ cup sugar, ⅓ cup water, and 1 tablespoon lemon juice in a large saucepan; bring to a boil, stirring constantly, until sugar dissolves. Continue cooking, uncovered, without stirring 15 minutes or until slightly thickened. Add rind or zest from 1 lemon, cut into julienne strips.

APPLE-NUT STRUDEL

It's always impressive—tissue-thin strudel dough twirled around
a buttery apple-nut filling.

Bake at 400° for 50 minutes.
Makes 8 servings.

3	cups *sifted* all-purpose flour	1	can (20 ounces) sliced apples, drained
¼	teaspoon salt		Or: 3 apples (approximately 2½ cups sliced)
1	egg		
¾	cup lukewarm water	¾	cup raisins
2	tablespoons vegetable oil	½	cup chopped walnuts
½	cup (1 stick) butter or margarine, melted	¾	cup granulated sugar
3	cups fresh white bread crumbs (6 slices)	1	teaspoon ground cinnamon 10X (confectioners') sugar

1. Sift flour and salt into a large bowl. Make a well in center of flour and add egg, water, and vegetable oil. Stir to make a sticky dough.
2. Place dough on a lightly floured board or pastry cloth. Slap dough down onto board; pick up; slap down again for 10 minutes to develop the gluten (as in bread), which gives the elasticity necessary for stretching dough. Cover dough with a bowl or towel and allow to rest 30 minutes.
3. Place a clean cloth or sheet on a kitchen or card table about 30 inches square. Sprinkle cloth with flour and rub in.
4. Roll out dough to as large a square as possible on floured cloth. Place hands, palm-sides down, under the dough and begin, gently, to stretch dough, moving around table until the dough has stretched over all corners of the table. (*Tip:* Remove your rings and watch to prevent making holes in the dough.)
5. Sprinkle dough with about 2 tablespoons of the melted butter. Measure 2 more tablespoons of the melted butter into a large skillet. Add bread crumbs and stir until crumbs are crisp and golden brown. Sprinkle crumbs over the entire surface of the dough. Preheat oven to 400°.
6. Combine apples, raisins, nuts, granulated sugar, and cinnamon in a large bowl. Spoon apple mixture in an even row down one end of dough, 2 inches in from the end of table.
7. Trim off thick parts of dough on all four overhanging sides with kitchen scissors.

8. Using the overhanging cloth to lift dough, roll dough just over filling. Fold the two parallel sides of dough toward center to enclose the filling completely.
9. Lift the cloth at filling end to allow dough to roll over and over on itself until completely rolled.
10. Line a large cookie sheet with a double thickness of heavy-duty aluminum foil. Ease filled roll onto cookie sheet, shaping roll into horseshoe shape. Turn up the ends of foil 1 inch all around cookie sheet to keep oven clean in case of spill-over.
11. Bake in a preheated hot oven (400°) for 50 minutes, brushing several times with remaining butter or until pastry is golden.
12. Allow pastry to cool 15 minutes and then slide onto serving board. Sprinkle with 10X sugar.

FLAKY STRUDEL DOUGH

The secret to light, flaky strudel is in stretching the dough paper-thin. (It should be so thin that you could slip a piece of newspaper underneath and be able to read it.) You may use either your fingers or fists to stretch the dough—whichever is easier.

ROLLING STRUDEL

Once the edge of the dough is covering the filling and the two adjacent sides are flipped over, roll up the strudel, exactly as you would a jelly roll.

FREEZING STRUDEL

Wrap cooled strudel in foil or plastic wrap; then freeze. To reheat, place frozen strudel on cookie sheet; cover loosely with foil. Place in moderate oven (350°) for 30 minutes; remove foil and heat 10 to 15 minutes longer.

BAKLAVA

Bake nuts at 350° for 10 minutes.
Bake at 325° for 50 minutes.
Makes about 3½ dozen pieces.

3   cups walnuts (about ¾ pound)
½   cup sugar
1½ teaspoons ground cinnamon
1   package (16 ounces) phyllo or strudel pastry leaves

½   cup (1 stick) unsalted butter or margarine, melted
1   tablespoon water
Honey Syrup (recipe follows)

1. Preheat oven to 350°. Place walnuts on a 15½ x 10 x 1-inch jelly roll pan; toast in a moderate oven (350°) for 10 minutes. Whirl walnuts, while still warm, ½ cup at a time, in the container of an electric blender until finely ground. (You may use a food grinder or food processor, if you wish.) Remove ground walnuts to a medium-size bowl. Repeat this procedure until all of the walnuts are ground. Mix in the sugar and ground cinnamon; set aside. Lower oven temperature to 325°.

2. Brush bottom of a 13 x 9 x 2-inch baking pan with some of the melted butter. Fold 2 phyllo leaves in half; place on the bottom of pan; brush with butter. Place 2 more folded leaves in pan; brush with butter. (Keep rest of pastry leaves covered with a clean damp kitchen towel to prevent drying out.)

3. Sprinkle top with ½ cup nut mixture. Add 2 more folded leaves; brush with butter.

4. Repeat step 3 five more times. Stack remaining leaves, brushing every other one. Brush top leaf with remaining butter; sprinkle with the 1 tablespoon water.

5. With a sharp knife, mark off the baklava. Cut through the top layer of the phyllo only, making 5 lengthwise cuts, 1½ inches apart (you will have 6 equal strips). Then cut diagonally again at 1½-inch intervals, making diamonds (9 strips).

6. Bake in a slow oven (325°) for 50 minutes or until top is golden. While baklava is baking, prepare Honey Syrup. Remove to a wire rack. Cut all the way through the diamonds, separating slightly. Pour cooled Honey Syrup over. Cool thoroughly in a pan on rack. Cover with aluminum foil; let stand at room temperature overnight for syrup to be absorbed. Baklava will keep in refrigerator up to 2 weeks.

HONEY SYRUP

Makes 2 cups.

1	small lemon	2	whole cloves
1	cup sugar	1	cup honey
1	cup water	1	tablespoon brandy (optional)
1	two-inch piece stick cinnamon		

1. Grate the rind from the lemon (the thin, yellow skin only) and reserve. Squeeze out 1½ teaspoons lemon juice into a small cup; set aside.

2. Place lemon rind, sugar, water, cinnamon stick, and cloves in a heavy medium-size saucepan. Bring to a boil. Lower heat; continue cooking, without stirring, 25 minutes or until mixture is syrupy (230° on a candy thermometer).

3. Stir in honey; pour through strainer into a 2-cup measure. Stir in reserved lemon juice and brandy. Cool.

CANNOLI

Cannoli shells are filled with creamy ricotta cheese and chocolate bits.

Makes 16 to 18 pastries.

1¾	cups *sifted* all-purpose flour	1	teaspoon vanilla
1	tablespoon granulated sugar	⅓	cup finely chopped candied orange peel
¼	teaspoon salt		
1	teaspoon ground cinnamon	3	squares semisweet chocolate, coarsely chopped
3	tablespoons wine vinegar		
3	tablespoons water	⅓	cup orange-flavored liqueur
1	egg	1	teaspoon ground cinnamon (optional)
2	tablespoons butter or margarine, softened		
		1	egg white
1	container (3 pounds) ricotta cheese		Vegetable oil for frying
		¼	cup chopped pistachio nuts
1½	cups sifted 10X (confectioners') sugar	1	tablespoon 10X (confectioners') sugar

1. Combine 1 cup of the flour, sugar, salt, and cinnamon in a medium-size bowl. Make a well in center of dry ingredients; add vinegar (it makes dough tender) and water; blend well. Beat in egg and butter.

2. Add remaining flour, ¼ cup at a time, until dough becomes a solid mass that can be easily lifted out of the bowl.

3. Knead dough on a lightly floured surface until it is soft and smooth, about 8 minutes, adding flour if necessary to prevent dough from sticking.

4. Wrap dough in plastic wrap. Chill in refrigerator for at least 1 hour.

5. Combine ricotta cheese, 10X sugar, vanilla, orange peel, chocolate, liqueur, and cinnamon, if using, in a large bowl; blend well. Chill until shells have been prepared.

6. Divide dough into 16 equal-size pieces. Roll each piece on a lightly floured surface to a round about ¹⁄₁₆ inch thick. *Tip:* If dough pulls back, allow it to relax for 2 minutes, then roll again.

7. Cut 4½-inch diameter circles from each piece using a saucer or lid for a pattern. When circles are all rolled, roll each again just before they ar placed on cannoli tube to give each circle an oval shape, about 5 inches long and 4½ inches wide.

8. Using metal cannoli tubes, place dough lengthwise on tube. Brush edges of dough with egg white, then press firmly to seal. *Note:* If cannoli forms are unavailabe, tear 18-inch wide heavy-duty aluminum foil into sixteen 6-inch lengths. Roll each piece, starting with the 6-inch side, around a 1-inch diameter broom handle or other similar form to shape into tubes. Wrap dough around foil tubes as directed above.

9. Pour 3 inches of oil in a deep-fat fryer or heavy kettle and heat to 375° on a deep-fat frying thermometer. Fry 2 or 3 cannoli shells at a time, depending on the size of the fryer or kettle, until golden brown, turning once. Remove with tongs or slotted spoon to paper toweling. Gently remove cannoli from forms; cool completely.

10. Fill each shell with ⅓ cup filling using a small spoon or pastry bag fitted with a large plain tip. Dip ends into nuts. Sprinkle with 10X sugar.

3

Cookies

Awell-filled cookie jar is always a delightful sight not only for children but for grownups as well. Cookies are ideal to keep on hand for a simple after-meal treat or lunchtime dessert. Cookies are a perfect accompaniment with light desserts such as ice cream or pudding.

Almost all cookies are easy to make and to store. The easiest ones to bake are bar-type cookies. They may be mixed in one bowl or sauce-pan and baked in one pan, and there's no rolling or cutting or greasing cookie sheets to deal with. No wonder they are so popular with cooks.

Drop and bake cookies include the popular chocolate chip and oatmeal raisin. Drop cookies are made from a soft dough which is pushed off a spoon onto a cookie sheet. Because of this, their shape tends to be irregular so space the cookies far enough apart on the sheet to allow for expansion or spreading.

Rolled cookies require a stiff dough that is rolled out and cut into cookies. For a tender cookie, chill dough well so that additional flour is not necessary when rolling. The dough should be handled as little as possible with unused portions left chilling in the refrigerator.

Cut out the cookies as close together as possible to get more from the first rolling. Cookies made from the trimmings will not be as tender as those cut from the first rolling.

Shaped or molded cookies are time consuming because each must be formed. The soft dough may be molded into balls, piped through a pastry bag, or pressed through a cookie gun. Spritz cookies, shortbread, and cookie pretzels are all examples of this type of cookie.

Refrigerator cookies, which are also called slice-and-bake cookies, are made of a stiff dough that is formed into a roll and refrigerated until firm enough to slice easily. This dough can be made ahead and baked when needed. You can roll two flavors of dough together to make pinwheel cookies or stack different flavors to form striped cookies.

In this cookie chapter, you'll find a deep-fried cookie called Swedish Rosettes. Though Scandinavian in origin, these delicate pastry-like cookies are popular all over the country. During the warm summer months you may want to make no-bake cookies, which rely on cookie crumbs. They may be molded into balls or pressed into a pan and cut into bars and are great for children to make.

This collection of cookie recipes will appeal to all ages, and some are ideal for holiday baking. More cookie recipes can be found in the Chocolate and Cake and Cookie Decorating chapters.

CARROT BROWNIES

Bake at 350° for 30 minutes.
Makes 32 squares.

½ cup (1 stick) butter	2 eggs
1½ cups firmly packed light brown sugar	2 cups finely grated carrots
	½ cup chopped walnuts
2 cups *sifted* all-purpose flour	Cream Cheese Frosting
2 teaspoons baking powder	(recipe below)
½ teaspoons salt	Walnut halves (optional)

1. Melt butter in a large saucepan. Add brown sugar; stir until blended. Remove from heat; cool slightly.

2. Sift flour, baking powder, and salt onto wax paper. Grease two 8 x 8 x 2-inch baking pans. Preheat oven to 350°.

3. Beat eggs into cooled butter mixture 1 at a time. Stir in flour mixture, blending well. Add carrots and walnuts, mixing well. Pour into prepared pans.

4. Bake in a preheated moderate oven (350°) for 30 minutes or until centers spring back when lightly pressed with fingertip. Cool 10 minutes in pans on wire racks. Remove from pans; cool completely.

5. Frost tops with Cream Cheese Frosting. Cut into squares and top each square with a walnut half, if you wish.

Cream Cheese Frosting: Combine 2 ounces (⅔ of a 3-ounce package) softened cream cheese with ⅓ cup softened butter; beat until smooth. Stir in 1 teaspoon vanilla and 1½ cups 10X (confectioners') sugar until fluffy and smooth. Makes 1 cup.

CRACKING WALNUTS

For perfect walnut halves, try opening walnuts using a clam knife instead of a nutcracker. A nutcracker tends to crush not only the shell but the nut kernel.

SOUTHERN-STYLE BUTTERSCOTCH BROWNIES

Bake at 350° for 30 minutes, then at 550° for 3 minutes.
Makes 16 squares.

¾ cup *sifted* all-purpose flour
1 teaspoon baking powder
½ teaspoon salt
¼ cup (½ stick) butter or margarine
¾ cup firmly packed light brown sugar

2 eggs
1 teaspoon vanilla
½ cup coarsely chopped walnuts
Coconut Topping (recipe below)

1. Grease a 8 x 8 x 2-inch baking pan. Preheat oven to 350°. Sift flour, baking powder, and salt onto wax paper.

2. Melt butter in a medium-size saucepan over moderate heat. Remove from heat; stir in brown sugar with a spoon until blended; beat in eggs and vanilla.

3. Stir in flour mixture and walnuts until thoroughly combined. Pour into prepared pan.

4. Bake in a preheated moderate oven (350°) for 30 minutes or until center springs back when lightly pressed with fingertip. Remove from oven; raise temperature to broil (550°). Prepare Coconut Topping and spread evenly on warm brownies. Place pan of brownies with tops 3 inches from broiler heat; broil for 3 minutes or just until sugar is melted and top is a light golden brown. Cut into squares. Serve warm or at room temperature.

Coconut Topping: Combine ¼ cup (½ stick) butter or margarine, ½ cup firmly packed light brown sugar, and 1 cup shredded coconut in a small bowl.

PEANUT BUTTER BROWNIES

Bake at 350° for 35 minutes.
Makes 24 squares.

1 cup peanut butter
½ cup (1 stick) butter or margarine, softened
2 cups firmly packed light brown sugar

3 eggs
1 teaspoon vanilla
1 cup *sifted* all-purpose flour
½ teaspoon salt

1. Grease a 13 x 9 x 2-inch baking pan. Preheat oven to 350°.
2. Beat peanut butter and butter in a large bowl with an electric mixer until well blended. Add sugar, eggs, and vanilla; beat until fluffy and light. Stir in flour and salt until well blended. Spread batter in prepared baking pan.
3. Bake in a preheated moderate oven (350°) for 30 to 35 minutes or until golden brown. Cool in pan on a wire rack. Cut into 24 brownies.

LINZER TARTS

Easy-to-make little pan cookie versions of the famous torte from Austria.

Bake at 350° for 30 minutes.
Makes 5 dozen bars.

1¼ cups (2½ sticks) butter or margarine, softened	2⅔ cups *sifted* all-purpose flour
¾ cup sugar	1 cup ground unblanched almonds (about ⅔ cup whole almonds)
1 teaspoon grated lemon rind	2½ cups raspberry preserves
¼ teaspoon ground cinnamon	
1 egg	
5 hard-cooked egg yolks, sieved	

1. Beat butter, sugar, lemon rind, cinnamon, egg, and sieved yolks in a medium-size bowl until light and fluffy. Stir in flour and almonds until well blended. Cover; refrigerate 1 hour or until dough is cold and firm enough to handle easily.
2. Preheat oven to 350°.
3. Press ⅔ of the dough in an even layer on bottom and up sides of an ungreased 15½ x 10½ x 1-inch jelly roll pan. Spread preserves evenly over dough. Roll remaining dough, a small portion at a time, with palms of hands on a floured surface into very thin strips, about ¼ inch in diameter. Arrange strips on preserves to form a diamond pattern.
4. Bake in a preheated moderate oven (350°) for 30 minutes or until pastry is golden brown. Cool in pan on a wire rack. Cut into 2 x 1¼-inch rectangles to serve.

HONEY DATE-NUT BARS

Bake at 350° for 35 minutes.
Makes 28 bars.

1½ cups *sifted* all-purpose flour
1 teaspoon baking powder
½ teaspoon salt
1 package (8 ounces) pitted dates, snipped into tiny pieces
1 cup coarsley chopped walnuts
2 tablespoons chopped crystallized ginger
3 eggs
1 cup honey
Cream Cheese Topping (recipe below)
⅓ cup chopped walnuts

1. Sift flour, baking powder, and salt onto wax paper. Combine dates, 1 cup walnuts, and ginger in a bowl; coat with 2 tablespoons of the flour mixture. Grease a 13 x 9 x 2-inch baking pan. Preheat oven to 350°.
2. Beat eggs in a large bowl until frothy; stir in honey. Stir in flour mixture just until well blended. Fold in date and nut mixture. Pour into prepared pan.
3. Bake in a preheated moderate oven (350°) for 35 minutes or until center springs back when lightly pressed with fingertip. Cool on a wire rack. Cover; let stand overnight.
4. Spread with Cream Cheese Topping; sprinkle with nuts.

Cream Cheese Topping: Beat 1 package (8 ounces) softened cream cheese with 2 tablespoons honey.

LONDON FRUIT BARS

Bake at 350° for 35 minutes.
Makes 4 dozen bars.

2 containers (8 ounces each) candied fruits
2 cups raisins, chopped
¾ cup port, sherry, or Madeira
1½ cups *sifted* all-purpose flour
½ teaspoon baking soda
2½ teaspoons apple pie spice
Or: combination of ground cinnamon, cloves, and nutmeg
6 tablespoons butter, softened
1 cup firmly packed light brown sugar
2 eggs

1. Combine fruits, raisins, and wine in a large bowl; cover; let stand overnight.
2. Grease and flour a 15½ x 10½ x 1-inch jelly roll pan. Preheat oven to 350°. Sift flour, baking soda, and spice onto wax paper. Beat butter, sugar, and eggs until fluffy. Stir in flour and fruit mixtures. Spread batter in prepared jelly roll pan.
3. Bake in a preheated moderate oven (350°) for 35 minutes. Cool on a wire rack; cut into bars.

PRUNE-OATMEAL BARS

Bake at 350° for 35 to 40 minutes.
Makes about 18 bars.

1 package (12 ounces) pitted prunes	¾ cup *sifted* all-purpose flour
⅓ cup granulated sugar	¼ teaspoon salt
1 teaspoon grated orange rind	¼ teaspoon ground cloves
1 tablespoon orange juice	¼ teaspoon ground cinnamon
1½ cups quick oats	½ cup (1 stick) butter or margarine
½ cup firmly packed light brown sugar	

1. Cook prunes following label directions; drain; chop and mix with granulated sugar, orange rind, and juice in a medium-size heavy saucepan. Cook, stirring constantly, over low heat until thick. Cool. Preheat oven to 350°.
2. Combine oats, brown, sugar, flour, salt, cloves, and cinnamon in a bowl; blend in butter until mixture is crumbly.
3. Press 1½ cups crumb mixture into bottom of an 8 x 8 x 2-inch baking pan, using spatula. Spread with prune mixture; then sprinkle remaining crumbs over, pressing down lightly.
4. Bake in a preheated moderate oven (350°) for 35 to 40 minutes. Cool completely on a wire rack; cut into bars.

MICROWAVE BUTTER OR CREAM CHEESE

To soften butter or cream cheese in a hurry, put it on a plate in a microwave oven for a few seconds.

DANISH SPICE COOKIES

Bake at 350° for 30 minutes.
Makes about 4 dozen cookies.

2	cups *sifted* all-purpose flour	1	cup firmly packed brown
½	teaspoon salt		sugar
¼	teaspoon baking soda	½	cup dairy sour cream
1	teaspoon ground cinnamon	1	egg
¼	teaspoon ground cloves	1	teaspoon vanilla
½	cup (1 stick) butter or	1	cup chopped dates
	margarine	½	cup finely chopped walnuts

1. Grease a 15½ x 10½ x 1-inch jelly roll pan. Preheat oven to 350°. Sift flour, salt, baking soda, cinnamon, and cloves onto wax paper.
2. Melt butter in a medium-size saucepan over moderate heat. Remove from heat. Add sugar and beat with a wooden spoon until combined. Beat in sour cream, egg, and vanilla until smooth.
3. Stir in flour mixture until thoroughly combined; stir in dates and nuts. Spread evenly in prepared jelly roll pan.
4. Bake in a preheated moderate oven (350°) for 30 minutes or until center springs back when lightly touched with fingertip. Cool in pan on a wire rack. Cut into diamond shapes.

APPLE SQUARES

Bake at 350° for 30 minutes.
Makes 16 squares.

1	cup *sifted* all-purpose flour	½	cup granulated sugar
1	teaspoon baking powder	1	egg
¼	teaspoon salt	1	teaspoon vanilla
¼	teaspoon ground cinnamon	½	cup chopped, pared cooking
¼	cup (½ stick) butter or		apple
	margarine	½	cup finely chopped walnuts
½	cup firmly packed light		Cinnamon Sugar
	brown sugar		(recipe below)

1. Grease an 8 x 8 x 2-inch baking pan. Preheat oven to 350°. Sift flour, baking powder, salt, and cinnamon onto wax paper.
2. Melt butter in a medium-size saucepan over moderate heat. Remove from heat. Beat in both sugars, egg, and vanilla with a wooden spoon until smooth.

3. Stir in flour mixture, apple, and walnuts until thoroughly combined. Spread in prepared pan. Sprinkle with 1 tablespoon of the Cinnamon Sugar mixture.

4. Bake in a preheated moderate oven (350°) for 30 minutes or until center springs back when lightly pressed with fingertip. Cool completely in pan on a wire rack. Cut into squares.

Cinnamon Sugar: Combine ½ cup granulated sugar with 1½ teaspoons ground cinnamon in a small jar with a screw-top lid. Cover; shake thoroughly. Store remainder for future use for French toast, pancakes, fruit topped desserts, etc.

COCONUT MACAROONS

Bake at 300° for 20 minutes.
Makes 3 dozen.

2	egg whites	1	cup chopped walnuts
¼	teaspoon salt	½	cup quick oats
½	cup granulated sugar	8	maraschino cherries,
½	cup firmly packed dark		chopped
	brown sugar	½	teaspoon vanilla
1	can (3½ ounces) flaked		
	coconut		

1. Beat egg whites and salt with an electric mixer in a medium-size bowl until foamy-white and double in volume; add both sugars, 1 tablespoon at a time, beating until stiff peaks form. Grease 2 cookie sheets. Preheat oven to 300°.

2. Fold coconut, walnuts, oats, cherries, and vanilla into meringue. Drop by teaspoonfuls, 1 inch apart, on prepared cookie sheets.

3. Bake in a preheated slow oven (300°) for 20 minutes or just until set. Cool on cookie sheets 2 minutes; then remove carefully with spatula to wire racks; cool.

FRESHENING DRIED COCONUT

To freshen up dried-out shredded coconut, place coconut in a vegetable steamer over boiling water. It will become moist and fresh enough to use.

AMARETTI

Bake at 325° for 45 minutes.
Makes 3 dozen cookies.

1 can or package (8 ounces) almond paste
2 egg whites
Pinch salt
1 teaspoon vanilla

1 cup *sifted* 10X (confectioners') sugar
1 tablespoon coarse sugar crystals

1. Grease 2 large cookie sheets; dust with flour; tap off any excess. Preheat oven to 325°.

2. Break up almond paste with fingers into a small bowl. Add egg whites, salt, and vanilla. Beat with an electric mixer on low speed until mixture is smooth. Add 10X sugar slowly, beating on low speed until a soft dough forms.

3. Fit a pastry bag with a small round tip. Fill with dough. Pipe dough out in small rounds or drop by teaspoonfuls on prepared cookie sheets.

4. For a cracked top: Dip fingertip into water; pat over tops; sprinkle with coarse sugar crystals.

5. Bake in a preheated slow oven (325°) for 45 minutes or until golden brown. Remove to wire racks with a spatula to cool. Store in an airtight tin.

STORING COOKIES

Store *soft* cookies in a container with a tight-fitting lid. *Bar* cookies can be kept in their baking pan, but seal the pan in a plastic bag. If the cookies dry out, add a piece of apple or bread to the container. Store *crisp* cookies in a container with a loose-fitting cover if you live in an area with low humidity. In muggy weather or areas of high humidity, store crisp cookies in an airtight container. If cookies do soften, heat in a 300° oven about 5 minutes to crisp them.

SUNFLOWER-OATMEAL COOKIES

Bake at 350° for 12 minutes.
Makes about 2 dozen jumbo cookies.

1½ cups *sifted* all-purpose flour
½ cup instant nonfat dry milk powder
1 teaspoon baking soda
½ teaspoon salt
1 cup (2 sticks) butter or margarine
1 cup granulated sugar

1 cup firmly packed light brown sugar
2 eggs
1 teaspoon vanilla
3 cups quick oats
¾ cup dry-roasted sunflower seeds

1. Lightly grease 2 cookie sheets. Preheat oven to 350°. Sift flour, dry milk powder, baking soda, and salt onto wax paper.
2. Beat butter and both sugars in a large bowl with an electric mixer until light and fluffy; beat in eggs, 1 at a time; add vanilla.
3. Add flour mixture, blending well; fold in oats and sunflower seeds.
4. Measure out cookie mix with a ¼-cup metal measure onto prepared cookie sheets (4 to a cookie sheet). Flatten to a 3½-inch round with a fork.*
5. Bake in a preheated moderate oven (350°) for 12 minutes or until golden. Remove from oven; let stand 1 minute on cookie sheet. Remove with wide spatula to a wire rack. Cool completely.

Note: Cookie dough can be store, covered, in the refrigerator up to a week and baked when convenient.

*Cookies can be dropped by teaspoonfuls onto greased cookie sheets. Bake at 350° for 10 minutes or until golden. Makes about 7 dozen.

SOFTENING HARD BROWN SUGAR

To soften brown sugar that has hardened, wrap in foil and put in a preheated 350° oven for 5 minutes, or wrap in plastic and put in a microwave oven for 2 minutes on low power. The sugar will soften enough to measure and use, but it will quickly harden again. To store it, place in an airtight container with a heel of bread or slice of apple.

SUGAR AND SPICE JUMBO COOKIES

Bake at 400° for 10 minutes.
Makes 2 dozen four-inch cookies.

4	cups *sifted* all-purpose flour	1	cup (2 sticks) butter or
3	teaspoon baking powder		margarine
1	teaspoon baking soda	2	cups sugar
1	teaspoon salt	2	eggs
½	teaspoon ground cinnamon	¼	cup milk
½	teaspooon ground nutmeg	2	teaspoons vanilla

1. Sift flour, baking powder, baking soda, salt, cinnamon, and nutmeg onto wax paper.

2. Beat butter, sugar, and eggs in a large bowl with an electric mixer until light and fluffy. Beat in milk and vanilla. Stir in flour mixture until well blended.

3. Turn dough out onto a large board. Divide in half, shape into equal balls; wrap each half in wax paper and chill 3 hours or until firm enough to roll.

4. Preheat oven to 400°. Roll dough, one half at a time, to ¼-inch thickness on a lightly floured surface. Cut into rounds with a 4-inch scalloped cutter. (You can use the top of a 3-pound vegetable shortening can, cutting around with a small sharp knife.)

5. Place cookies on an ungreased large cookie sheet (5 to a sheet).

6. Bake in upper third of a preheated hot oven (400°) for 10 minutes or until lightly browned. Cool on wire racks.

CHOOSING A COOKIE SHEET

Choose shiny cookie sheets rather than dark ones for baking cookies. Dark ones absorb heat quickly causing cookies to overbrown on the bottom. For even baking, use cookie sheets about 2 inches smaller or shorter than your oven to allow space all around the edges for heat circulation. When baking one sheet at a time, place oven rack in center; if baking two sheets, place racks so they divide oven in thirds. If you run out of cookie sheets, use inverted baking pans or cut a piece of foil or parchment paper to fit your cookie sheet. While the cookie sheet of cookies bakes, drop more dough onto foil or parchment; then place foil or parchment on cookie sheet as it comes from the oven and is emptied.

LEMON TUILES

These delicate cookies are shaped to resemble the curved roof tiles on European buildings.

Bake at 325° for 6 minutes.
Makes 5 dozen cookies.

1	can (6 ounces) sliced blanched almonds	¼	cup *unsifted* all-purpose flour
4	egg whites, at room temperature	6	tablespoons clarified butter*
½	cup sugar	2	teaspoons grated lemon rind
		¼	teaspoon almond extract

1. Lightly grease 3 cookie sheets. Preheat oven to 325°.

2. Grind ½ cup of the almonds in the container of an electric blender. Reserve remaining sliced almonds for step 6.

3. Beat egg whites in a medium-size bowl until foamy; beat in sugar, 1 tablespoon at a time, until meringue forms soft peaks.

4. Sift flour over meringue, folding in gently.

5. Fold in butter a little at a time. Fold in the ground almonds, lemon rind, and almond extract; blend thoroughly.

6. Drop batter by slightly rounded teaspoonful onto prepared cookie sheets 3 inches apart (6 to a sheet). Spread each with a small metal spatula to a 2½-inch circle. Sprinkle cookies with a little of the reserved sliced almonds.

7. Bake in a preheated slow oven (325°) for 6 minutes or until lightly browned around edges. Remove from oven. Using metal spatula, carefully loosen cookies from sheet, one at a time, and curve, almond side up, over a rolling pin (set rolling pin on grooves of a wire rack to prevent rolling). Remove when cool. Repeat with remaining batter.

*To clarify butter: Melt ½ cup (1 stick) butter in a small saucepan; cool slightly. Measure out 6 tablespoons of the clear oily liquid, leaving milky solids in the cup.

COOLING COOKIES

When cookies are baked, remove from sheets onto a wire rack to cool. Do not overlap cookies until they are firm and cool.

BUTTER COOKIE STARS

Bake at 375° for 10 minutes.
Makes about 8 dozen cookies.

2¼ cups *sifted* all-purpose flour
¼ teaspoon baking soda
¼ teaspoon salt
½ cup (1 stick) unsalted butter, softened
½ cup sugar
1 egg
1 tablespoon lemon juice
Butter Cookie Frosting (page 276)
Silver dragees

1. Combine flour, baking soda, and salt on wax paper. Beat butter, sugar, egg, and lemon juice in a large bowl until fluffy. Stir in flour mixture until well blended. Cover; refrigerate 1 hour or until dough is cold and firm enough to handle easily.

2. Grease cookie sheets. Preheat oven to 375°.

3. Roll dough, ¼ at a time, on a lightly floured surface to ⅛-inch thickness. Cut out with a star-shaped cookie cutter. Place 1 inch apart on prepared cookie sheets.

4. Bake in a preheated moderate oven (375°) for 10 minutes or until lightly browned around edges. Remove from cookie sheets; cool on wire racks. Decorate with Butter Cookie Frosting, tinted or plain, piped around edges, and silver dragees.

CINNAMON CARDS

Bake at 350° for 10 minutes.
Makes about 4½ dozen cookies.

1 cup plus 2 tablespoons *sifted* all-purpose flour
1 teaspoon ground cinnamon
¼ cup (½ stick) unsalted butter, softened
⅓ cup sugar
1 egg yolk
1 tablespoon dark corn syrup
2 ounces (1½ package) sweet cooking chocolate, grated
Vanilla Sugar Glaze (page 287)
Miniature semisweet chocolate pieces

1. Combine flour and cinnamon on wax paper. Beat butter, sugar, egg yolk, and corn syrup in a medium-size bowl until fluffy. Stir in flour mixture and grated chocolate until well blended. Cover; refrigerate about 1 hour or until dough is cold and firm enough to handle easily.

2. Lightly grease 2 cookie sheets. Preheat oven to 350°.

3. Roll dough, ¼ at a time on a lightly floured surface, until slightly less than ⅛ inch thick. Cut dough into 2 x 1¼-inch rectangles. Place 1 inch apart on prepared cookie sheets.

4. Bake in a preheated moderate oven (350°) for 10 minutes or until lightly browned. Remove from cookie sheets; cool on wire racks. Spread cooled cookies with Vanilla Sugar Glaze; decorate with chocolate pieces to resemble playing cards.

NUTMEG LEAVES

Bake at 350° for 8 minutes.
Makes 8 dozen cookies.

1½ cups *sifted* all-purpose flour	½ cup sugar
1 teaspoon baking powder	1½ tablespoons milk
½ teaspoon baking soda	1 teaspoon vanilla
½ teaspoon ground nutmeg	4 squares semisweet
½ cup (1 stick) butter or	chocolate, melted
margarine, softened	½ cup chopped pistachio nuts
1 egg	

1. Sift flour, baking powder, baking soda, and nutmeg onto wax paper.

2. Beat butter, egg, and sugar in a large bowl with an electric mixer until fluffy, about 3 minutes. Stir in milk and vanilla. Stir in flour mixture until blended and smooth. Chill several hours or overnight.

3. Preheat oven to 350°.

4. Roll out ¼ of the dough on a lightly floured surface to a ¼-inch thickness. Cut out dough with a small floured leaf-shape cookie cutter. Re-roll scraps of dough and cut out as many leaves as you can. Arrange on an ungreased cookie sheet, 1 inch apart. Repeat with remaining dough.

5. Bake in a preheated moderate oven (350°) for 8 minutes or until cookies are set and lightly browned. Cool on wire racks. Decorate with the melted chocolate and chopped pistachios.

GINGERBREAD COOKIES

Bake at 350° for 8 minutes.
Makes 6 dozen cookies.

5½ cups *sifted* all-purpose flour
1   teaspoon baking soda
1   teaspoon salt
2   teaspoons ground cinnamon
1   teaspoon ground ginger
1   teaspoon ground cloves
½   teaspoon ground nutmeg

1   cup vegetable shortening
1   cup sugar
1   cup molasses
1   egg
1   teaspoon vanilla
     Royal Frosting (page 277)

1. Sift flour, baking soda, salt, and spices onto wax paper.

2. Beat vegetable shortening with sugar until fluffy-light in a large bowl; beat in molasses, egg, and vanilla.

3. Stir in flour mixture, ⅓ at a time, blending well after each addition, to make a soft dough. Wrap dough in foil and chill 4 hours or overnight.

4. Preheat oven to 350°. Roll out dough, ¼ at a time, to a ⅛-inch thickness on a lightly floured surface. Cut with 3-inch cookie cutter.

5. Place 1 inch apart on ungreased cookie sheets.

6. Bake in a preheated moderate oven (350°) for 8 minutes or until cookies are firm but not too dark. Remove to wire racks with spatula; cool. Decorate with Royal Frosting and allow frosting to harden before storing.

PREPARING COOKIE SHEETS

Grease cookie sheets only when recipes instruct you to. Use shortening or nonstick cooking sprays. To avoid hard-to-wash brown patches baking onto your cookie sheets, grease only the spots where dough is to be placed, allowing space for spreading.

LEBKUCHEN

Store these spicy, fruited morsels a week or so to mellow and soften.
*Bake at 350° for 12 minutes for small cookies,
and 15 minutes for large cookies.
Makes 24 small cookies or 12 large cookies.*

¾	cup honey	½	teaspoon ground ginger
¾	cup firmly packed dark brown sugar	¼	teaspoon ground cloves
		½	teaspoon baking soda
1	egg	1	container (8 ounces) candied orange peel, chopped
2	teaspoons grated lemon rind		
3	tablespoons lemon juice	1	cup chopped unblanched almonds
3½	cups *sifted* all-purpose flour		
1	teaspoon salt		Lebkuchen Icing (page 285)
1	teaspoon ground cinnamon		Pecan halves
1	teaspoon ground nutmeg		Candied red cherries
½	teaspoon ground allspice		10X (confectioners') sugar

1. Heat honey to a boil in a small saucepan; pour into a large bowl; cool about 30 minutes.

2. Stir brown sugar, egg, lemon rind, and lemon juice into cooled honey, blending well.

3. Sift flour, salt, cinnamon, nutmeg, allspice, ginger, cloves, and baking soda onto wax paper. Stir into honey mixture, ⅓ at a time, until well blended. Stir in candied orange peel and almonds. Dough will be stiff, but sticky. Wrap in plastic wrap or foil; refrigerate several hours or overnight.

4. Grease 2 cookie sheets. Preheat oven to 350°. Roll out ¼ of the dough on a lightly floured surface to a 9 x 7-inch rectangle. (Keep remaining dough refrigerated.) Even sides of dough, then cut crosswise into 3 equal strips, each about 7 x 3 inches (for large cookies). Or, for small cookies, cut the same way, but cut each rectangle in half to make two 3½ x 3-inch rectangles. Repeat with remaining chilled dough, working with ¼ at a time. Place cookies 1 inch apart on prepared cookie sheets.

5. Bake in a preheated moderate oven (350°) for about 12 minutes for the small cookies and 15 minutes for the large cookies or until firm. Remove cookies to wire racks. Brush hot cookies with hot Lebkuchen Icing. Decorate small cookies with pecans and candied red cherries. Decorate the large cookies with Santa Claus cutouts using a "glue" of 10X sugar and water. Store cookies in a tightly covered container with wax paper between layers for a week or two to mellow.

ALMOND SPRITZ COOKIES

Bake at 400° for 7 minutes.
Makes about 5 dozen cookies.

1	cup (2 sticks) butter, softened	1	teaspoon vanilla
⅔	cup sugar	2½	cups *sifted* all-purpose flour
3	egg yolks	1	egg white
		1	cup sliced almonds

1. Preheat oven to 400°. Beat butter, sugar, egg yolks, and vanilla in a medium-size bowl until well blended. Blend in flour gradually until soft dough forms.

2. Using a cookie press or a pastry bag fitted with a large plain tip, pipe cookie dough out onto ungreased cookie sheets. Brush unbaked cookie dough with slightly beaten egg white; press sliced almonds into dough.

3. Bake in a preheated hot oven (400°) for 7 minutes or until golden brown. Remove to wire racks; cool.

MULTIPLE CHOICE COOKIES

With only one batch of dough, you can make a whole panful of different-looking cookies. After shaping the dough, leave some plain, press others crisscross fashion with a fork. Make a hollow in some with your thumb or the handle of a wooden spoon to fill with jam after baking or top with a nice walnut half.

BEAR PAWS

Bake at 350° for 12 minutes.
Makes about 8 dozen cookies.

2⅔ cups *sifted* all-purpose flour
2½ cups ground unblanched almonds (about 1 ⅔ cups whole almonds)*
1 teaspoon ground cinnamon
¼ teaspoon salt

1 cup (2 sticks) unsalted butter, softened
1 cup granulated sugar
1 teaspoon grated lemon rind
10X (confectioners') sugar

1. Combine flour, almonds, cinnamon, and salt on wax paper. Beat butter, sugar, and lemon rind in a large bowl until well blended. Stir in flour mixture until thoroughly combined. Cover; refrigerate about 1 hour or until dough is cold and firm enough to handle easily.
2. Lightly grease madeleine molds (fluted scallop-shaped molds, about 12 to a pan). Preheat oven to 350°.
3. Break off pieces of dough about the size of large marbles. Press dough into molds.
4. Bake in a preheated moderate oven (350°) for 12 minutes or until lightly browned. Remove molds from oven to wire racks; cool 2 minutes. Invert molds; lightly tap out cookies onto wire racks; cool completely. Sprinkle lightly with 10X sugar just before serving.

*Or use half almonds and half hazelnuts (filberts).

A SCOOP ON COOKIE DOUGHS

When making dropped cookies, use a tiny ice cream scoop or two teaspoons, one to scoop and the other to push dough off.

TO MAKE EVEN-SIZE COOKIES

To make round or molded cookies the same size, try patting the dough into a rectangle about an inch thick. Then divide and cut the dough into as many pieces as the yield of the recipe. Shape each piece into a perfect ball.

SHORTBREAD

Bake at 325° for 25 minutes.
Makes 2 dozen cookies.

1 cup (2 sticks) butter, softened	½ cup sugar
	2½ cups *sifted* all-purpose flour

1. Preheat oven to 325°. Beat butter and sugar in a large bowl until creamy and smooth. Work in flour with a wooden spoon until a stiff dough forms.
2. Divide dough into 3 parts. Working with one part at a time, roll out to about a 5-inch circle on an ungreased cookie sheet. Score circle with knife into 8 equal wedges. Pierce dough along the score lines with tines of a fork. Make sure the tines go through the entire thickness to facilitate breaking later. Press back of fork around edge of cookie to decorate. Repeat with remaining dough.
3. Bake in a preheated slow oven (325°) for 25 minutes or until cookies are faintly golden brown. They should be quite pale.
4. Remove from oven to wire racks. While still warm break along score lines. Remove cookies to racks to cool. Store in covered containers.

COOKIE PRETZELS

You have a choice of frostings for these almond-scented little delicacies.

Bake at 350° for 10 minutes.
Makes 4½ dozen cookies.

1 cup (2 sticks) butter, softened	2⅓ cups *sifted* all-purpose flour
	Vanilla Icing (page 285)
⅔ cup sugar	Chocolate Icing (page 285)
3 egg yolks	Multi-colored sprinkles
1 teaspoon almond extract	Silver dragees

1. Beat butter, sugar, egg yolks, and almond extract in a medium-size bowl with an electric mixer until fluffy-light. Stir in flour, blending well. Wrap dough in plastic wrap or foil; refrigerate overnight.
2. Preheat oven to 350°. Roll dough, 1 teaspoonful at a time, into balls slightly less than 1 inch. Roll each ball with palms of hands on a lightly floured surface to a 9-inch length. Pick up one end in each hand, cross over, fold back onto the circle and press down, forming pretzel shape.

Gently transfer each pretzel to an ungreased cookie sheet with a spatula, spacing them 2 inches apart.

3. Bake in a preheated moderate oven (350°) for 10 minutes or until firm (cookies will be pale). Remove from oven; cool slightly. Transfer to wire racks.

4. When thoroughly cooled, dip cookies, top-side down, into Vanilla or Chocolate Icing. Remove with a fork and place, right-side up, on wire racks placed over wax paper, to catch drips. Before icing sets, sprinkle with multi-colored sprinkles or dragees.

SWEDISH ROSETTES

These crispy star-shaped cookies are made on a special rosette iron and plunged into deep fat to brown. Giving the iron with the cookies would make a wonderful gift.

Makes about 3 dozen cookies.

1	cup *sifted* all-purpose flour	1	cup milk
2	tablespoons granulated sugar	2	tablespoon vegetable oil
½	teaspoon salt	1	teaspoon vanilla
2	eggs		Vegetable oil for frying
			10X (confectioners') sugar

1. Sift flour, sugar, and salt into a medium-size bowl.

2. Beat eggs, milk, the 2 tablespoons oil, and the vanilla in a small bowl until blended. Stir into flour mixture until batter is smooth.

3. Pour enough oil in a medium-size saucepan to fill half full; heat to 400° on a deep-fat frying thermometer.

4. Heat rosette iron in hot oil for 30 seconds; remove and shake off excess oil. Dip hot iron into batter just up to rim; immerse in hot oil. Leave iron immersed in oil until rosette begins to brown, so it will hold its shape. Shake rosette off iron; turn over; brown on other side. Lift out rosette with a slotted spoon; drain on paper toweling; cool. Repeat with remaining batter. Rosettes may be stored in a tightly covered container for up to 2 weeks. Sprinkle with 10X sugar before serving.

APRICOT PINWHEELS

A lightly spiced sugar cookie with a swirl of tangy apricot.

Bake at 350° for 10 minutes.
Makes 8 dozen cookies.

1 cup chopped dried apricots	⅛ teaspoon ground cloves
¾ cup water	1 cup vegetable shortening
½ cup granulated sugar	2 cups firmly packed light
1 cup finely chopped pecans	brown sugar
3½ cups *sifted* all-purpose flour	2 eggs
½ teaspoon salt	Butter Cookie Frosting
½ teaspoon baking soda	(page 276)
¼ teaspoon ground nutmeg	

1. Combine apricots, water, and sugar in a small saucepan. Bring to a boil; lower heat; simmer 10 minutes. Remove from heat; puree in the container of an electric blender. Cool; stir in nuts.

2. Sift flour, salt, baking soda, nutmeg, and cloves onto wax paper.

3. Beat shortening, sugar, and eggs in a large bowl with an electric mixer until fluffy-light. Stir in flour mixture until well blended. Wrap in plastic wrap or foil; refrigerate 2 hours or overrnight.

4. Divide chilled dough in half. Roll out between sheets of lightly floured wax paper to a 13 x 9-inch rectangle. (Moisten counter top with water to hold bottom sheet in place.) Lift onto a cookie sheet; place in refrigerator for 30 minutes.

5. Remove top sheet of wax paper. Spread dough with ½ the apricot filling to within ¼ inch of the edges. Roll dough, jelly roll style, from one of the long sides, lifting up dough with bottom sheet of wax paper to start rolling. Wrap roll in plastic wrap or foil; chill several hours or overnight. Repeat with remaining half of dough and filling.

6. Lightly grease cookie sheets. Preheat oven to 350°. Cut chilled dough in ¼-inch-thick slices. Place 2 inches apart on prepared cookie sheets.

7. Bake in a moderate oven (350°) for 10 minutes or until lightly browned. Cool on wire racks.

8. Pipe Butter Cookie Frosting onto cookies following the spiral shape.

GINGER SNAPPY TURTLES

Makes 2 dozen cookies,

1½ cups pecan halves
¾ cup vegetable shortening
2 egg whites
1 teaspoon vanilla
3 cups 10X (confectioners') sugar

1 package (16 ounces) gingersnaps
1 package (6¼ ounces) caramels
1 tablespoon water

1. Reserve 24 whole pecan halves; cut remaining pecans in half lengthwise.
2. Beat shortening, egg whites, and vanilla in a medium-size bowl with an electric mixer until smooth. Beat in 10X sugar until thick and creamy.
3. Spread a generous tablespoon of frosting on the bottom of one gingersnap. Press another cookie on top so that frosting oozes out slightly. Press in cut pecan pieces to resemble legs and one whole pecan half to resemble head of turtle. Repeat to make 23 more sandwich cookies.
4. Melt 14 caramels with water in small saucepan over low heat; stir until smooth. Drizzle about ½ teaspoon melted caramel on the back (top of gingersnap) of each turtle. Let stand until firm.
5. Store with wax paper between layers in a container with tight-fitting lid.

REFRIGERATOR COOKIE MOLDS

Small juice cans make good molds for refrigerator cookies. Pack dough in the can and chill. At baking time, open the bottom of the can with a can opener. Press the can bottom against the dough to push dough out the top and cut with a sharp knife into slices.

ALMOND CRESCENTS

These little nutted gems literally melt in your mouth.

Bake at 350° for 15 minutes.
Makes 4 dozen cookies.

2 cups *sifted* all-purpose flour
¼ teaspoon salt
1 cup (2 sticks) unsalted butter, softened
¼ cup granulated sugar
½ teaspoon almond extract

1 cup whole blanched almonds (about 4½ ounces), finely ground
10X (confectioners') sugar
3 squares semisweet chocolate
1 tablespoon butter

1. Sift flour and salt onto wax paper.

2. Beat the 1 cup butter, sugar, and almond extract in a medium-size bowl until smooth. Stir in flour until well blended. Stir in almonds. Wrap dough in plastic wrap or foil; refrigerate several hours or overnight.

3. Lightly grease 2 cookie sheets. Preheat oven to 350°. Roll dough, a heaping teaspoonful at a time, into 1-inch balls. Roll each ball with palms of hands on a lightly floured surface to a 3-inch length. Form into a crescent shape and place 2 inches apart on prepared cookie sheets.

4. Bake in a preheated moderate oven (350°) for 15 minutes. Remove from oven; cool slightly; transfer to wire racks. Sift 10X sugar through a fine sieve over the warm cookies or roll in 10X sugar, tapping off excess.

5. Melt chocolate and 1 tablespoon butter over hot, not boiling, water. Drizzle mixture over cookies with a small spoon. Store cookies in a tightly covered container with wax paper between layers.

GOLDEN FIG NUGGETS

Makes 20 cookies.

¼ cup (½ stick) butter or margarine, softened
¼ cup firmly packed brown sugar
1 teaspoon grated lemon rind
1 cup graham cracker crumbs (7 double crackers, crushed)

1 cup finely chopped dried figs, stems removed
¼ cup honey
2 tablespoons grated orange rind
¼ cup orange juice

1. Generously grease 20 miniature (1¾ inches) muffin cups. Press a 3-inch square of wax paper into each.

2. Beat butter, sugar, and lemon rind in a large bowl with an electric mixer until creamy, blending thoroughly. Stir in graham cracker crumbs until well combined.

3. Press a rounded tablespoon of crumb mixture firmly over the bottom and partly up the side of each lined muffin cup. Refrigerate until firm, about 1 hour.

4. Combine figs, honey, orange rind, and orange juice in a small saucepan. Bring to a boil; lower heat; cook, stirring constantly, until thickened, about 2 minutes. Cool.

5. Spoon a rounded teaspoon of fig mixture into graham cracker shells. Remove cookies from muffin cups by pulling up wax paper; serve in miniature muffin cup liners. Store, covered, in refrigerator.

ROCKY ROAD BROWNIES

Makes about 24 bars.

6	tablespoons (¾ stick) butter or margarine, cut up	1	package (11 ounces) tea cookies, each broken into 12 pieces (5 cups)
3	squares unsweetened chocolate	1	cup miniature marshmallows
1	teaspoon vanilla	¾	cup coarsely chopped walnuts
3	egg yolks		
⅓	cup sugar		
1	egg white		

1. Melt butter and chocolate in a heavy medium-size saucepan over moderate heat. Remove from heat; stir in vanilla. Reserve. Grease a 8 x 8 x 2-inch baking pan.

2. Beat egg yolks with sugar in a large bowl with an electric mixer until thick and light. Gradually stir in chocolate mixture.

3. Beat egg white in a small bowl with electric mixer until soft peaks form; fold into chocolate mixture until no streaks of white remain. Stir in cookie pieces, marshmallows, and walnuts until thoroughly combined.

4. Spread evenly into prepared pan. Refrigerate, covered, for at least 1 hour. Cut into bars of approximately 2 x 1½ inches.

4

Chocolate

There's no question that one of America's most beloved flavors is chocolate. Chocolate has a unique, satisfying, and sensuous taste, and is enjoyed in many forms.

Chocolate is a product of the New World. As early as the 16th century, Mexicans were already enjoying a frothy chocolate drink and the Spanish invaders under Cortez took the dark brown mystery product back to Europe. Hot chocolate in particular became an instant favorite. It wasn't long before there were chocolate shops galore where people went to enjoy a cup of the brew.

Chocolate is produced from cacao beans. Cacao beans are the seeds of a large, oval fruit. The fruit grows directly on the main branches of the cacao tree. Each fruit contains about 25 to 40 olive-size seeds or beans. The seeds are removed from the pulp and dried. Then they are roasted and ground until the fat in them liquifies. The rich dark liquid is unsweetened chocolate. Cacao beans are also called cocoa beans.

In Colonial America, chocolate was imported from Europe until the first chocolate factory in Massachusetts started production in 1765. No other people in the world have explored cooking with chocolate to the extent that Americans have. We pride ourselves on our lusious, mind-boggling recipes for chocolate cakes, pies, desserts, and cookies. In this chapter, you will find some of our best examples for the most mouth-watering chocolate goodies that any chocoholic could imagine!

VARIETIES OF CHOCOLATE

Unsweetened chocolate is the basic chocolate from which all other products are made. Roasted cocoa beans are pressed in special machines until the cocoa butter liquefies; the resulting chocolate liquor is then poured into molds to harden into cakes of pure chocolate, each weighing 1 ounce.

Cocoa is made by processing the chocolate liquor to remove most of the cocoa butter. The resulting mass is cooled, pulverized, and sifted to produce unsweetened cocoa. *Breakfast cocoa* has slightly more cocoa butter than plain cocoa. *"Dutch" cocoa* has been treated with an alkali that darkens the cocoa and gives it a characteristic taste.

Semisweet chocolate is a blend of unsweetened chocolate, sugar, and cocoa butter.

Semisweet chocolate pieces, also called bits or chips, are a blend of unsweetened chocolate, sugar, and cocoa butter, specially formulated to hold their shape softly when baked. Milk chocolate pieces are also available.

Sweet cooking chocolate is a lighter and milder blend of unsweetened chocolate, sugar, and cocoa butter. It's sold as 4-ounce bars.

Liquid chocolate is an unsweetened liquid product with a cocoa base that is available in 1-ounce packets.

Chocolate syrup is a ready-to-use sweetened product with a cocoa base. *Cocoa beverage mixes* are generally a blend of cocoa, sugar, and dry milk. They are convenient for making hot or cold beverages.

Milk chocolate is sweet chocolate with milk added and comes in the familiar candy bar.

Chocolate substitutes such as chocolate-flavored chips are fairly new products that do not contain chocolate but do have a cocoa base and vegetable fats added. Check labels for uses.

MELTING AND STORING CHOCOLATE

Chocolate scorches easily, so melt it over hot, not boiling water. A double boiler is best, but you can improvise by using a cup or bowl in a small saucepan. Either way, keep the water just below simmering. If steam gets into melting chocolate it will thicken the mixture and make it difficult to mix with the other ingredients. However, if this happens, simple soften the chocolate by adding 1 to 2 tablespoons vegetable shortening (not butter) and stir vigorously.

If there is liquid in a chocolate recipe such as milk, water, or spirits, melt the chocolate in the liquid in a small saucepan over direct heat. There should be at least ¼ cup liquid for every 6 ounces of chocolate. Stir constantly while melting to blend with the liquid.

You can also melt chocolate with the fat in the recipe directly over very low heat. Use a heavy saucepan and watch mixture carefully.

When chocolate is stored in too warm a place, or during hot weather, it often developes a whitish film known as "bloom." This is caused by the cocoa butter rising to the surface. It will not affect the eating quality. Chocolate keeps best stored at a temperature of from 60°F to 70°F, with a low humidity factor.

Store cocoa in a tightly covered container at moderate temperature and humidity to keep it from forming lumps or hardening.

DECORATING WITH CHOCOLATE

Cakes, pies, cookies, candies, puddings, and ice-cream desserts take on a professional look with a garnish of grated chocolate or chocolate curls.

To grate: Start with cold chocolate, a dry grater, and cold hands. Rub the square up and down over the grating surface, working quickly and handling the chocolate as little as possible.

To make curls: Warm a square of chocolate slightly at room temperature; then, for little curls, shave thin strips from the narrow side with a vegetable parer; for large ones, from the bottom. Pick up the curls with a wooden pick (otherwise they shatter) and chill until firm before arranging on food.

CHOCOLATE FUDGE CAKE

Bake at 350° for 35 minutes.
Makes 12 servings.

3   squares unsweetened chocolate
2¼   cups *sifted* cake flour
2   teaspoons baking soda
½   teaspoon salt
½   cup (1 stick) butter or margarine
2¼   cups firmly packed light brown sugar

3   large eggs
1½   teaspoons vanilla
1   container (8 ounces) dairy sour cream
1   cup boiling water
     Chocolate Fudge Frosting (page 279)

1. Melt chocolate in a small bowl over hot, not boiling, water; cool.
2. Grease and flour two 9 x 1½-inch layer-cake pans; tap out excess flour. (Or use cocoa in place of flour to keep cake dark on outside.)
3. Sift flour, baking soda, and salt onto wax paper. Preheat oven to 350°.
4. Beat butter until soft in a large bowl. Add brown sugar and eggs; beat with an electric mixer on high speed until light and fluffy, 5 minutes. Beat in vanilla and cooled melted chocolate.
5. Stir in dry ingredients alternately with sour cream, beating well with a wooden spoon after each addition until batter is smooth. Stir in boiling water. (Batter will be thin.) Pour at once into prepared pans.
6. Bake in a preheated moderate oven (350°) for 35 minutes or until centers spring back when lightly pressed with fingertip.
7. Cool layers in pans on wire racks for 10 minutes. Loosen around edges with a small knife or spatula; turn out onto wire racks. Cool completely.
8. Prepare Chocolate Fudge Frosting. Place 1 cake layer on a serving plate; spread with about ¼ of frosting; place second layer over. Gently brush off loose crumbs and spread a thin coat of frosting over top and sides; let set. Spread remaining frosting, making swirls with spatula.

DEEP DARK DEVIL'S FOOD CAKE

Bake at 350° for 40 minutes.
Makes 12 servings.

2 cups *sifted* cake flour	**2** teaspoons vanilla
⅔ cup unsweetened cocoa powder	**1¼** cups water
¾ teaspoon baking powder	**Fluffy 7-Minute Frosting** (page 281)
1¼ teaspoons baking soda	**1** square unsweetened chocolate
1 teaspoon salt	
⅔ cup vegetable shortening	**1** tablespoon butter or margarine
1⅓ cups sugar	
3 large eggs	

1. Sift flour, cocoa, baking powder, baking soda, and salt onto wax paper. Grease two 9 x 1½-inch layer-cake pans. Preheat oven to 350°.
2. Beat shortening, sugar, eggs, and vanilla in a large bowl with an electric mixer on high speed until light and fluffy, about 5 minutes. Beat in flour mixture alternately with water on low speed. Do not overbeat. Pour into prepared pans.
3. Bake in a preheated moderate oven (350°) for 40 minutes or until centers spring back when lightly pressed with fingertip. Cool in pans on wire racks for 10 minutes. Remove from pans; cool.
4. Make Fluffy 7-Minute Frosting. Place 1 cake layer on a serving plate; spread with about ¼ of the frosting; place second layer over. Gently brush off loose crumbs and spread a thin coat of frosting over top and sides; let set. Spread remaining frosting, making swirls with spatula.
5. Melt chocolate square with the butter in a cup over hot water; stir until smooth. Drizzle over top of cake, letting mixture drip down side, if you wish.

DUST WITH COCOA

To keep cocoa and chocolate cakes brown on the outside, grease pans and dust with cocoa instead of flour.

CHOCOLATE ROLL WITH CREAMY PRALINE FILLING

A luscious make-ahead dessert, perfect for a special dinner party.

Bake at 375° for 20 minutes.
Makes 8 servings.

⅔	cup *sifted* cake flour	¼	teaspoon baking soda
½	teaspoon baking powder	3	tablespoons cold water
¼	teaspoon salt		10X (confectioners') sugar
2	squares unsweetened chocolate		Creamy Praline Filling (page 282)
4	eggs	½	recipe Chocolate Fudge
⅔	cup granulated sugar		Frosting (page 279)
1	teaspoon vanilla		Chopped pistachio nuts
2	tablespoons granulated sugar		

1. Preheat oven to 375°. Grease a 15½ x 10½ x 1-inch jelly roll pan; line bottom with wax paper; grease paper.

2. Sift flour, baking powder, and salt onto another piece of wax paper.

3. Melt chocolate in top of double boiler over hot, not boiling, water.

4. Beat eggs in a medium-size bowl until thick and creamy. Gradually add the ⅔ cup sugar, beating constantly, until very thick. Fold in flour mixture and vanilla.

5. Stir the 2 tablespoons sugar, baking soda, and cold water into chocolate until thickened; fold into batter. Spread batter in prepared pan.

6. Bake in a preheated moderated oven (375°) for 15 to 20 minutes or until center springs back when lightly pressed with fingertip.

7. Loosen cake around edges with a knife; invert pan onto clean towel dusted with 10X sugar; peel off wax papers. Starting at short end, gently roll up cake and towel together. Place seam side down on a wire rack; cool completely.

8. When cake is cool, unroll carefully. Spread evenly with Creamy Praline Filling. Reroll. Place seam side down on serving plate.

9. Spread outside of roll evenly with Chocolate Fudge Frosting, pulling frosting into swirls. Sprinkle with chopped pistachios. Refrigerate until ready to serve.

CHOCOLATE-RUM ICEBOX CAKE

An updated version of an old favorite that is still easy to make ahead
for a special occasion.

Makes 10 servings.

2 cups heavy cream	Dash salt
6 tablespoons unsweetened cocoa powder	32 chocolate wafer cookies (from an 8½-ounce package)
6 tablespoons sugar	Rum Cream (page 288)
2 tablespoons rum	Chocolate curls (optional)

1. Combine cream, cocoa, sugar, rum, and salt in a small deep bowl; refrigerate 2 hours.

2. Beat chilled mixture with an electric mixer on high speed until stiff peaks form.

3. Frost each wafer with about 1 tablespoon cocoa-cream mixture, making 4 stacks of 8 cookies each. Set aside remaining cocoa mixture. Place 1 stack on its side on a serving plate. Press another stack of wafers onto the frosted end of the first stack to make a long roll.

4. Arrange remaining 2 stacks, end to end, to make another long roll. Place second roll adjacent to first roll on plate.

5. Frost rolls together with remaining cocoa mixture to make 1 cake, swirling top in a decorative pattern. Refrigerate at least 4 hours or overnight before serving.

6. When ready to serve prepare Rum Cream. Decorate cake with rosettes of cream; garnish with chocolate curls, if you wish. To serve: Cut icebox cake in ½-inch slices on the diagonal.

TRIPLE CHOCOLATE DELIGHT

The ultimate chocolate dessert! Fudgy layers of cake hold whipped chocolate cream and are glazed with pure rich chocolate. A perfect make-ahead.

Bake at 350° for 15 minutes.
Makes 12 servings.

Cake Layers:
2½ squares unsweetened chocolate
3   eggs, separated
⅓   cup superfine sugar
½   cup (1 stick) butter, softened
1   teaspoon vanilla
½   cup *sifted* cake flour

Filling:
1   package (8 ounces) semisweet chocolate squares
2   squares unsweetened chocolate
2   cups heavy cream
2   tablespoons brandy or coffee-flavored liqueur (optional)

Glaze and Decorations:
4   squares semisweet chocolate
½   cup heavy cream
3   to 4 teaspoons hot coffee or water
2   tablespoons butter, softened
2   to 3 tablespoons chopped pistachio nuts

1. Prepare Layers: Melt unsweetened chocolate in a small bowl placed over hot water; cool to lukewarm.

2. Grease two 9 x 1½-inch layer-cake pans; line bottoms with wax paper; grease paper. Preheat oven to 350°.

3. Beat egg whites in a medium-size bowl until foamy. Beat in 3 tablespoons of the sugar, 1 tablespoon at a time, until meringue forms soft peaks.

4. Beat butter in a large bowl with same beaters until creamy; beat in remaining sugar and the egg yolks until light and fluffy; beat in cooled chocolate and vanilla. Stir in flour just until blended.

5. Fold meringue into chocolate mixture ⅓ at a time until no streaks of white remain. Divide batter evenly in prepared pans. Smooth tops.

6. Bake in a preheated moderate oven (350°) for 15 minutes or until centers spring back when lightly pressed with fingertip. Cool in pans on wire racks for 10 minutes; turn out; cool completely. Wrap and chill layers.

7. Prepare Filling: Chop semisweet and unsweetened chocolate coarsely; place in heavy saucepan with cream. Cook, stirring constantly, over medium heat until chocolate melts and mixture just comes to a boil. Pour into large deep bowl; stir in brandy, if using.

Cool, stirring often; then chill until mixture starts to thicken and set, about 45 minutes.

8. Beat chocolate mixture with electric mixer on high speed until it becomes light and fluffy and about doubled in volume, about 3 to 5 minutes. Immediately spoon onto chilled cake layer placed on a small cookie sheet. Spread quickly to a layer about 1¼ inches thick; top with second cake layer, pressing lightly with your hand; smooth side with spatula. Chill at least 1 hour or until firm.

9. Prepare Glaze: Heat 4 squares semisweet chocolate and cream in a small saucepan over low heat, stirring constantly until chocolate is melted and mixture just comes to boil. Remove from heat; cool to lukewarm. Add a little hot water or coffee if too thick or mixture separates.

10. Transfer chilled cake to a rack over a pan to catch excess glaze. Pour chocolate glaze on top of cake. Spread with long spatula, letting glaze run down side of cake to coat completely. Chill cake until glaze is set. Place on a serving plate.

11. Beat 2 tablespoons butter with about 4 tablespoons of the excess chocolate glaze until stiff enough to pipe onto cake; chill briefly, if necessary. Spoon into pastry bag with small star tip. Pipe small rosettes in circles over center of cake. Sprinkle with pistachio nuts. Press nuts around base of cake.

RASPBERRY CREAM CHOCOLATE CAKE

For the whipped-cream-and-chocolate-cake lover. The center of the cake is filled with raspberries and cream; the outside is gilded with whipped cream and chocolate curls.

Bake at 350° for 45 minutes.
Makes 12 servings.

1	package (18.5 ounces) Swiss chocolate cake mix	3	cups heavy cream
1	package (10 ounces) quick thaw raspberries, thawed	1	bar (8 ounces) milk chocolate candy
1½	teaspoons unflavored gelatin	¼	cup 10X (confectioners') sugar

1. Preheat oven to 350°. Grease an 11 x 4½ x 2¼-inch loaf pan. Line bottom and long sides with wax paper, letting paper extend ½ inch above top edge; grease paper.

2. Prepare cake mix following package directions. Pour batter into prepared pan.

3. Bake in a preheated moderate oven (350°) for 45 minutes or until center springs back when lightly pressed with fingertip. Cool in pan on a wire rack for 10 minutes. Loosen cake around edge with a knife; remove from pan; cool completely. Chill cake several hours (this makes it easier to hollow out later).

4. To prepare cake for filling: Cut a thin slice off top to even, if necessary. Cut a thicker slice, about ¾ inch thick from top of cake; reserve. With a sharp knife, cut out center of cake lengthwise, through both ends, hollowing out and leaving ¾ inch sides and bottom. Return cake shell to washed and dried loaf pan.

5. Drain raspberries and reserve juice. Press berries through a fine sieve to puree and remove seeds. Sprinkle gelatin over 2 tablespoons of the reserved juice in a small bowl; let stand 5 minutes to soften. Place over simmering water, stirring until gelatin is dissolved; stir in remaining raspberry juice and pureed raspberries. Cool; chill just until mixture starts to thicken.

6. Beat 1¼ cups of the cream in a medium-size bowl until stiff; fold in thickened raspberry mixture.

7. Spoon raspberry cream into cavity of cake; replace top. Cover; refrigerate several hours or overnight, until filling is firm.

8. For chocolate curls: Draw a thin-bladed flexible knife across the smooth side of the candy bar, letting chocolate curl up in front of the knife. Reserve large curls for top of cake. Shave or grate chocolate for side of cake. Refrigerate chocolate until ready to garnish.

9. Beat remaining cream with 10X sugar in a medium-size bowl until stiff. Fit a pastry bag with a star tip; fill with 1½ cups of the whipped cream. Frost top and sides of cake with remaining cream. Press chocolate shavings against sides of cake. Pipe border of whipped cream along each top edge. Place chocolate curls on top of cake. Dust lightly with additional 10X sugar. Refrigerate until ready to serve.

CHOCOLATE MERINGUE GLACÉ

A meringue and ice cream sandwich topped with a layer of smooth sweet chocolate and flurry of whipped cream.

Bake at 275° for 50 minutes.
Makes 10 servings.

4	egg whites, at room temperature	1	package (4 ounces) sweet cooking chocolate
⅛	teaspoon cream of tartar	1	tablespoon butter
1	cup superfine sugar	3	tablespoons light corn syrup
½	cup very finely chopped blanched almonds	2	tablespoons milk
2	squares unsweetened chocolate, grated	1	tablespoon rum, brandy, or Amaretto
2	pints chocolate or coffee ice cream	1½	cups heavy cream

1. Preheat oven to 275°. Line a large cookie sheet with aluminum foil. Mark off two 10 x 6-inch rectangles on the foil.

2. Beat egg whites and cream of tartar in a large bowl with an electric mixer on high speed until foamy. Beat in sugar, 1 tablespoon at a time, until mixture forms stiff glossy peaks (this will take 8 to 10 minutes). Gently fold in almonds and chocolate. Divide meringue mixture in half; spread each within marked rectangles on cookie sheet.

3. Bake in a preheated very slow oven (275°) for 50 minutes or until layers are firm. Turn off oven heat. Leave in oven 30 minutes. Cool on a wire rack. Peel off aluminum foil. 30 minutes. Cool on a wire rack. Peel off aluminum foil.

4. If ice cream is frozen very hard, place in refrigerator to soften slightly. Spread ice cream carefully in an even layer on one meringue layer. Top with second layer. Wrap and freeze. (This can be done a day ahead.)

5. Combine sweet chocolate, butter, corn syrup, and milk in a small saucepan. Stir over low heat until chocolate is melted and sauce is smooth; stir in rum; cool.

6. Beat cream in a medium-size bowl until stiff.

7. Spoon chocolate sauce over top meringue to form a thin layer. Frost sides with part of the whipped cream. Pipe remaining cream through pastry bag with star tip over top in lattice pattern. Place in freezer until serving time. Cut into 3 x 2-inch pieces to serve.

CHOCOLATE FONDUE

Makes 2½ cups.

2   bars (8 ounces each) milk
    chocolate candy
¾   to 1 cup heavy cream
3   tablespoons brandy

For dipping: strawberries,
pear and apple slices,
seedless grapes, banana
chunks, tangerine and orange
sections, pound cake
squares, angel food cake
squares

1. Combine chocolate candy and ¾ cup heavy cream in a heavy saucepan. Cook over low heat, stirring constantly, until chocolate is melted. Add brandy. Remove from heat.
2. Pour into a small fondue pot; surrround by fruit and cake. Spear pieces of fruit or cake on fondue forks; twirl into sauce; provide small plates to catch drippings. If mixture becomes too thick, stir in additional cream.

"INSTANT" MOUSSE AU CHOCOLAT

It's just as smooth and velvety as the longer version.

Makes 8 servings.

1   package (6 ounces)
    semisweet chocolate pieces
⅓   cup hot brewed coffee
4   egg yolks
2   tablespoons apricot brandy
    or other fruit-flavored brandy

4   egg whites, at room
    temperature
3   tablespoons sugar
    Whipped cream (optional)

1. Combine chocolate pieces and hot coffee in the container of an electric blender; cover. Whirl at high speed for 30 seconds or until smooth.
2. Add egg yolks and brandy; cover. Whirl at high speed for 30 seconds.
3. Beat egg whites in a small bowl with an electric mixer until foamy and double in volume; beat in sugar, 1 tablespoon at a time, until meringue stands in firm peaks. Gently fold in chocolate mixture until no streaks of white remain. Spoon into 8 parfait glasses or a serving bowl.
4. Chill at least 1 hour. Serve with whipped cream, if you wish.

POTS DE CRÈME AU CHOCOLAT

Bake at 325° for 20 minutes.
Makes 4 to 6 servings.

4   squares semisweet chocolate
1¼ cups light or heavy cream
3   egg yolks
2   tablespoons light brown
    sugar

Whipped cream (optional)
Candied violets (optional)

1. Place four 4-ounce or six 3-ounce pots de crème cups, custard cups, or individual soufflé dishes in a shallow baking pan. Preheat oven to 325°.

2. Chop the chocolate coarsely. Place in a small, heavy saucepan; add cream. Cook, stirring constantly, over medium-high heat until chocolate melts and mixture comes to a boil.

3. Beat egg yolks and sugar with wire whisk in a medium-size bowl until blended; gradually beat in hot cream mixture. Strain into 4-cup measure; pour into cups.

4. Set shallow baking pan on oven rack. Pour boiling water into pan, about halfway up the sides of cups.

5. Bake in a preheated slow oven (325°) for 20 minutes or just until mixture begins to set around edges. Remove cups from water to a wire rack; let cool 30 minutes. Cover with lids or plastic wrap; refrigerate at least 4 hours. Decorate with rosettes of whipped cream and candied violets, if you wish.

CHOPPING CHOCOLATE

To chop chocolate squares for melting, hit the unwrapped square with the textured end of a metal or wooden meat mallet. The paper wrapper will keep the pieces together.

CHOCOLATE FLOATING ISLAND

Smooth, rich chocolate custard with a touch of rum holds a light-as-a-cloud meringue island topped with a fantasy of spun sugar.

Bake at 275° for 25 minutes.
Makes 6 servings.

4 **eggs, separated**	**2** **cups milk**
½ **cup superfine sugar**	**1** **tablespoon rum or Amaretto**
⅓ **cup unsweetened cocoa powder**	**Spun Sugar (recipe below), optional**
⅓ **cup granulated sugar**	**Candied violets (optional)**
½ **cup water**	

1. Lightly butter a 4-cup mold or ovenproof bowl. Sprinkle with sugar, tapping out excess. Preheat oven to 275°.

2. Beat egg whites in a large bowl until foamy and double in volume. Beat in superfine sugar, 1 tablespoon at a time, until meringue forms stiff glossy peaks. Spoon into prepared milk; smooth top.

3. Bake in preheated slow oven (275°) for 25 minutes or until puffed and firm. Cool in pan; unmold into shallow serving dish.

4. Combine cocoa, granulated sugar, and water in a medium-size saucepan, stirring until smooth. Cook over medium heat, stirring constantly until mixture comes to a boil; lower heat; simmer 2 minutes. Gradually stir in milk; bring to a boil again.

5. Beat egg yolks in a medium-size bowl; gradually beat hot cocoa mixture into yolks until well blended. Pour back into saucepan; cook, stirring constantly over low heat, until custard thickens slightly and coats a spoon. Pour into bowl; cool. Stir in rum; chill.

6. When ready, pour custard around meringue "island" until it floats; garnish with Spun Sugar and candied violets.

Spun Sugar: Combine 1 cup sugar and ¼ cup water in small saucepan. Cook over low heat, stirring constantly until sugar is melted; bring to a boil. With a pastry brush dipped in water, dissolve any sugar crystals from sides of pan. Boil, without stirring, until mixture turns a pale amber color, about 8 minutes. Remove from heat; cool slightly by placing saucepan in cold water for 1 to 2 minutes. Place dish with floating island close to syrup; cover edge of bowl with strips of foil. With a fork, lift some of syrup high over saucepan, then quickly wave over meringue "island" to form sugar threads. Continue dipping fork in syrup and waving it over dessert until you have a considerable "halo" of sugar threads over the "island."

CHOCOLATE ZABAGLIONE MOUSSE

Makes 8 servings.

⅓	cup sugar	1	tablespoon sugar
¾	cup sweet Marsala wine	2	egg whites
1½	teaspoons unflavored gelatin		Pinch salt
4	large egg yolks	⅛	teaspoon cream of tartar
1	tablespoon sugar	1½	cups heavy cream, whipped
3	squares semisweet chocolate, melted	2	squares semisweet chocolate, coarsely chopped
1	teaspoon vanilla		

1. Combine the ⅓ cup sugar, Marsala, gelatin, and egg yolks in a medium-size saucepan. Beat over low heat 2 to 3 minutes until mixture is foamy, hot, and gelatin is dissolved. *Do not boil or yolks will curdle.*

2. Remove from heat and continue beating 2 minutes to cool.

3. Stir in melted chocolate and vanilla. Set saucepan in bowl of cold water and ice to speed cooling.

4. Meanwhile, beat egg whites with the 1 tablespoon sugar, the salt, and cream of tartar in a small bowl until soft peaks form.

5. Fold whites and all but 1 cup of the whipped cream into the chocolate mixture. Refrigerate remaining cream until later for garnish. Spoon mousse into 8 demitasse or teacups or small wine glasses. Cover and chill at least 2 hours.

6. Just before serving, garnish each serving with the reserved whipped cream and the chopped chocolate.

Note: Dessert is best prepared up to, but no more than, 8 hours in advance.

PECAN-FUDGE TART

Wickedly delicious, divinely chocolate. A tiny sliver is pure bliss!

Bake at 400° for 5 minutes, then at 350° for 35 minutes.
Makes 12 servings.

½	package piecrust mix	1	cup sugar
3	squares unsweetened chocolate	1	cup light or dark corn syrup
		2	cups pecan halves
¼	cup (½ stick) butter		Coffee Whipped Cream
4	eggs		(page 287)

1. Preheat oven to 400°. Prepare piecrust mix following label directions. Roll out to a 13-inch round; fit into a 9-inch tart pan with removable bottom (or fit into a 9-inch pie plate, forming a stand-up fluted edge).
2. Melt chocolate and butter in a small saucepan over low heat; cool.
3. Beat eggs slightly in a medium-size bowl; blend in sugar and corn syrup. Stir in chocolate-butter mixture and 1⅓ cups of the pecans. Pour into prepared tart shell. Arrange remaining pecans in a design.
4. Bake in a preheated hot oven (400°) for 5 minutes. Lower oven temperature to moderate (350°); continue baking 35 minutes or until filling is set. Cool completely in pan on a wire rack. Remove side of pan. Spoon Coffee Whipped Cream on top just before serving.

HOT FUDGE PIE

This easy crustless pie is a chocolate lover's delight.

Bake at 400° for 20 minutes.
Makes 8 servings.

½	cup (1 stick) butter	¼	cup all-purpose flour
2	squares semisweet chocolate	1	teaspoon vanilla
1	cup sugar	½	teaspoon salt
2	eggs, lightly beaten		

1. Grease a 9-inch pie plate. Preheat oven to 400°.
2. Melt butter and chocolate in the top of a double boiler over simmering water.
3. Stir in sugar off heat. Cool slightly. Stir in eggs, flour, vanilla, and salt. Pour into prepared pie plate.

4. Bake in a preheated hot oven (400°) for 20 minutes or until set. Lower heat to 350° after minutes if edges begin to brown too quickly. Cool slightly on a wire rack.

CHOCOLATE MOUSSE PIE

A unique pie that uses part of the mixture to form its shell.

Bake at 350° for 25 minutes.
Makes 8 servings.

	Packaged unseasoned bread crumbs	1	**teaspoon vanilla**
		⅛	**teaspoon salt**
8	**squares semisweet chocolate**	½	**cup cherry preserves**
¼	**cup boiling water**	1	**cup heavy cream, whipped**
8	**eggs, separated (whites should be at room temperature)**		**Chocolate curls (optional)**
			Maraschino cherries (optional)
⅔	**cup sugar**		

1. Grease a 9-inch pie plate; dust with bread crumbs.

2. Place chocolate in top of a double boiler over hot, not boiling, water. Add boiling water. Cook over low heat, stirring occasionally, until chocolate is almost melted. Remove from heat and continue to stir until smooth. Cool slightly.

3. Beat egg yolks in a small bowl with an electric mixer on high speed until thick and pale lemon-colored, about 5 minutes. Gradually add sugar; continue beating 5 minutes longer until very thick. Blend in vanilla and melted chocolate.

4. Preheat oven to 350°. Beat egg whites and salt in a large bowl with clean beaters until stiff but not dry. Gradually fold ½ the whites into chocolate mixture, then fold chocolate into remaining whites, folding only until no streaks of white remain. Spoon part of mousse mixture into prepared pie plate so it just comes level with edge of plate.

5. Bake in a preheated moderate oven (350°) for 25 minutes. Turn off oven heat and leave pie in oven 5 minutes longer. Remove and cool on a wire rack 2 hours. As pie cools, mixture will form a shell.

6. Cover and refrigerate remaining uncooked mousse. When the shell has cooled completely, spread cherry preserves over bottom; fill with chilled mousse; chill 2 to 3 hours. Pipe cream through pastry bag around edge. Garnish with chocolate curls and maraschino cherries, if you wish.

CHOCOLATE CREAM PIE

Rich and smooth, the luscious chocolate filling is topped with fluffy whipped cream.

Makes 6 servings.

1 baked 9-inch pastry shell	½ teaspoon salt
2 squares unsweetened chocolate	2¾ cups milk
½ cup milk	4 egg yolks
1⅓ cups sugar	1 tablespoon vanilla
⅓ cup cornstarch	1 cup heavy cream

1. Prepare pastry shell from your own recipe or from a mix, with a high fluted edge to hold the filling.

2. Heat chocolate and the ½ cup of milk in a small saucepan over low heat, stirring constantly, until chocolate is melted.

3. Combine sugar, cornstarch, salt, 2¾ cups milk, and egg yolks in a large saucepan. Beat with rotary beater or wire whisk until mixture is well blended. Stir in chocolate mixture.

4. Cook over medium heat, stirring constantly, until mixture thickens and comes to a boil. Cook 1 minute. Remove from heat; stir in vanilla. Pour into prepared shell. Put a piece of plastic wrap directly on surface of hot filling to keep skin from forming. Refrigerate pie at least 3 hours.

5. Just before serving, remove plastic from pie. Whip cream in a small bowl until stiff. Spread over pie in a smooth layer.

CHOCOLATE-ALMOND SNOWDROPS

Delicate mounds to serve with tea.

Bake at 325° for 20 minutes.
Makes about 5 dozen mounds.

1 can (4 ounces) slivered, blanched almonds	⅔ cup *sifted* all-purpose flour
½ cup (1 stick) butter or margarine, softened	⅓ cup unsweetened cocoa powder
3 tablespoons 10X (confectioners') sugar	10X (confectioners) sugar

1. Place ⅓ of the almonds in an electric blender. Cover; whirl until smooth; turn out onto wax paper. Repeat until all almonds are blended.
2. Beat butter with the 3 tablespoons 10X sugar in a medium-size bowl until light and fluff; work flour, cocoa, and almonds into dough with a wooden spoon until dough begins to clean sides of bowl. Cover with plastic wrap. Refrigerate at least 2 hours or until firm enough to handle.
3. Preheat oven to 325°. Shape dough, 1 teaspoonful at a time (use teaspoon from measuring spoon set), into marble-size balls. Place on ungreased cookie sheets 1 inch apart.
4. Bake in a preheated slow oven (325°) for 20 minutes or until firm. Remove carefully from cookie sheets. While still warm, roll in 10X sugar to generously coat; cool completely on wire racks. Store with wax paper between layers in tightly covered container.

CHOCOLATE-ALMOND MERINGUES

Crackly-crisp with a light touch of chocolate. Best made on a dry day.

Bake at 275° for 20 minutes.
Makes about 7 dozen meringues.

3	egg whites, at room temperature	4	squares unsweetened chocolate, coarsely grated
1	teaspoon vinegar		Chocolate Glaze (page 287)
½	teaspoon salt		Chopped pistachio nuts
1	cup sugar		
1	cup finely chopped blanched almonds		

1. Grease cookie sheets. Preheat oven to 275°. Beat egg whites, vinegar, and salt in a large bowl with an electric mixer on high speed until foamy. Add sugar, 1 tablespoon at a time, and continue beating until mixture forms stiff glossy peaks, about 8 to 10 minutes. Fold in almonds and chocolate very gently.
2. Spoon mixture by teaspoonfuls 1 inch apart onto prepared cookie sheets.
3. Bake in a preheated very slow oven (275°) for 20 minutes or until just set. Remove from cookie sheets with metal spatula to wire racks. Cool completely. Swirl tops of cooled meringues with Chocolate Glaze; sprinkle with pistachio nuts.

CHOCOLATE CHIP COOKIES

In 1940, the owner of a Masachusetts restaurant, the Toll House, dropped chopped chocolate pieces into her cookie dough when she ran out of raisins—and thus, the birth of the chocolate chip cookie! Today there are hundreds of variations; ours includes nuts as well as chocolate.

Bake at 350° for 8 minutes.
Makes about 4 dozen cookies.

1¾ cups *sifted* all-purpose flour	1 egg
½ teaspoon baking soda	1 teaspoon vanilla
¼ teaspoon salt	1 cup chopped walnuts or pecans
¾ cup (1½ sticks) butter or margarine, softened	1 package (6 ounces) semisweet chocolate pieces
½ cup granulated sugar	
¼ cup firmly packed light or dark brown sugar	

1. Sift flour, baking soda, and salt onto wax paper. Grease cookie sheets.

2. Beat butter, both sugars, egg, and vanilla in a large bowl with an electric mixer until fluffy. Preheat oven to 350°.

3. Stir in flour mixture by hand until mixed. Stir in nuts and chocolate.

4. Drop dough by rounded teaspoonsful, 1 inch apart, onto prepared cookie sheets.

5. Bake in a preheated moderate oven (350°) for 8 minutes or until cookies are golden brown. Remove from cookie sheets; cool on wire racks. When thoroughly cool, store in covered containers.

Note: For larger cookies, drop dough by rounded tablespoonsful onto greased cookie sheets. Increase baking time to 10 to 12 minutes.

CREAM CHEESE BROWNIES

Bake at 350° for 40 minutes.
Makes 16 squares.

3	tablespoons butter	2	teaspoons vanilla
4	squares semisweet chocolate	½	cup *unsifted* all-purpose
2	tablespoons butter, softened		flour
1	package (3 ounces) cream	½	teaspoon baking powder
	cheese, softened	½	teaspoon salt
1	cup sugar	½	cup chopped walnuts
3	eggs	¼	teaspoon almond extract
1	tablespoon all-purpose flour		

1. Melt the 3 tablespoon butter with the chocolate in top of a double boiler over hot water. Remove and cool.

2. Grease a 9 x 9 x 2-inch baking pan.

3. Blend remaining 2 tablespoons butter with the cream cheese in a medium-size bowl with an electric mixer until fluffy. Beat in ¼ cup of the sugar, 1 egg, the 1 tablespoon flour, and 1 teaspoon of the vanilla. Preheat oven to 350°.

4. Beat remaining 2 eggs in a large bowl with an electric mixer until foamy. Slowly add remaining ¾ cup sugar, beating until blended. Stir in the ½ cup flour, the baking powder, and salt until smooth. Add chocolate mixture, walnuts, 1 teaspoon vanilla, and almond extract.

5. Spread half of chocolate mixture evenly in prepared pan. Spread cream cheese mixture on top. Drop spoonfuls of remaining chocolate mixture on top of cream cheese. Swirl top of batter.

6. Bake in a preheated moderate oven (350°) for 40 minutes. Cool in pan on a wire rack.

DOUBLE CHOCOLATE-WALNUT BROWNIES

Bake at 350° for 35 minutes.
Makes about 24 bars.

1	cup (2 sticks) butter or margarine	1	teaspoon vanilla
4	squares unsweetened chocolate	1	cup *sifted* all-purpose flour
2	cups sugar	1½	cups coarsely chopped walnuts
3	eggs	1	package (6 ounces) semisweet chocolate pieces

1. Melt butter and chocolate in a medium-size saucepan over moderate heat. Remove from heat. Grease a 13 x 9 x 2-inch pan. Preheat oven to 350°.

2. Beat in sugar gradually with a wooden spoon until thoroughly combined. Add eggs, 1 at a time, beating well after each addition; stir in vanilla. Stir in flour until thoroughly combined. Stir in 1 cup of the walnuts. Spread into prepared pan. Combine remaining ½ cup walnuts with chocolate pieces; sprinkle over top of brownie mixture, pressing down lightly.

3. Bake in a preheated moderate oven (350°) for 35 minutes or until center springs back when lightly pressed with fingertip. Cool completely in pan on a wire rack. Cut into bars or squares.

CHOCOLATE-RASPBERRY BOMBE

Pretty, colorful, and an easy make-ahead dessert.

Makes 8 servings.

2	packages ladyfingers, split	1	tablespoon seedless raspberry preserves or currant jelly (optional)
1½	pints chocolate ice cream		
1	pint frozen raspberry yogurt		Raspberry Sauce (page 290)

1. Line a 9 x 5 x 3-inch loaf pan with wax paper. Arrange the ladyfingers around the sides and bottom of the pan. Place in freezer to chill.

2. Soften 1 pint chocolate ice cream in a medium-size bowl in refrigerator for 30 minutes.

3. Spread 1 pint of the softened ice cream along the bottom and up the long sides of the chilled pan with the back of a spoon to a ½-inch thickness. Return to freezer until firm.

4. Meanwhile, soften yogurt and remaining chocolate ice cream in refrigerator. Spread yogurt into center of ice cream-lined pan, leveling top. Gently spread the remaining chocolate ice cream over the entire top. Return to freezer until solid, at least 3 hours.

5. Melt jelly in a small saucepan over low heat; cool slightly. Unmold bombe; peel off wax paper. Gently brush ladyfingers with jelly. Serve with Raspberry Sauce.

REFRIGERATOR CHOCOLATE ICE CREAM

Makes 3 quarts.

1½	cups sugar	4	squares unsweetened
¼	teaspoon salt		chocolate
3	tablespoons all-purpose	4	eggs, slightly beaten
	flour	1	quart (4 cups) heavy cream
2	cups milk	1	tablespoon vanilla

1. Combine sugar, salt, and flour in a large saucepan; gradually stir in milk and chocolate. Cook over medium heat, stirring constantly, until chocolate is melted and mixture thickens. Remove from heat.

2. Stir half the chocolate mixture slowly into eggs in a medium-size bowl; stir back into chocolate mixture in saucepan. Cook over low heat, stirring constantly, 1 minute; do not boil. Pour into large bowl; cool. Stir in 2 cups heavy cream and vanilla. Refrigerate about 2 hours or until chilled.

3. Pour into 13 x 9 x 2-inch metal pan. Freeze until partially frozen, about 1 hour.

4. Beat remaining cream in bowl until stiff. Beat partially frozen chocolate mixture in chilled bowl with chilled beaters until smooth. Fold in whipped cream quickly. Return to metal pan; cover. Freeze until firm, stirring once or twice, 4 hours.

CHOCOLATE-MARBLED CHEESECAKE

This spectacular cheesecake has a walnut-chocolate crumb crust and a creamy orange-accented cheese filling marbled with semisweet chocolate.

Bake crust at 350° for 10 minutes.
Makes 12 servings.

1 cup chocolate wafer crumbs (18 to 20 wafers)	1 tablespoon grated orange rind
½ cup finely chopped walnuts	½ cup dairy sour cream
2 tablespoons sugar	3 tablespoons sugar
¼ cup (½ stick) butter, melted	1 package (6 ounces) semisweet chocolate pieces, melted and cooled
½ cup sugar	
1 envelope unflavored gelatin	
⅔ cup milk	Mandarin orange segments (optional)
2 eggs, separated	
2 packages (8 ounces each) cream cheese, softened	

1. Lightly butter an 8-inch springform pan. Preheat oven to 350°.

2. Combine chocolate wafer crumbs, walnuts, and the 2 tablespoons sugar in a small bowl; blend in melted butter. Press mixture over bottom and partly up side of prepared pan.

3. Bake in a preheated moderate oven (350°) for 10 minutes. Cool completely; chill.

4. Combine the ½ cup sugar and the gelatin in small saucepan; beat in milk until well blended. Beat in egg yolks until mixture is smooth. Let stand 3 minutes.

5. Cook over medium heat, stirring constantly, until gelatin is dissolved and mixture is slightly thickened, about 5 minutes. (Do not allow mixture to boil.) Remove from heat; cool completely.

6. Beat cream cheese in a large bowl until smooth; beat in orange rind and sour cream. Gradually add cooled gelatin mixture, beating on low speed just until blended. Chill over ice and water until mixture mounds slightly when spooned.

7. Beat egg whites until foamy and double in volume. Gradually beat in remaining 3 tablespoons sugar until meringue forms soft peaks. Fold meringue into cheese mixture. Add about 2 cups of the cheese mixture to cooled semisweet chocolate; stir until blended. Spoon plain and chocolate mixtures, alternately, into prepared crumb crust. Swirl mixtures with a small knife to marbleize.

8. Chill until firm, at least 4 hours or overnight. Remove from pan; garnish with orange segments, if you wish.

CHOCOLATE-ESPRESSO CHEESECAKE

Bake at 350° for 1 hour.
Makes 16 to 20 servings.

3	packages (8 ounces each) cream cheese	2	tablespoons hot water
26	packaged chocolate wafers, crushed (1½ cups)	1	cup sugar
2	tablespoons sugar	3	tablespoon all-purpose flour
¼	cup (½ stick) butter or margarine, melted	3	whole eggs
1	package (12 ounces) semisweet chocolate pieces	2	egg yolks
2	tablespoons instant espresso coffee	1	cup heavy cream
			Whipped cream (optional)
			Chocolate curls (optional)

1. Let the cream cheese soften to room temperature in a large bowl. Lightly butter a 9-inch springform pan.

2. Blend chocolate wafer crumbs, 2 tablespoons sugar, and butter in a medium-size bowl. Press firmly over the bottom and halfway up the side of prepared springform pan. Chill before filling. Preheat oven to 350°.

3. Melt chocolate in top of double boiler over hot, not boiling, water. Dissolve espresso in 2 tablespoons hot water.

4. Beat cream cheese with an electric mixer on medium speed just until smooth. Add 1 cup sugar gradually, beating just until light and fluffy; sprinkle flour over mixture; blend thoroughly. Add eggs and egg yolks, 1 at a time; beat well after each addition.

5. Beat in melted chocolate, dissolved espresso, and cream on low speed. Pour into prepared pan.

6. Bake in a preheated moderate oven (350°) for 1 hour. Turn off oven heat and let cake remain in oven, with door closed, 40 mintues longer.

7. Remove cake from oven; let cake cool completely on a wire rack. Refrigerate several hours or overnight.

8. To serve: Loosen cake around edge with metal spatula; remove side of springform pan. Serve at room temperature, but keep leftover cake in refrigerator. Garnish with whipped cream rosettes and chocolate curls, if you wish.

5

Puddings
and Custards

Puddings are soft, creamy desserts which may be thickened with cornstarch, flour, tapioca, or cornmeal, or made of rice or bread. They may be stirred and cooked on top of the stove or baked in the oven. Custards and *flans* (which comes from Spain) are puddings thickened by cooking or baking eggs or egg yolks with milk. Steamed puddings are really steamed fruitcakes rather than soft, creamy mixtures. Mousses, Bavarian creams, and sweet soufflés are placed in this chapter because they too have a soft creamy consistency and are based on a custard mixture.

Homemade puddings thickened with cornstarch or flour are almost as easy to prepare as the packaged cooked pudding mixes. When making these cooked puddings, be sure to use a heavy saucepan over low heat to prevent scorching the mixture. Constant stirring is recommended to prevent lumps from forming. Cooked custards are made in a similar manner except that no starch is used for thickening; rather eggs or egg yolks are used as the thickening agent. Custards must be cooked slowly to avoid curdling the mixture. A double boiler is best for cooking stirred custards. A baked custard or flan should be placed in a water bath to prevent overbaking.

Besides traditional puddings and custards in this chapter, we have included some desserts, such as trifle, which are based on pudding.

VANILLA PUDDING

Makes 4 servings.

1¾ cups milk
⅓ cup sugar
3 tablespoons cornstarch

½ cup cold milk
1 teaspoon vanilla

1. Heat the 1¾ cups milk in top of a double boiler over boiling water until bubbles appear around edge of milk. Combine sugar and cornstarch in a small bowl; stir in the ½ cup cold milk until smooth. Gradually stir mixture into the heated milk.
2. Cook over boiling water, stirring constantly, until mixture thickens. Cover; cook over simmering water 20 minutes, stirring occasionally.
3. Remove from heat; stir in vanilla. Pour into a serving dish; place a piece of plastic wrap directly on surface of pudding to prevent skin from forming. Cool to room temperature; refrigerate until cold.

Chocolate Pudding: Increase sugar to ½ cup; add ⅓ cup unsweetened cocoa powder and ⅛ teaspoon ground cinnamon with the cornstarch.

PRUNE PUDDING

Makes 6 servings.

1 package (12 ounces) pitted prunes
2 cups water
⅔ cup sugar
½ teaspoon ground cinnamon
¼ cup cornstarch

½ cup water
1 teaspoon grated lemon rind
¼ cup lemon juice
½ cup heavy cream
Toasted almonds

1. Cook prunes in 2 cups water in a medium-size saucepan until very soft, about 15 minutes. Drain; reserve liquid. Measure ⅓ cup liquid; pour remaining into a 1-cup measure.

2. Press prunes and the ⅓ cup liquid through food mill or strainer to puree (do not use blender). Return to saucepan.

3. Combine the remaining prune liquid with enough water to make 1 cup. Stir into prunes; add sugar and cinnamon. Cook over medium heat, stirring occasionally, for 5 minutes or until mixture thickens.

4. Mix cornstarch with ½ cup water; stir into prune mixture. Cook, stirring constantly, until mixture is very thick, about 10 minutes.

5. Remove from heat; stir in lemon rind and juice. Pour into a serving bowl. Cool; then chill.

6. Whip cream in a small bowl until soft peaks form; spoon whipped cream onto pudding; sprinkle with toasted almonds.

CREAMY TAPIOCA PUDDING

Makes 6 servings.

¼	cup quick-cooking tapioca	2	cups milk
½	cup sugar	1	teaspoon vanilla
⅛	teaspoon salt		Strawberry-Wine Sauce
2	eggs, separated		(page 290)

1. Combine tapioca, ¼ cup of the sugar, salt, and egg yolks in a medium-size saucepan. Stir in milk. Let stand 5 minutes to soften tapioca.

2. Cook tapioca mixture over medium heat, stirring constantly, about 6 minutes or until thickened and bubbly. Remove from heat, stir in vanilla; cover surface with wax paper. Chill until cold.

3. Prepare Strawberry-Wine Sauce.

4. Just before serving, beat egg whites in a small bowl until foamy. Gradually beat in remaining ¼ cup sugar, 1 tablespoon at a time, until meringue forms soft peaks.

5. Stir chilled tapioca until softened; fold in meringue until no streaks of white remain. Spoon into stemmed wineglasses; top with sauce.

CUSTARD STORAGE

Puddings and custards made from milk or cream should always be stored in the refrigerator because they spoil easily.

INDIAN PUDDING

Bake at 325° for 3 hours.
Makes 6 servings.

5	cups milk	¼	cup (½ stick) butter or
½	cup yellow cornmeal		margarine
½	cup sugar	1	teaspoon salt
½	cup molasses	1	teaspoon pumpkin pie spice

1. Combine 2 cups of the milk with the cornmeal, sugar, molasses, butter, salt, and pumpkin pie spice in a large, heavy saucepan. Heat slowly until bubbling; then simmer, stirring often, 5 minutes or until creamy-thick. Butter a 2-quart baking dish. Preheat oven to 325°.
2. Pour pudding into prepared dish; stir in 2 more cups milk.
3. Bake in a preheated slow oven (325°) for 1 hour; stir in remaining 1 cup milk. Bake 2 hours longer or until pudding sets. Serve warm with cream or ice cream, if you wish.

CARAMEL-PEAR UPSIDE-DOWN PUDDING

Bake at 350° for 35 minutes.
Makes 6 servings.

1	can (29 ounces) pear halves	1	cup milk
3	slices white bread, cubed	1	cup light or heavy cream
1	cup sugar	4	eggs
¼	cup water	2	teaspoons vanilla

1. Drain pears, reserving 6 tablespoons juice. Sprinkle reserved juice over bread cubes on a plate.
2. Heat ¾ cup of the sugar and the water slowly in a large, heavy saucepan, stirring until sugar melts; cook without stirring just until mixture turns golden. Quickly rinse a 6- or 8-cup soufflé or other straight-sided baking dish with hot water; dry thoroughly.
3. Pour hot caramel into heated dish; tip and turn dish quickly to coat bottom and side thinly. Set aside while preparing custard.
4. Heat milk and cream in same saucepan (no need to wash pan) until bubbles form around edge. Beat eggs with remaining ¼ cup sugar in a medium-size bowl; slowly add hot milk and vanilla while beating constantly.
5. Arrange pears in caramel-lined dish, to cover completely, pointed

ends toward center and round sides up. Arrange bread over pears. Pour egg mixture over bread. Let stand for 15 minutes.

6. Preheat oven to 350°. Set dish in a deep baking pan on oven rack; pour water into pan to within 1 inch from top of baking dish.

7. Bake in a preheated moderate oven (350°) for 35 minutes or until a knife inserted ½ inch in from edge comes out clean. Cool. Chill at least 4 hours.

8. To unmold, loosen around edge with small knife; invert onto a serving plate with a rim. Serve with whipped cream, if you wish.

SUMMER PUDDING SURPRISE

Makes 8 servings.

3	cups sliced fresh strawberries	1	package (10 ounces) frozen raspberries, partially thawed
1	pint fresh or frozen unsweetened blueberries	10	slices firm white bread
⅓	to ½ cup sugar	1	cup heavy cream

1. Place strawberries and blueberries in large bowl; stir in sugar. Let stand, stirring often, until juicy and sugar is dissolved, about 30 minutes. Stir in raspberries.

2. Meanwhile, remove crusts from bread slices. Line a 1½-quart deep mixing bowl with 6 or 7 overlapping bread slices. Cut one slice to fit bottom. Fill bowl with berry mixture; cover top completely with remaining bread. Cover with wax paper; set a small flat plate or pie plate on top and place a 3- to 4-pound weight on the plate. (Several large cans of fruit or vegetables will do.) The weighted plate presses on the bread to compact the mixture. Refrigerate overnight.

3. To serve: Invert pudding onto a chilled serving plate. Garnish with a few extra berries, if you wish. Cut pudding in wedges to serve. Beat the cream just until softly whipped. Serve with the pudding.

BAKED CUSTARD TEST

With baked custards, the test of doneness is to insert a knife into the custard midway between the edge and the center. The center should remain soft because the custard will continue to cook even after it has been removed from the oven. The custard is done when the knife comes out clean.

APPLE-BREAD PUDDING

Bake at 350° for 35 minutes.
Makes 6 servings.

¼ cup dried currants or raisins	1¾ cups milk
2 tablespoons apple cider or juice	½ cup heavy cream
1 large tart cooking apple (Rome Beauty or Granny Smith)	½ cup granulated sugar
	½ teaspoon vanilla
	2 cups *unseasoned* croutons
¼ cup (½ stick) butter or margarine, melted	⅓ cup slivered almonds
4 eggs, beaten	2 tablespoons light or dark brown sugar

1. Soak currants in the apple cider while preparing other ingredients.

2. Peel, core, and cut apple into very thin slices. Cook slices in 2 tablespoons of butter in a small skillet just until soft and translucent; spoon into a 1½-quart casserole.

3. Beat eggs in a medium-size bowl. Add milk, cream, granulated sugar, and vanilla and stir to blend well.

4. Add croutons, remaining butter and currant mixture to casserole; stir gently to mix with apples.

5. Pour custard mixture into casserole and let stand 20 minutes until croutons are soaked with custard. Sprinkle with almonds and brown sugar. Preheat oven to 350°.

6. Place casserole in a large, shallow baking pan; place on oven shelf. Pour boiling water into pan to a depth of 1 to 2 inches.

7. Bake in a preheated moderate oven (350°) for 35 minutes or until a thin-bladed knife comes out clean when inserted 1 inch from edge. Serve warm or cold with heavy cream, if you wish.

QUEEN OF PUDDINGS

Bake at 350° for 1 hour.
Makes 6 servings.

4 cups cubed very dry white bread (about 10 slices)	1 tablespoon butter
4 cups milk	4 eggs
¾ cup sugar	2 teapoons vanilla
⅛ teaspoon salt	½ cup apple jelly
¼ teaspoon ground cinnamon	½ cup currant jelly (optional)

1. Lightly butter a 2-quart baking dish. Add bread cubes.

2. Heat milk, ½ cup of the sugar, salt, cinnamon, and butter in a large saucepan, stirring occasionally, just until butter is melted. Remove from heat; cool slightly.

3. Separate 2 of the eggs; reserve whites. Beat the 2 egg yolks and the 2 whole eggs in a medium-size bowl until frothy; stir in vanilla. Stir in warm milk mixture until well blended. Pour over bread cubes; let stand 15 minutes for bread to absorb custard. Preheat oven to 350°. Set dish in a large, shallow baking pan; place on oven rack. Pour boiling water into pan to a depth of 1 inch.

4. Bake in a preheated moderate oven (350°) for 50 minutes or until knife inserted 1 inch from edge of pudding comes out clean. (Center will be almost set, but still soft. Do not overbake, for custard will set as it cools.) Remove dish from oven, but leave oven on.

5. Beat reserved egg whites with an electric mixer until foamy. Beat in remaining ¼ cup sugar, 1 tablespoon at a time, until meringue forms stiff, glossy peaks.

6. Spoon apple jelly evenly over top of hot pudding. Press meringue through a pastry bag fitted with a large star tip onto pudding, covering as much of the top as possible. Return dish to baking pan.

7. Bake in a preheated moderate oven (350°) for another 10 minutes or just until peaks turn golden. Cool on a wire rack. Just before serving, melt the currant jelly in a small saucepan. Drizzle jelly over meringue. Serve pudding warm or cold, with cream to pour over, if you wish.

CINNAMON-RAISIN BREAD PUDDING

Bread puddings were invented by our thrifty ancestors to make good use of stale bread.
Bake at 350° for 50 minutes.
Makes 6 to 8 servings.

8	to 10 slices firm white bread	¼	teaspoon salt
¼	cup (½ stick) butter or margarine, melted	4	eggs
		4	cups milk
½	cup golden or dark raisins	1	teaspoon vanilla
¾	cup sugar	¼	cup apple jelly
1	teaspoon ground cinnamon		

1. If bread is very fresh, place in single layer on a cookie sheet to dry out for about 1 hour at room temperature. Brush 1 side of each slice with melted butter; cut into quarters. Arrange bread, overlapping, in shallow 2-quart baking dish; sprinkle with raisins. Mix sugar and cinnamon; sprinkle half over bread.

2. Combine remaining sugar-cinnamon mixture, salt, and eggs in a large bowl; beat with a wire whisk or rotary beater, just until combined. Stir in milk and vanilla; ladle over bread. Preheat oven to 350°.

3. Set baking dish in a large shallow pan; place pan on oven shelf; pour boiling water into pan to a depth of 1 inch.

4. Bake in a preheated moderate oven (350°) for 50 minutes or until center is almost set, but still soft; remove baking dish from water to a wire rack.

5. Melt apple jelly in small saucepan; brush over top of bread pudding. Serve hot or warm; pass whipped cream or Creamy Custard Sauce (page 291) to spoon over each serving, if you wish.

DANISH ALMOND RICE

Makes 6 servings.

¼ **cup uncooked long-grain rice**
2¼ **cups milk**
⅓ **cup sugar**
¼ **teaspoon salt**
1 **teaspoon vanilla**
¼ **teaspoon almond extract**

1 **cup heavy cream**
¼ **cup finely chopped almonds**
   Sweet Cherry Sauce
   (page 289) or Raspberry
   Sauce (page 290)

1. Rinse rice with hot water. Bring milk to a boil in a medium-size saucepan; stir in rice; lower heat. Simmer over low heat, covered, stirring often, 50 to 60 minutes or until milk is almost absorbed and rice is tender and creamy.

2. Stir in sugar, salt, vanilla, and almond extracts; cover; chill.

3. Just before serving, whip cream; fold into pudding with almonds. Serve with Sweet Cherry Sauce.

WARMING EGGS

If you need room temperature eggs for a pudding and have forgotten to remove them from the refrigerator ahead of time, put the uncracked eggs in a small bowl of warm water while you are assembling the rest of the ingredients for the recipe.

CRÈME BRÛLÉE

Makes 6 servings.

3	cups heavy or light cream	1	tablespoon vanilla
7	egg yolks	½	cup firmly packed light
2	tablespoons cornstarch		brown sugar
¼	cup granulated sugar		

1. Heat the cream in a medium-size saucepan. Beat egg yolks, cornstarch, and sugar in a small bowl with an electric mixer until mixture is thick and pale. Gradually beat in the heated cream.
2. Return cream mixture to saucepan and cook over moderate heat, stirring constantly and taking care to reach entire bottom and sides of the pan, until custard thickens and bubbles for 1 minute. Remove immediately from heat, while still stirring. Stir in vanilla.
3. Pour into a 6-cup heatproof serving bowl; cover; chill overnight.
4. To serve: Preheat broiler and cover the surface of the cream with brown sugar. Surround bowl with aluminum foil and place 3 inches from broiler heat. Broil for 2 to 3 minutes or until brown sugar is melted and caramelized. Refrigerate until ready to serve.

CARAMEL-COCONUT FLAN

Bake at 350° for 1 hour.
Makes 8 servings.

1½	cups sugar	⅛	teaspoon salt
8	large eggs	½	cup flaked coconut
2	cans (13 ounces) evaporated milk, undiluted		

1. Preheat oven to 350°. Place a 6-cup mold in a large, shallow baking pan filled with 1 inch of hot water. Place in a preheated moderate oven (350°) for 10 minutes to warm.
2. While mold is warming, heat 1 cup of the sugar in a small saucepan, stirring constantly until melted and golden. Remove mold from water with pot holder. Pour melted sugar into mold and swirl to coat bottom and sides with the caramel; cool slightly.
3. Beat eggs until foamy in a large bowl. Beat in the remaining ½ cup of the sugar, milk, and salt until blended; stir in coconut. Pour mixture into caramel-lined mold. Replace mold in water bath.
4. Bake in a preheated moderate oven (350°) for 1 hour or until knife

inserted 1 inch from edge comes out clean. (Center will still be soft.) Remove from water bath; cool on a wire rack 10 minutes.

5. Refrigerate until cold. To serve: Loosen flan around edge with knife. Place rimmed serving dish upside-down over mold. Holding mold and dish, turn dish upright and lift off mold. Caramel will flow out to form sauce.

EGGS IN SNOW

Makes 6 servings.

Soft Custard:
1   large navel orange
2   cups milk
3   egg yolks
2   whole eggs
¼   cup sugar
1   teaspoon vanilla
2   tablespoons Grand Marnier
    Or: 2 tablespoons frozen
    orange juice concentrate

Meringue:
3   egg whites
6   tablespoons sugar
    Candied Orange Rind
    (recipe below)

1. To make Soft Custard: Pare orange thinly with a vegetable parer, cutting only the bright orange part and none of the white. Reserve rind and the orange.

2. Scald milk with a 3-inch piece of rind in top of a double boiler placed over direct heat. Beat egg yolks, eggs, and ¼ cup sugar with a wire whisk or rotary beater until light and fluffy; gradually stir in scalded milk; pour mixture back into top of double boiler.

3. Cook, stirring constantly, over simmering water for 10 minutes or until custard thickens slightly. Remove from heat; strain into a small bowl; stir in vanilla and Grand Marnier. Cover; chill.

4. To make Meringue: Bring 1 quart lightly salted water to a simmer in a large skillet.

5. Beat egg whites in a medium-size bowl with an electric mixer until foamy-white and double in volume. Beat in 6 tablespoons sugar, 1 at a time, until meringue stands in firm peaks.

6. Scoop meringue with large spoon into 6 large egg-shaped puffs. Float, not touching, on simmering water; cover skillet. Cook over very low heat 5 minutes. Lift from water with slotted spoon; drain on cookie sheet covered with paper toweling; chill.

7. To serve: Pare all white from reserved orange and cut orange into thin slices. Press slices against sides of shallow glass bowl; carefully pour in custard sauce. Float meringue islands gently on top; spoon a little candied orange rind and syrup over each.

Candied Orange Rind: Cut the remaining rind removed from the orange into match-like strips. Simmer in water 5 minutes; drain. Combine ½ cup sugar and ¼ cup water in small saucepan; bring to a boil, stirring constantly until sugar is melted. Boil 2 minutes; add orange rind; continue cooking 5 minutes. Cool completely. When covered, will keep in refrigerator several weeks.

RICE IMPERATRICE

Makes 10 servings.

½	cup uncooked long-grain rice	1	cup milk
2	cups water	1	teaspoon vanilla
1¼	cups milk	1	cup heavy cream, whipped
1	envelope unflavored gelatin		Sweet Cherry Sauce
¼	cup cold water		(page 289)
2	eggs		Whipped cream (optional)
½	cup sugar		Cherries (optional)

1. Cook rice in 2 cups water in a medium-size saucepan, stirring occasionally, for 30 minutes or until all the water is absorbed. Add 1¼ cups of the milk to rice; simmer 30 minutes longer or until milk is absorbed. Cool.
2. Soften gelatin in cold water.
3. Beat eggs lightly in top of a double boiler; add sugar and 1 cup milk. Cook over simmering water, stirring constantly, until mixture coats a spoon. Add vanilla and softened gelatin; stir until the gelatin is completely dissolved. Turn into a large bowl; stir in the rice.
4. Chill custard mixture over ice and cold water, or in refrigerator, stirring often, until mixture starts to thicken. Fold in whipped cream. Turn into a 6- or 8-cup mold. Refrigerate 3 hours or until firm. Unmold on a serving plate. Garnish with additional whipped cream and cherries from Sweet Cherry Sauce, if you wish. Serve with Sweet Cherry Sauce.

STEAMED APPLE-DATE PUDDING

Makes 6 servings.

3	medium-size Rome Beauty apples, pared, cored, and diced	1½	teaspoons baking soda
1	package (8 ounces) pitted dates, coarsely chopped (1 cup)	1	teaspoon baking powder
		2	teaspoons ground cinnamon
		1	teaspoon ground nutmeg
		1	teaspoon ground allspice
1	cup coarsely chopped walnuts	¾	teaspoon ground cloves
1¼	cups *sifted* all-purpose flour	3	eggs
1	cup sugar	¼	cup vegetable oil
1	teaspoon salt		Granulated sugar
			Creamy Custard Sauce or Custard Sauce (page 291)

1. Combine apples, dates, and walnuts in a large bowl. Combine flour, sugar, salt, baking soda, baking powder, cinnamon, nutmeg, allspice, and cloves on wax paper. Sprinkle over fruits and nuts; toss until they are evenly coated.

2. Beat eggs and oil in a small bowl until well blended. Pour over floured fruit mixture. Stir until well blended.

3. Generously butter a 6-cup decorative mold. Turn pudding into prepared mold. Cover securely with a double thickness of aluminum foil.

4. Place mold on a wire rack or trivet in a large kettle; pour in boiling water to half the height of the mold; cover the kettle. Keep water boiling gently, adding more if necessary.

5. Steam pudding for 2 hours. Remove pudding from kettle; let cool 5 minutes; remove foil. Unmold onto heated serving plate and serve with Creamy Custard Sauce or Custard Sauce.

HOW TO SERVE STEAMED PUDDING

To serve steamed pudding, cut into wedges or pieces (as you would a cake) and top with a sauce.

PLUM PUDDING

A modern, light, and easy-to-make version of Tiny Tim's favorite pudding.
Though this English pudding does not contain plums,
it has a lot of dried fruit.

Makes 6 to 8 servings.

¾ cup *sifted* all-purpose flour
½ teaspoon baking soda
½ teaspoon salt
1 teaspoon ground cinnamon
½ teaspoon ground nutmeg
½ teaspoon ground allspice
½ teaspoon ground mace
¾ cup packaged unseasoned bread crumbs
½ cup (1 stick) butter or margarine, softened
¾ cup firmly packed dark brown sugar
3 eggs
1 pound (2 cups) mixed chopped candied fruit
1 cup raisins
½ cup slivered almonds
Brandy Hard Sauce (page 291)

1. Butter a 6-cup mold; dust evenly with granulated sugar, tapping out any excess.

2. Sift flour, baking soda, salt, cinnamon, nutmeg, allspice, and mace into a small bowl; stir in bread crumbs.

3. Cream butter or margarine with brown sugar until fluffy in a large bowl; beat in eggs one at a time.

4. Stir in flour mixture until blended; fold in candied fruits, raisins, and almonds. Spoon into prepared mold. Cover with buttered lid of mold or with aluminum foil; fasten with string to hold tightly.

5. Place on a rack or trivet in a kettle or steamer; pour in boiling water to half the height of pudding mold; cover tightly.

6. Steam 3 hours or until pudding is firm and a long skewer inserted in center comes out clean. (Keep water boiling *gently* during entire cooking time, adding more boiling water, if needed.)

7. Cool pudding in mold 10 minutes. Loosen around edge with a knife; invert onto a serving plate. Let stand about 15 minutes to cool. Serve with Brandy Hard Sauce.

CRANBERRY-PINEAPPLE MOUSSE

Makes 6 servings.

1 can (8 ounces) crushed pineapple in pineapple juice	⅛ teaspoon ground ginger
1¼ cups fresh or frozen cranberries (about ½ package)	2 eggs, separated
	½ teaspoon cornstarch
¾ cup sugar	¾ cup half and half
1 teaspoon grated orange rind	1½ teaspoons unflavored gelatin
¼ teaspoon ground cinnamon	¼ cup water
⅛ teaspoon ground nutmeg	3 tablespoons orange liqueur
	½ cup heavy cream

1. Drain pineapple; measure ⅓ cup crushed pineapple and ¼ cup pineapple juice. Combine with cranberries, ½ cup of the sugar, orange rind, cinnamon, nutmeg, and ginger in a large saucepan. Cook, stirring often, until cranberries burst and mixture is thickened. Transfer mixture to the container of an electric blender; cover; whirl until pureed.

2. Combine egg yolks, cornstarch, and the remaining ¼ cup sugar in top of a double boiler; beat until blended. Stir in half and half. Place over simmering water, beating constantly with a portable hand mixer, until mixture thickens, about 10 minutes. (Mixture will coat a spoon heavily.) Remove custard from heat.

3. Sprinkle gelatin over water; let stand 5 minutes to soften; stir into hot custard until dissolved. Stir in liqueur. Pour into large bowl; refrigerate just until custard thickens and will mound on spoon when stirred.

4. Beat cream in a small bowl until stiff. Beat egg whites in a medium-size bowl until soft peaks form. Fold cranberry mixture, then cream, and finally egg whites into the custard mixture until no streaks of white remain. Turn into a serving bowl; chill until softly set, at least 2 hours.

COOKED CUSTARD TEST

The test of doneness for custard is to cook it until the mixture thickens and "coats a metal spoon." Unfortunately *uncooked* custard will also coat a metal spoon. What you are looking for in a cooked custard is a thick, translucent coating about the consistency of gravy. Uncooked custard will be thin and opaque. If you see tiny clumps forming in the custard, it is on the verge of curdling. Remove from heat quickly and plunge the pan into a sink of cold water to stop further cooking.

MAPLE BAVARIAN

Use maple or maple-blended syrup to add flavor and sweetness
to this dessert.

Makes 8 servings

1 envelope unflavored gelatin	¾ cup milk
¼ cup cold water	½ cup heavy cream, whipped
3 eggs, separated	Canned fruit (optional)
½ cup maple or maple-blended syrup	Fresh green grapes (optional)
Dash salt	

1. Soften gelatin in water.

2. Combine egg yolks, syrup, and salt in top of a double boiler. Stir in milk. Cook over hot, not boiling, water, stirring constantly, until mixture thickens and coats a metal spoon. Add softened gelatin; stir until dissolved.

3. Pour mixture into a bowl; place in another bowl filled with ice and cold water. Stir gently until mixture mounds a bit.

4. Beat egg whites until stiff; fold into chilled mixture with whipped cream. Pour into a 4-cup mold that has been rinsed with cold water. Refrigerate 4 hours or until firm.

5. Unmold on a serving plate. Garnish with well-drained canned fruits or clusters of green grapes, if you wish.

PEACH MELBA-TOPPED RASPBERRY SOUFFLÉ

Makes 8 servings.

2 packages (10 ounces each) frozen raspberries, thawed	⅔ cup sugar
2 envelopes unflavored gelatin	1 cup heavy cream
½ cup water	2 cups peeled, sliced fresh peaches, sweetened with
4 egg whites	2 tablespoons sugar
½ teaspoon cream of tartar	Melba Sauce (recipe below)

1. To fit a 4-cup soufflé or other straight-sided dish with a wax paper collar, measure two lengths of wax paper long enough to encircle dish. Fold in half lengthwise (wax paper should be about 2 inches higher than the rim of the dish); fasten collar with tape or string.

2. Drain syrup from one package of the raspberries into a cup (you should have about ½ cup syrup); reserve for Melba Sauce. Place drained raspberries and second package of raspberries with syrup into the container of an electric blender; cover; whirl until thick. To remove seeds, press puree through sieve into a large bowl.

3. Sprinkle gelatin over water in a small saucepan to soften; let stand 10 minutes. Place saucepan over very low heat until gelatin dissolves (mixture will be clear). Remove from heat; cool. Stir into raspberry puree; chill until mixture mounds when spooned.

4. With an electric mixer, beat egg whites and cream of tartar until foamy-white and double in volume in a large bowl. Beat in the sugar, 1 tablespoon at a time, until stiff peaks form.

5. Whip cream in a small bowl until soft peaks form. Fold whipped cream, then egg whites, into thickened raspberry mixture with a rubber spatula until no streaks of white remain; pour into prepared dish. Refrigerate at least 3 hours or until set.

6. To assemble: Remove collar gently, freeing soufflé from wax paper, if necessary, with a small paring knife. Drain peach slices; garnish top of soufflé. Top with Melba Sauce.

Melba Sauce: Combine 1 teaspoon cornstarch with the reserved ½ cup raspberry juice in a small saucepan. Cook, stirring constantly, until sauce thickens and clears; cool.

ESPRESSO SOUFFLÉ

Makes 8 servings.

1	envelope unflavored gelatin	¼	sugar
⅓	cup sugar	1½	cups heavy cream
3	tablespoons instant espresso coffee		Lemon strips or lemon peel roses (optional)
4	eggs, separated		Candied violets (optional)
1⅔	cups milk		Fresh mint (optional)
¼	teaspoon grated lemon rind		

1. Combine gelatin, the ⅓ cup sugar, coffee, and egg yolks in a medium-size saucepan. Beat with an electric mixer or rotary beater until well blended. Beat in milk slowly until mixture is smooth.

2. Cook over medium heat, stirring constantly, until gelatin and sugar are dissolved. Remove from heat; stir in lemon rind. Chill over a bowl of ice and cold water to speed setting until mixture mounds when stirred with a spoon.

3. Beat egg whites in a large bowl until foamy-white; gradually beat in the ¼ cup sugar until meringue forms soft peaks.

4. Whip 1 cup of the cream in a small bowl. Fold gelatin mixture and whipped cream into meringue until no streaks of white remain. Turn into a 1-quart soufflé dish with a 2-inch wax paper collar. Chill 4 hours or until set.

5. Whip remaining ½ cup cream in a small bowl. Pipe around edge of soufflé. Garnish with lemon strips or lemon peel roses, candied violets, and mint leaves, if you wish.

APRICOT SOUFFLÉ PUDDINGS

These individual desserts should be served immediately.

Bake at 350° for 30 minutes.
Makes 8 servings.

3	tablespoons butter or margarine	4	eggs, separated
6	tablespoons all-purpose flour	3	tablespoons sugar
¾	cup milk, scalded		Dash salt
½	teaspoon vanilla	1½	teaspoons sugar
		½	cup apricot preserves

1. Combine butter and flour in a medium-size saucepan; work with a wooden spoon until smooth. Pour in scalded milk; stir rapidly with wire whisk over medium-low heat until mixture leaves sides of pan and is very thick. Remove from heat; add vanilla.

2. Preheat oven to 350°. Beat egg yolks with the 3 tablespoons sugar and salt until very light in color and thick. Stir into milk mixture.

3. Beat egg whites until stiff; beat in 1½ teaspoons sugar. Fold into batter.

4. Butter eight 5-ounce custard cups. Spoon 1 tablespoon apricot preserves in to each cup. Fill cups ¾ full with batter. Place cups in a large, shallow pan. Pour in hot water to half the height of filled cups.

5. Bake in a preheated moderate oven (350°) for 30 minutes or until puffed and brown. Remove from oven; let settle for a minute. Loosen pudding from cups; turn out onto individual dessert plates. The apricot preserves will form a sauce over each pudding. Serve at once.

FRESH APPLE-NOUGAT SOUFFLÉ

Makes 8 servings.

3	to 4 medium-size apples	5	eggs, separated
½	cup apple juice or water	½	cup heavy cream, whipped
1	envelope unflavored gelatin	1	cup crushed Walnut Nougat
½	cup sugar		(recipe below)
½	teaspoon ground cinnamon		Whipped cream (optional)
⅛	teaspoon ground nutmeg		Apple slices (optional)

1. Prepare a 5-cup soufflé or other straight-sided glass dish with a collar this way: Fold a 24-inch length of wax paper in half lengthwise; wrap around dish to make a 2-inch collar. Fasten with tape or string.

2. Pare, quarter, core, and slice apples to make about 4 cups. Sprinkle with ¼ cup of the apple juice. Cook in a large skillet, covered, over low heat, just until apples are tender, about 10 minutes.

3. While apples are cooking, sprinkle gelatin over remaining apple juice in a medium-size bowl. Let stand 5 minutes to soften.

4. Beat ¼ cup of the sugar, the cinnamon, nutmeg, and egg yolks into softened gelatin. Beat mixture well; add to apples all at once, beating constantly. Remove from heat; pour into medium-size bowl. Chill, stirring often, just until mixture mounds slightly when spooned.

5. Beat egg whites in a large bowl until foamy-white. Gradually beat in remaining ¼ cup sugar until meringue stands in soft peaks. Fold meringue, then whipped cream, into chilled apple mixture until no streaks of white remain. Fold in nougat. Pour into prepared dish. Refrigerate until firm, about 4 hours.

6. To serve: Gently remove collar. Garnish with additional whipped cream and apple slices, if you wish. Sprinkle edge with crushed Walnut Nougat.

Walnut Nougat: Combine 5 tablespoons butter, ½ cup sugar, 1 tablespoon honey, and 1 tablespoon water in a small heavy saucepan. Cook, stirring often, over medium-high heat until candy thermometer reaches 300° to 305°, about 5 minutes. Add ½ cup coarsely chopped walnuts; mix well. Pour onto a buttered cookie sheet. Cool completely. When candy is cooled and hardened, chop or crush into small pieces. Makes about 1½ cups crushed.

Note: Keep any extra Walnut Nougat in a tightly covered jar to sprinkle on ice cream or breakfast cereal.

ALMOND-SHERRY TORTE

Pretty trifle in a ladyfinger shell that uses pudding mix for quick fixing.

Makes 12 servings.

1 envelope unflavored gelatin	½ cup cherry preserves
1 quart milk	½ cup sliced blanched almonds,
2 packages (3¾ ounces each) vanilla pudding and pie filling mix	toasted
	1 cup heavy cream
	½ teaspoon almond extract
1½ packages (3 ounces each) ladyfingers, split	2 tablespoons 10X (confectioners') sugar
⅓ cup cream sherry or cherry brandy	

1. Sprinkle gelatin over milk in a large saucepan; let stand to soften 5 minutes. Blend in pudding mix; cook stirring constantly, over low heat, until mixture thickens and comes to a boil. Remove from heat; press a piece of wax paper directly onto surface to keep skin from forming. Cool; refrigerate about 45 minutes.

2. Line bottom and sides of a 9 x 5 x 3-inch pan with wax paper, leaving about 2 inches of excess paper over edge of pan, for easy removal of torte.

3. Brush ladyfingers with 4 tablespoons of the sherry. Arrange one layer of ladyfingers, rounded-sides out, around sides and bottom of pan.

4. Spread half the cherry preserves on the bottom layer of lady-fingers; sprinkle half the almonds (¼ cup) on top of preserves.

5. Whip ½ cup of the cream in a small bowl until stiff. Fold into cooled pudding mixture along with the remaining 1⅓ tablespoons sherry and the almond extract. Spoon mixture carefully over the almonds and preserves. Top with the remaining ladyfingers. Cover; refrigerate 4 hours or overnight.

6. Just before serving, whip the remaining ½ cup cream in small bowl. Stir in the 10X sugar. Remove torte from pan with the help of the extra wax paper; peel off paper. Garnish torte with the sweetened cream, the remaining cherry preserves, and remaining toasted almonds.

6

Ice Creams and Other Frozen Desserts

Everyone indulges at one time or another on ice cream. Where ice cream originated is uncertain; some say ancient China. As early as the 16th century, it appeared on the tables of Romans, perhaps introduced by Marco Polo; and Italian ices and frozen creams became popular throughout Europe soon thereafter. Thomas Jefferson sampled some while he was traveling abroad and introduced them to America. Today, Americans devour billions of gallons in cones, sodas, sundaes, splits, and cups.

Making ice cream at home can be a very enjoyable family activity. Homemade ice cream can be made with or without an ice cream machine or freezer. In this chapter, you'll find recipes for both types of homemade ice cream. You'll also find ices, which are frozen desserts made of water, sugar, and fruit puree or juice, and sherbet— similar to ices except that milk, gelatin, or egg white may be added. Frozen yogurt is light and has become a popular frozen dessert. Included are several fruit-flavored frozen versions.

You can make sensational desserts using store-bought ice cream. They're great for entertaining because you can prepare them ahead of time. Put together a festive combination of ice cream, sherbet, or ice in a decorative mold and you'll have a spectacular dessert called a *bombe*. With commercial ice cream, you can create sensational pies, mousses, even cheesecakes.

With so many kinds of frozen desserts, you'll never run out of delicious flavors.

MACAROON ICE CREAM

A delicate, almondy variation of vanilla ice cream.

Makes about 1½ quarts

½	cup sugar	2	cups light cream
2	tablespsoons cornstarch	¼	cup almond-flavored liqueur
½	teaspoon salt	¾	cup crushed macaroon cookies
2	cups milk		
½	cup light corn syrup	¼	cup toasted almonds, chopped
2	eggs, slightly beaten		

1. Combine sugar, cornstarch, and salt in a large saucepan; gradually stir in milk and corn syrup. Cook over medium heat, stirring constantly, until mixture comes to a boil; boil 1 minute; remove from heat.

2. Stir 1 cup of the mixture slowly into beaten eggs; stir back into remaining mixture in saucepan. Cook over low heat, stirring constantly, until mixture thickens and coats a metal spoon. (Do not boil.) Remove from heat. Pour into a large bowl; cover surface with plastic wrap or wax paper to prevent skin from forming; chill about 2 hours.

3. Stir in light cream and almond-flavored liqueur. Pour mixture into a 13 x 9 x 2-inch metal baking pan. Freeze until mixture is partly frozen, 1 hour or more.

4. Beat frozen mixture in a chilled large bowl with an electric mixer until smooth. Quickly fold in macaroon crumbs and almonds. Pour back into metal pan; cover. Return to freezer; freeze until firm, stirring once or twice, about 4 hours.

HONEY-ALMOND CRUNCH ICE CREAM

Makes 1 quart.

1 cup honey	3 eggs, separated
2 cups heavy cream	½ cup Almond Crunch
2 cups milk	(recipe below)
1 tablespoon vanilla	

1. Combine honey, cream, and milk in a medium-size saucepan. Cook over medium heat, stirring, until mixture just begins to bubble. Remove from heat; stir in vanilla.

2. Set pan in a bowl of ice water to chill, stirring occasionally, until mixture is cold.

3. Beat egg yolks in a large bowl until frothy; stir in chilled honey-cream mixture.

4. Beat egg whites in a medium-size bowl just until soft peaks form; fold into honey mixture with a wire whisk or rubber spatula.

5. Pour mixture into a 4- to 6-quart ice cream freezer can; freeze, following manufacturers's directions.

6. Fold Almond Crunch quickly into soft ice cream. Pack in plastic containers; freeze until firm.

Almond Crunch: Toast ½ cup chopped almonds on a cookie sheet in a preheated moderate oven (350°) for 10 minutes until lightly browned. Combine ¼ cup (½ stick) butter or margarine, 3 tablespoons honey, 3 tablespoons sugar, and 1 tablespoon water in a small saucepan. Cook over medium heat, stirring constantly, until mixture reaches 300° on candy thermometer (hard crack). Remove from heat; stir in almonds; pour immediately onto a buttered cookie sheet, spreading as thin as possible with a spatula. Let cool completely, then crush with a hammer. Store leftover crunch in a screw-top jar; it will make a delicious topping for ice cream, pudding, fruit desserts, or cakes. Makes 1½ cups.

HOMEMADE ICE

When you need ice for making ice cream, freeze water in washed quart-size waxed milk cartons. Use a hammer to break the ice into chunks.

PEACH ICE CREAM

Makes about 1½ pints.

5	large peaches	¼	teaspoon almond extract
¾	cup sugar		Dash salt
1	teaspoon unflavored gelatin	1	cup heavy cream
2	teaspoons lemon juice		

1. Dip peaches into boiling water for 30 seconds, then into ice water for 1 minute. Peel, halve, pit, and slice. Puree enough peaches in the container of an electric blender or food processor to measure ¾ cup. Finely chop remaining peaches.
2. Combine pureed peaches, sugar, and gelatin in a small saucepan. Heat, stirring often, until mixture bubbles and is very hot. Remove from heat. Add chopped peaches, lemon juice, almond extract, and salt. Pour into a 9 x 9 x 2-inch baking pan. Freeze until mixture is firm throughout, but not hard, about 1½ hours.
3. Beat cream in a small bowl with an electric mixer until soft peaks form. Scoop peach mixture into large bowl. Beat with an electric mixture until all frozen lumps are gone, but do not allow it to become watery. Add whipped cream; continue to beat until mixture is fluffy and well blended. Return to baking pan. Freeze overnight until firm.

STRAWBERRY ICE CREAM

Makes 3 quarts.

1½	cups sugar	2	cups milk
¼	teaspoon salt	3	eggs, slightly beaten
3	tablespoons all-purpose flour	2	pints (4 cups) strawberries
		3	cups heavy cream

1. Combine 1 cup of the sugar, salt, and flour in a medium-size saucepan; gradually stir in milk. Cook over medium heat, stirring, until mixture thickens and bubbles. Remove from heat.
2. Stir half of the mixture slowly into beaten eggs in a medium-size bowl; stir back into the remaining mixture in saucepan. Cook, stirring constantly for 1 minute. Remove from heat; pour into a large bowl; cool.
3. Wash, hull, dry, and halve strawberries into another large bowl.

Toss with the remaining ½ cup sugar. Let stand 10 minutes. Remove 1 cup of the strawberries and chop coarsely. Place remainder in the container of an electric blender or food processor. Cover; whirl until pureed. Add chopped strawberries, pureed strawberries, and 1½ cups of the heavy cream to the custard mixture. Chill about 2 hours.

4. Pour mixture into a 13 x 9 x 2-inch metal baking pan. Freeze until mixture is partly frozen, 1 hour or more.

5. Whip the remaining cream in a medium-size bowl until stiff. Beat frozen mixture in a chilled large bowl with an electric mixer until smooth. Quickly fold in whipped cream. Pour back into metal pan; cover. Return to freezer; freeze until firm, stirring once or twice, about 4 hours.

ICE-CREAM MAKER VANILLA ICE CREAM

Makes 2 quarts.

2	cups heavy cream	1	cup sugar
2	cups light cream or half and half	1½	teaspoons vanilla
		⅛	teaspoon salt

1. Pour heavy and light creams into freezer can of an electric ice-cream maker. Stir in sugar, vanilla, and salt until sugar is dissolved.

2. Freeze, following manufacturer's directions. Serve immediately or spoon into freezer storage container; store in freezer.

VARIATIONS:

Mocha Chip: Add 1½ tablespoons instant coffee powder with the 1 cup sugar, in above recipe. Stir in 1 cup semisweet mini-chocolate pieces before storing ice cream in freezer.

Banana: Add 2 cups pureed bananas (about 4 medium size), 2 tablespoons lemon juice, and ½ teaspoon ground nutmeg with the sugar in above recipe.

Chocolate-Chocolate Chip: Add 6 tablespoons unsweetened cocoa powder or ½ cup chocolate syrup with the sugar in the above recipe. Stir in 1 cup semisweet mini-chocolate pieces before storing in freezer.

FROZEN PAPAYA CREAM

Simple to make and so good! Serve it alone or with fragrant
ripe strawberries or peaches.

Makes about 1 quart.

2	medium-size papayas	1	cup light cream or half and
¼	cup lemon juice		half
½	cup sugar		

1. Cut papayas in half lengthwise; scoop out and discard seeds; then
scoop out pulp (about 2 cups). Puree papaya with lemon juice and
sugar in container of an electric blender or food processor until
smooth. Stir in cream. Pour mixture into a 9 x 9 x 2-inch pan.
2. Place in freezer for 1 hour or until frozen 1 inch in from edges. Stir
with a spoon until smooth. Return to freezer another 30 minutes to 1
hour or until softly frozen. Spoon into a chilled medium-size bowl;
beat with an electric mixer until smooth, 1 to 2 minutes. Spoon into
plastic container or bowl; cover. Freeze until firm, about 6 hours or
overnight.

HONEYDEW ICE

Makes about 1½ quarts.

1	cup sugar	4	to 5 tablespoons lemon juice
1½	teaspoons unflavored gelatin		Green and yellow food
1½	cups water		coloring
1	large honeydew melon		

1. Combine sugar and gelatin in a small saucepan. Stir in water. Bring
to a boil, stirring until sugar is dissolved; lower heat. Cook, uncovered,
5 minutes. Cool completely.
2. Cut honeydew in half; scoop out and discard seeds. Scoop out pulp
and puree in the container of an electric blender or food processor.
3. Pour pureed honeydew, sugar, and gelatin mixture and 4
tablespoons lemon juice (taste and add more if you like) into ice-
cream freezer can or 13 x 9 x 2-inch pan. Tint a pale green with food
coloring.
4. If using ice-cream freezer, adjust dasher and top of can. Freeze
following manufacturer's directions.

5. If not using ice cream freezer, place pan in freezer. Freeze mixture stirring several times, until firm, about 4 hours. Chill a large bowl and beaters. Break frozen honeydew ice into chunks into chilled bowl; beat with an electric mixer until very smooth.

6. Spoon ice cream from can of ice-cream freezer or bowl of mixer into a plastic container; cover. Freeze until firm, at least 6 hours or overnight.

LEMON SHERBET

Makes 1½ quarts.

1¼	cups sugar	½	cup lemon juice
1	envelope unflavored gelatin	1½	cups milk
2¼	cups water	2	egg whites
1	tablespoon grated lemon rind	¼	cup sugar

1. Combine the 1¼ cups sugar and unflavored gelatin in a medium-size saucepan; stir in water and lemon rind.

2. Heat, stirring often, until mixture comes to a boil; lower heat and simmer 5 minutes. Remove saucepan from heat; stir in lemon juice. Strain mixture into a 13 x 9 x 2-inch metal pan.

3. Cool at room temperature for 30 minutes. Stir in milk until well blended. Freeze mixture, stirring several times so that sherbet freezes evenly, until almost frozen, about 4 hours.

4. Beat egg whites until foamy and double in volume in a small bowl. Beat in the ¼ cup of sugar, 1 tablespoon at a time, until meringue forms soft peaks.

5. Spoon frozen mixture into a chilled large bowl. Beat with an electric mixer until mixture is very smooth.

6. Fold in meringue quickly. Spoon into a 6-cup mold or bowl; cover with aluminum foil or plastic wrap.

7. Freeze at least 6 hours or overnight. Unmold or scoop directly from bowl to serve.

SPICY ACCOMPANIMENT

For a spicy complement to cakes and pies, stir some ground cinnamon into softened vanilla ice cream and refreeze until firm. Then serve with your dessert.

ORANGE SHERBET IN ORANGE CUPS

A most appealing and attractive dessert.

Makes 8 servings.

8	navel or Valencia oranges	3	tablespoons orange-flavored
1	envelope unflavored gelatin		liqueur
1¼	cups sugar	1	teaspoon almond extract
1	cup milk	2	egg whites
¼	cup ground blanched almonds		

1. Cut oranges in half; squeeze and strain juice. Measure and reserve 2¾ cups of the juice. Remove crushed pulp from 8 of the orange shells for serving cups; scallop edges with a paring knife. Wrap in foil or plastic; refrigerate.

2. Combine gelatin and 1 cup of the sugar in a medium-size saucepan. Stir in 1½ cups of the orange juice. Heat, stirring constantly, until mixture just comes to a boil. Lower heat; simmer, stirring occasionally, for 5 minutes.

3. Remove from heat; cool. Stir in remaining 1¼ cups orange juice, milk, almonds, orange liqueur, and almond extract. (Mixture will look curdled.) Pour into a 13 x 9 x 2-inch metal pan. Freeze until mixture is almost solidly frozen, about 4 hours.

4. Beat egg whites in a small bowl with an electric mixer until foamy. Gradually beat in remaining ¼ cup sugar until meringue forms soft peaks.

5. Break up frozen mixture into chunks; turn into a chilled large bowl. Beat with an electric mixer until smooth. Quickly fold in meringue. Cover with foil; freeze overnight.

6. To serve: Spoon frozen sherbet into reserved orange shells.

CRANBERRY ICE

Makes 2½ quarts.

1	envelope unflavored gelatin	1	pound fresh or frozen
2	tablespoons grated orange rind		cranberries, washed and stemmed (4 cups)
½	cup orange juice	2¼	cups sugar
1	tablespoon grated lemon rind	3	cups cold water
¼	cup lemon juice		

1. Combine gelatin with orange and lemon rinds and juices.

2. Simmer cranberries with sugar and water about 5 minutes over moderate heat, stirring now and then, until skins pop. Set a food mill or large fine sieve over a large heatproof bowl and pour in cranberries and their liquid. Puree cranberries in the food mill or by forcing as much pulp as possible through the sieve. Stir gelatin mixture into hot cranberry puree; if it does not dissolve completely, pour mixture into a large, heavy saucepan and heat and stir over low heat until gelatin does dissolve, 2 to 3 minutes. Cool.

3. Pour mixture into a 13 x 9 x 2-inch pan and freeze for 2 hours until mushy-firm. Break up semifrozen mixture; beat in a chilled large bowl with an electric mixer until fluffy.

4. Pack into freezer containers and store in the freezer. Soften the cranberry ice slightly before serving.

GRAPEFRUIT ICE

For best results, use pink or naturally sweet grapefruit for making this recipe. You can, of course, substitute canned or bottled grapefruit juice for the fresh, but it will have a more bitter, acid flavor.

Makes 1¼ quarts.

1 envelope unflavored gelatin	3 cups strained fresh
1¼ cups sugar	grapefruit juice (about 3
1 cup water	large grapefruit)
2 teaspoons finely grated	
grapefruit rind	

1. Combine gelatin, sugar, and water in a small, heavy saucepan. Heat and stir over low heat until gelatin and sugar are both completely dissoved, about 5 minutes. Stir in rind and let steep 2 to 3 minutes. Mix with grapefruit juice.

2. Pour into a 13 x 9 x 2-inch pan and freeze for 2 hours or until mushy-firm. Break up semifrozen mixture; beat in a chilled large bowl with an electric mixture until fluffy.

3. Pack into freezer containers and store in the freezer. Soften ever so slightly before serving.

FROZEN PEACH YOGURT

Smooth and mellow and especially good when eaten just at the "soft-frozen" stage. Add topping of finely chopped crystallized ginger for a "peach of a treat."

Makes 1 quart.

1¼ pounds firm-ripe peaches (4 large)	3 egg whites, at room temperature
2 tablespoons lemon juice	1 container (16 ounces) plain yogurt
1 cup sugar	1 tablespoon vanilla
½ teaspoon ground ginger	
1 cup water	

1. Cut peaches into chunks. Put into container of electric blender; add lemon juice; cover. Whirl until smooth, stopping blender once or twice to press fruit down. (You will have 2 cups peach puree.)

2. Combine peach puree, ¼ cup of the sugar, and the ginger in a large bowl; blend thoroughly, Set aside.

3. Combine remaining ¾ cup sugar and water in a small saucepan; bring to a boil, stirring until sugar dissolves. Boil rapidly, without stirring until syrup registers 236° on a candy thermometer (the soft-ball stage; rapid flattening ball), 15 to 18 minutes.

4. Beat egg whites in a small bowl with an electric mixer until soft peaks forms; pour hot syrup in a thin stream over egg whites while beating constantly. Continue beating until meringue forms very stiff peaks and mixture cools, about 15 minutes in all.

5. Blend yogurt and vanilla into peach puree. Add ¼ of the meringue to peach mixture; stir to blend will. Fold in remaining meringue. Pour into a 13x9x2-inch pan. Freeze, stirring occasionally so mixture freezes evenly, until partially frozen, 2 to 3 hours.

6. Spoon into a chilled large bowl. Beat with an electric mixer until very smooth. Spoon into freezer containers or bowl; cover; freeze until softly-firm, 3 to 4 hours, or freeze solid. If frozen solid, remove from freezer 15 to 30 minutes before serving to soften.

FROZEN VANILLA YOGURT

Makes about 7 cups.

1	cup sugar	3	containers (8 ounces each) plain yogurt
⅓	cup water		
3	egg whites	1	tablespoon vanilla
⅛	teaspoon cream of tartar	1	teaspoon grated lemon rind
1	package (3 ounces) cream cheese		

1. Combine sugar and water in a small sauce pan; bring to a boil, stirring until sugar dissolves. Boil rapidly, without stirring, 5 to 8 minutes or until syrup registers 236° on a candy thermometer.

2. Beat egg whites with cream of tartar in a small bowl with an electric mixer until soft peaks form; pour hot syrup in a thin stream over egg whites while beating constantly. Continue beating until very stiff peaks form and mixture cools.

3. Soften cream cheese in a large bowl; gradually blend in yogurt; stir in vanilla and lemon rind. Add ¼ of meringue to yogurt mixture; stir to combine well. Fold in remaining meringue.

4. Pack into freezer containers and freeze until firm, 4 to 6 hours.

PINEAPPLE-YOGURT SHERBET

This easy-to-make and refreshing dessert can be served alone or with fresh berries.

Makes about 1 quart.

2	cans (8 ounces each) crushed pineapple in pineapple juice	1	teaspoon vanilla
		⅛	teaspoon salt
½	cup honey		Fresh mint or fresh berries (optional)
1	container (16 ounces) plain yogurt		

1. Drain juice from pineapple (about ½ cup) into a small saucepan; add honey. Bring to a boil uncovered, over low heat for 5 minutes. Pour into a large bowl; cool. Stir in pineapple, yogurt, vanilla, and salt.

2. Spoon mixture into a 9x9x2-inch pan. Freeze, stirring several times, until mushy, about 3 hours.

3. Turn partially frozen mixture into a chilled bowl; beat with an electric mixer until smooth. Return to pan and freeze until firm, at least 6 hours. Leave at room temperature for 15 to 30 minutes before serving. Scoop into sherbet glasses; garnish with fresh mint or fresh berries, if you wish.

FROZEN PEAR CREAM MOLD

Very simple to make, a cool creamy topper for a great dinner.

Makes 8 servings.

1	can (29 ounces) pear halves in syrup	Raspberry Sauce or Strawberry Sauce (page 290)
¼	cup sugar	
1	thin slice lemon	Whipped cream (optional)
1	quart vanilla ice cream	Strawberries (optional)
2	tablespoons mixed candied fruits, chopped	

1. Drain pears; reserve syrup. Measure 1 cup into a small saucepan; add sugar and lemon slice; stir until sugar is dissolved. Bring to a boil; boil, uncovered, until syrup is reduced to half its volume, about 10 minutes. Remove and discard lemon slice.
2. Select 3 pear halves for garnish; place in small bowl with remaining syrup and cover. Chill.
3. Puree enough of the remaining pears in the container of an electric blender to make 1½ cups. Stir in lemon-sugar syrup. Pour into a 9 x 9 x 2-inch baking pan. Freeze, stirring several times, until almost frozen, 1 to 3 hours, depending on your freezer.
4. Spoon into a chilled large bowl. Beat with chilled beaters until smooth, 3 to 4 minutes. Gradually beat in slightly softened vanilla ice cream.
5. Spoon pear cream into a chilled 8-cup mold; cover; freeze 6 hours or overnight.
6. Unmold onto rimmed serving plate. Garnish with reserved pears; sprinkle candied fruits over center. Return cream to freezer until ready to serve. Just before serving, spoon a little Raspberry or Strawberry sauce around mold; garnish with whipped cream and strawberries, if you wish.

PEACH MELBA-ICE CREAM FLAN

Makes 12 servings.

1 ready-to-use-sponge cake shell (7.1 ounces)	1 cup water
2 tablespoons dry sherry	1 package (10 ounces) frozen raspberries, thawed
½ cup raspberry preserves	⅓ cup dry sherry
1½ quarts strawberry ice cream	1 can (29 ounces) cling peach halves, drained
2 tablespoons cornstarch	1 cup heavy cream
¼ cup sugar	

1. Place cake on serving platter. Sprinkle with the 2 tablespoons dry sherry. Spread preserves evenly over bottom of cake. Soften ice cream in a large chilled bowl. Spoon into cake shell, spreading evenly to edge and mounding slightly in center. Freeze.
2. To make raspberry sauce, combine cornstarch and sugar in a medium-size saucepan. Gradually stir in water, raspberries, and ⅓ cup sherry. Cook over medium heat, stirring constantly, until mixture thickens and clears. Cool to room temperature. Set aside.
3. To assemble, arrange peach halves, rounded-side up, over ice cream. Beat heavy cream in a small bowl until stiff. Spoon into pastry bag. Pipe rosettes between peach halves. Return to freezer for 15 minutes.
4. Spoon some raspberry sauce over peaches; serve remaining sauce separately.

BANANAS FOSTER-ICE CREAM CAKE

Makes 12 servings.

1 ready-to-use sponge cake shell (7.1 ounces)	4 ripe bananas, peeled and sliced in rounds
1 quart vanilla ice cream	⅛ teaspoon ground cinnamon
2 cups heavy cream	1 kiwi, peeled and sliced
½ cup chopped pecans	6 strawberries, washed
½ cup firmly packed light brown sugar	½ cup light rum
¼ cup (½ stick) butter	¼ cup banana liqueur

1. Place cake shell on serving platter. Arrange 12 small scoops of vanilla ice cream around outer edge of cake. Spread remaining ice cream evenly in center, up to ice cream balls. Freeze until firm.

2. Beat heavy cream in a medium-size bowl until stiff. Spread around side of cake up to ice cream balls. Press chopped pecans into cream. Freeze until very firm.

3. Just before serving, melt sugar and butter in skillet, stirring until bubbly. Add bananas; heat until soft (do not overcook). Sprinkle with cinnamon.

4. Remove cake from freezer. Arrange kiwi slices and strawberries between ice cream scoops.

5. Heat rum and banana liqueur in saucepan. Pour over bananas, still over low heat, but do not stir into sauce. Carefully ignite with long match; spoon sauce over bananas. Carefully spoon flaming sauce and bananas into center of cake.

HOW TO WORK WITH ICE CREAM

• Chill bowl and beaters well.

• Make sure you have adequate freezer space before you start. Pans of ice cream should rest directly on freezer surface.

• Beat ice cream with an electric mixer or work with a wooden spoon to soften. Do not allow to melt or ice crystals will form when ice cream refreezes.

• Fill ice cream cake layers in either of two ways:

   1. Spoon the softened ice cream over cake; then spread evenly and gently with a spatula to keep from lifting crumbs from cake. Return to freezer.

   2. Smooth softened ice cream into foil-lined layer-cake pans the same size as the cake layers. Freeze until firm, then turn out onto cake layers, all the while peeling off pieces of aluminum foil as you go.

• Plan to make ice cream desserts a day or two before serving, so they have plenty of time to freeze firm.

• If you plan to keep the decorated cake longer than a day, freeze it until frim and wrap in plastic wrap or aluminum foil.

BAKED ALASKA BOMBE

Bake brownie layer at 350° for 30 minutes;
bake bombe at 500° for 5 minutes.
Makes 12 servings.

1	package (15½ ounces) double-fudge brownie mix	4	eggs whites
⅓	cup chopped walnuts	½	teaspoon cream of tartar
1	quart pistachio ice cream	⅛	teaspoon salt
½	cup raspberry preserves	½	cup sugar
1	pint strawberry ice cream	¼	cup unsweetened cocoa powder
⅓	cup finely chopped walnuts		Chocolate leaves (optional)
1	pint vanilla ice cream		

1. Grease an 8 x 1½-inch layer-cake pan. Preheat oven to 350°. Prepare the brownie mix with the added ⅓ chopped walnuts, following package directions. Pour into prepared pan. Bake in a preheated moderate oven (350°) for 30 minutes.

2. Line an 8-cup metal bowl with aluminum foil; place in freezer to chill. Soften pistachio ice cream slightly.

3. Spread ice cream evenly over inside of chilled aluminum foil-lined bowl; cover with plastic wrap; freeze until firm.

4. Spread raspberries preserves over pistachio ice cream; cover; freeze. Soften strawberry ice cream.

5. Spread strawberry ice cream in even layer over preserves. Press finely chopped nuts into ice cream; cover. Freeze until firm.

6. Soften vanilla ice cream slightly.

7. Spoon vanilla ice cream into hollow in bombe; smooth top; cover. Freeze until very firm.

8. Unmold bombe from bowl with aluminum foil. Place on brownie layer. Freeze until very firm, preferably overnight.

9. Preheat oven to 500°.

10. Beat egg whites, cream of tartar, and salt in a medium-size bowl until foamy; gradually beat in sugar and cocoa. Beat until meringue forms stiff, glossy peaks. Place brownie layer and bombe on an aluminum foil-lined cookie sheet. Remove foil from bombe. Quickly frost with chocolate meringue, covering brownie layer and bombe, and sealing to cookie sheet; swirl meringue into peaks.

11. Bake in a preheated extremely hot oven (500°) for 4 to 5 minutes or until browned. Remove to platter. Garnish base with chocolate leaves, if you wish.

PIÑA COLADA ICE CREAM CAKE ROLL

Bake at 375° for 12 minutes.
Makes 10 servings.

1   cup *sifted* cake flour
1   teaspoon baking powder
¼   teaspoon salt
3   eggs
¾   cup granulated sugar
1   teaspoon vanilla
⅓   cup water
     10X (confectioners') sugar
2   tablespoons light rum
1   tablespoon light corn syrup
1   quart vanilla ice cream
1   can (8 ounces) crushed
     pineapple, drained

⅔   cup (half of 15-ounce can)
     cream of coconut
1   jar (9½ ounces) kumquats,
     drained, seeded, and chopped
2   cups heavy cream
1   can (3½ ounces) flaked
     coconut, toasted
     Pineapple slices (optional)
     Cherries (optional)
     Kumquats (optional)

1. Preheat oven to 375°. Grease a 15½ x 10½ x1-inch jelly roll pan; line with wax paper; grease paper.

2. Sift flour, baking powder, and salt onto another piece of wax paper.

3. Beat eggs in a medium-size bowl until fluffy. Gradually beat in sugar until very thick, 5 minutes. Stir in vanilla and water. Gently fold in flour mixture. Spread batter in pan.

4. Bake in a preheated moderate oven (375°) for 12 minutes or until center springs back when lightly pressed with fingertip.

5. Loosen cake around edges with small spatula. Invert onto clean towel dusted with 10X sugar; peel off wax paper. Roll up cake and towel together from short end. Cool completely on a wire rack.

6. Unroll cooled cake. Combine rum and corn syrup sprinkle over cake. Soften vanilla ice cream in a chilled bowl. Quickly stir in crushed pineapple, cream of coconut, and kumquats. Spoon filling over cake; spread evenly. Reroll firmly. Wrap tightly in aluminum foil. Freeze until firm.

7. To decorate roll: Remove aluminum foil. Place cake seam side down, on serving dish. Beat heavy cream in a medium-size bowl until stiff; spread over roll. Sprinkle with toasted coconut. Return to freezer. Remove 20 minutes before serving. Garnish with pineapple slices, cherries, and kumquats, if you wish.

FROZEN VANILLA BAVARIAN CREAM

This delicious but easy-to-make dessert is pictured on the cover.

Makes 10 servings

1	baker's jelly roll	¼	teaspoon ground nutmeg
½	cup sugar	4	egg whites
1	envelope unflavored gelatin	1	cup heavy cream, whipped
2	teaspoons cornstarch		Whipped cream (optional)
6	egg yolks		Apricots (optional)
1	cup milk		Strawberries (optional)
1	tablespoon vanilla		

1. Cut jelly roll into 10 to 12 slices. Arrange slices against side and bottom of an 8-inch springform pan.

2. Combine ⅓ cup of sugar, gelatin, and cornstarch in a medium-size saucepan. Beat in egg yolks until well blended. Stir in milk slowly until smooth. Cook, stirring constantly, over medium heat just until mixture is slightly thickened. Remove from heat; stir in vanilla and nutmeg. Chill, stirring often, until mixture mounds when spooned.

3. Beat egg whites in a large bowl until foamy. Beat in remaining sugar gradually until meringue forms soft peaks.

4. Fold whipped cream, then meringue into gelatin mixture until no streaks of white remain. Pour into prepared pan. Wrap with aluminum foil or plastic wrap; freeze overnight until firm.

5. Remove carefully from pan. Garnish with additional whipped cream, apricots, and strawberries, if you wish.

TOASTING COCONUT

To toast shredded or flaked coconut for desserts, place coconut in a heavy skillet and heat until coconut is lightly browned, stirring constantly. Or toast coconut in a 350° oven for 15 minutes.

HOLIDAY ICE CREAM CAKE

Bake at 350° for 30 minutes.
Makes 8 servings

1 quart pistachio ice cream	1 package (15½ ounces)
1 pint vanilla ice cream	double-fudge brownie mix
½ cup chopped drained	2 cups heavy cream, whipped
maraschino cherries	Candied fruit (optional)
2 tablespoons grenadine syrup	

1. Line a 6-cup mold or bowl with aluminum foil; chill in freezer. Soften pistachio ice cream slightly; spoon into chilled mold, lining the side and leaving the center hollow; cover with plastic wrap; freeze.
2. Soften vanilla ice cream in a medium-size bowl; quickly stir in cherries and syrup; spoon into hollow in mold; smooth top; cover with plastic wrap; return to freezer several hours or overnight.
3. Grease an 8 x 1½-inch layer-cake pan. Preheat oven to 350°. Prepare brownie mix with nuts, following package directions. Pour into prepared pan. Bake in a preheated moderate oven (350°) for 30 minutes.
4. Put brownie layer on a serving plate. Unmold ice cream onto brownie layer.
5. Frost with part of the whipped cream. Pipe with remaining cream in a design. Decorate with candied fruits, if you wish.

MINCEMEAT-ICE CREAM PIE

Bake at 350° for 10 minutes.
Makes 8 servings.

1½ cups pecan halves, finely	½ teaspoon ground cinnamon
chopped (about 6 ounces)	½ teaspoon ground ginger
3 tablespoons sugar	¼ teaspoon ground allspice
2 tablespoons butter, melted	1 tablespoon grated orange
1 cup prepared bottled	rind
mincemeat	1 heavy cream, whipped
1 quart vanilla ice cream	

1. Grease a 9-inch pie plate. Preheat oven to 350°. Combine chopped pecans, sugar, and melted butter in a medium-size bowl; mix well. Press firmly and evenly onto the bottom and side of prepared 9-inch pie plate.

2. Bake in moderate oven (350°) for 10 minutes. Cool throughly.

3. Spread prepared mincemeat evenly onto the bottom of cooled prepared shell.

4. Soften ice cream in a chilled medium-size bowl; blend in cinnamon, ginger, allspice, and grated rind. Spread the ice cream evenly over mincemeat layer. Freeze until firm.

5. To serve: Remove pie from freezer 20 minutes before serving. Garnish with whipped cream.

FROZEN HONEY MOUSSE

Makes 8 servings.

4 eggs, separated	1½ cups heavy cream
¾ cup honey	Whipped cream (optional)
2 teaspoons grated lemon rind	Apricots (optional)
2 tablespoons lemon juice	Fresh mint (optional)
⅛ teaspoon cream of tartar	

1. Prepare a 4-cup soufflé dish or straight-sided dish with a wax paper collar: Measure a length of wax paper long enough to encircle dish. Fold in half lengthwise. (Wax paper should be about 2 inches higher than the rim of the dish). Fasten collar with tape or string.

2. Beat egg yolks in the top of a double boiler; stir in honey. Cook over simmering water, stirring frequently for 20 minutes until mixture is slightly thickened. Remove from heat. Stir in lemon rind and juice.

3. Set top part of double boiler in a bowl of ice water to chill; stir until mixture mounds slightly.

4. While honey mixture chills, beat egg whites and cream of tartar in a small bowl with an electric mixer just until soft peaks form. Whip cream in a large bowl until soft peaks form.

5. Gently fold whipped cream, then egg whites, into honey mixture until no streaks of white remain.

6. Turn into prepared soufflé dish; freeze overnight. When ready to serve, remove collar gently, freeing mousse from wax paper, if necessary, with small paring knife. Garnish with additional whipped cream, apricots, and mint, if you wish.

FROZEN SOUFFLÉ AMARETTO

Makes 8 to 10 servings.

5 egg yolks	1 cup finely crushed almond
3 whole eggs	macaroons
½ cup superfine sugar	2 cups heavy cream, whipped
⅓ cup Amaretto liqueur	

1. Prepare a 5-cup soufflé dish or other straight-sided dish with an aluminum foil collar 2 inches higher than rim of dish. Fasten foil with tape or string. Put dish in freezer.
2. Combine egg yolks, eggs, and sugar in a large bowl. Beat with an electric mixer on high speed until very thick and light. (This takes 10 to 12 minutes.) Turn mixer to low speed; add Amaretto and macaroons.
3. Fold in whipped cream with a rubber spatula until no streaks of white remain. Pour into prepared dish; freeze overnight. Remove collar from soufflé.

FROZEN RASPBERRY CREAM CHEESECAKE

Makes 12 servings.

1 cup graham cracker crumbs	2 packages (8 ounces each)
3 tablespoons sugar	cream cheese
½ teaspoon ground cinnamon	1 quart vanilla ice cream
3 tablespoons butter or	¾ cup red raspberry preserves
margarine, melted	½ cup heavy cream

1. Butter an 8-inch springform pan. Combine crumbs, sugar, cinnamon, and butter in a small bowl; blend well. Press firmly over bottom and sides of prepared springform pan; chill.
2. Beat cream cheese in a large bowl until soft. Soften ice cream in a chilled large bowl; beat into cream cheese just until blended.
3. Spoon about ¼ of the ice cream-cheese mixture into prepared pan; drizzle part of raspberry preserves over (use ½ cup of preserves for layering). Repeat until all of the cheese mixture and preserves are used; smooth top. Cover with plastic wrap. Freeze overnight or until firm.
4. Remove cake from freezer about ½ hour before serving. Spread the remaining ¼ cup of raspberry preserves over top. Whip cream in a small bowl. Pipe cream in a lattice design over preserves.

TORTONI ICE CREAM CAKE

Makes 12 servings.

½ cup boiling water
2 teaspoons instant espresso coffee or regular coffee
2 tablespoons dark or light rum
1 package (10¾ ounces) frozen pound cake
1 quart chocolate chip ice cream

½ cup chopped, toasted blanched almonds
½ cup chopped red and green candied cherries
½ teaspoon almond extract
1 cup heavy cream
   Candied red and green cherries

1. Stir water into coffee in a cup until dissolved; stir in rum.

2. Line a 2-quart bowl with aluminum foil or plastic wrap.

3. Cut pound cake into ¼-inch slices. Cut half the slices diagonally into triangles. Arrange triangles in bottom of lined bowl, pin-wheel fashion, with points toward center. Line side of bowl with whole cake slices. Sprinkle slices with ⅔ of the coffee mixture.

4. Soften ice cream slightly in a chilled large bowl. Work in almonds, the ½ cup cherries, and almond extract. Spoon evenly into cake-lined bowl, working quickly so ice cream does not melt. Cover ice cream with remaining cake slices, pressing down firmly; sprinkle slices with remaining coffee mixture. Cover bowl with plastic wrap or aluminum foil; freeze overnight or for up to 2 days.

5. Unmold cake onto serving plate about 2 hours before serving. Beat cream in a small bowl until stiff. Spread a thin layer of cream over surface of cake. Spoon remaining cream into pastry bag fitted with a star tip. Pipe rosettes of cream around bottom of cake and on top and side. Garnish with cherries. Return to the freezer until ready to serve.

7

Desserts for Special Occasions

S pecial occasions—a birthday wedding anniversary, new home, or family reunion—call for celebrations, and there's no better way to celebrate than with a fabulous dinner followed by a spectacular dessert. Some desserts in this chapter require a little bit more work, but they are well worth the extra effort. However, there are some simple ones too; they just *look* difficult.

There are fancy individual or small desserts you can put together for a dessert tray that will be just as enticing and tasty as those you'll find in the best bakeries or on a deluxe restaurant's pastry cart. Try the bite-size chocolate cheesecakes laced with coffee and cinnamon. Moist, tender pound cake is the basis of colorful petit fours. Ripe red strawberries dipped in vanilla frosting and speckled with green pistachio nuts make a stunning treat. Tender ladyfingers, coffee-almond chiffon cake squares, and small frosted cupcakes are other choices for your dessert tray assortment.

Cheesecakes, crêpes, and flaming desserts are big moment desserts you'll find in this chapter. For quiet holiday meals, perhaps a snowball cake or walnut cake log are fitting finales. Many desserts can be made well ahead so they are perfect for entertaining any time of the year from New Year's to Hanukkah and Christmas. There's very little last-minute fussing.

Though the desserts in other chapters may please or delight the palate as well as these, there is something special about the ones in this collection.

RASPBERRY-ALMOND PETIT FOURS

There is a moist, tender, almond pound cake in the center of these colorful little morsels.

Bake at 325° for 45 minutes.
Makes 4 dozen petit fours.

2½ cups *sifted* cake flour
1 teaspoon baking powder
½ cup almond paste (not almond filling or marzipan), from an 8-ounce can or package
⅔ cup butter, softened
1¼ cups sugar
4 eggs
½ cup milk

Raspberry Glaze (page 286)
2 container (16.5 ounces each) vanilla ready-to-spread frosting
Red food coloring
2 tubes red cake decorating gel
2 tubes green cake decorating gel

1. Grease a 13 x 9 x 2-inch pan; line bottom with wax paper; grease paper.

2. Preheat oven to 325°. Sift flour and baking powder onto wax paper.

3. Crumble almond paste into a large bowl; add butter. Beat with an electric mixer until creamy and smooth. Beat in sugar and eggs until mixture is fluffy and light, about 3 minutes.

4. Add flour mixture alternately with milk, beating after each addition with mixer on low speed, until batter is smooth. Pour into prepared pan.

5. Bake in a preheated slow oven (325°) for 45 minutes or until center springs back when lightly pressed with fingertip. Cool in pan on a wire rack for 10 minutes. Loosen around edges with small spatula; turn out onto wire rack; cool completely.

6. Trim top of cake with a large knife to make top flat and even. Cut cake into 48 rectangles, each about 2 x 1 inches (12 across, 4 down).

7. Prepare Raspberry Glaze. Hold cakes, 1 at a time, on a fork over saucepan of glaze. Dip to evenly coat top and sides. Place cakes on wire rack over wax paper to catch any drips. Let stand until sticky-firm, about 1 hour.

8. Spoon vanilla frosting into top of a double boiler; place over simmering water. Heat, stirring occasionally, just until frosting is melted. Stir in a few drops of red food coloring to tint a pale pink.

9. Holding glazed cakes, 1 at a time on a fork, spoon frosting over to coat top and sides, letting excess drip back into pan. Use a wooden pick to slide each cake onto a wire rack. Let stand until frosting is set. Decorate with decorating gels.

CHOCOLATE-CAPPUCINO CHEESECAKES

Bite-size cheesecakes laced with espresso coffee and cinnamon.

Bake at 350° for 18 minutes.
Makes 2½ dozen cheesecakes.

8 to 10 packaged chocolate wafers, crushed (½ cup)	2 teaspoons espresso coffee powder
1 teaspoon sugar	⅛ teaspoon ground cinnamon
1 tablespoon butter or margarine, melted	1 teaspoon vanilla
	Whipped cream (optional)
2 squares semisweet chocolate	Crystallized violets
1 package (8 ounces) cream cheese, softened	(optional)
	Fresh mint (optional)
¼ cup sugar	Ground cinnamon (optional)
1 egg	

1. Line 1¾-inch miniature muffin cups with paper liners.

2. Blend chocolate crumbs, the 1 teaspoon sugar, and butter in a small bowl. Press a scant ½ teaspoon of the chocolate crumbs into bottom of each paper-lined muffin cup. Preheat oven to 350°.

3. Melt chocolate in a 1-cup measure set in hot, not boiling, water.

4. Beat cream cheese with an electric mixer on medium-speed just until smooth. Add ¼ cup sugar gradually, beating until light and fluffy; beat in egg, espresso coffee, cinnamon, and vanilla.

5. Add melted chocolate; beat on low speed until blended, then on high speed for 1 minute until mixture thickens.

6. Fill muffin cups half full (2 level teaspoonsful).

7. Bake in a preheated moderate oven (350°) for 18 minutes or until centers are firm when lightly pressed with fingertip. Cool cheesecakes in pans on wire racks 15 minutes. Remove from pans; cool completely.

(Cheesecakes characteristically crack and sink upon cooling.) Refrigerate until ready to serve.

8. Garnish with whipped cream, crystallized violets, fresh mint, or a dusting of ground cinnamon, if you wish.

COFFEE-ALMOND SQUARES

Rich coffee butter cream frosts the delicate chiffon cake squares.

Bake at 350° for 45 minutes.
Makes 2 dozen cakes.

2¼ cups *sifted* cake flour	⅓ cup vegetable oil
1½ cups sugar	1 teaspoon almond extract
3 tablespoons baking powder	Apricot Glaze (page 286)
¾ teaspoon salt	Coffee Butter Cream Frosting
3 eggs, separated	(page 277)
1 cup milk	1½ cups sliced almonds

1. Sift four, 1 cup of the sugar, baking powder, and salt into large bowl; make a well in center. Grease and flour a 13 x 9 x 2-inch baking pan. Preheat oven to 350°.

2. Beat egg whites with remaining ½ cup sugar in a small bowl with an electric mixer until soft peaks form.

3. Pour ½ cup of the milk, vegetable oil, and almond extract into well of dry ingredients; beat on high speed with electric mixer for 1 minute. Add remaining ½ cup milk and egg yolks; beat 1 minute longer. Fold whites gently into yolk mixture until no steaks of white remain. Pour into prepared baking pan.

4. Bake in a preheated moderate oven (350°) for 45 minutes or until center springs back when lightly pressed with fingertip. Cool for 10 minutes on a wire rack; turn out. Cool completely.

5. Prepare Apricot Glaze. Split cake into two layers. Spread Apricot Glaze on the top of each cake layer. Cut each layer into 24 squares. Brush sides of each square with Apricot Glaze. Place cakes on wire rack set over wax paper; let stand 1 hour.

6. Prepare Coffee Butter Cream Frosting. Lightly frost sides of each cake square with frosting; let set about 15 minutes; frost again. Sprinkle sides of cakes with sliced almonds, pressing onto sides; place on a wire rack or cookie sheet; frost tops of cake. Use any remaining frosting to decorate tops of cakes.

FROSTED STRAWBERRIES

Ripe red stawberries dipped in vanilla frosting and sprinkled
with pistachio nuts.

Makes about 24 frosted strawberries.

1	quart large firm-ripe strawberries	2	teaspoons brandy
⅔	cup vanilla ready-to-spread frosting	6	tablespoons chopped pistachio nuts

1. Wash strawberries (do not hull); pat dry with paper toweling.

2. Place frosting and brandy in a small bowl. Place over hot, not boiling, water and stir until frosting is melted and smooth; cool slightly.

3. Hold berries by the hull and dip into melted frosting until they are three-fourths covered. Hold over bowl until excess frosting has dripped off.

4. Sprinkle coated strawberries with nuts over a piece of wax paper. Place dipped strawberries on a cookie sheet lined with wax paper. Chill until frosting hardens. (Prepare strawberries only a few hours in advance.)

LADYFINGERS

Bake at 300° for 20 minutes.
Makes about 30 ladyfingers.

3	eggs, separated	⅔	cup *sifted* cake flour
⅛	teaspoon salt	1	teaspoon grated lemon rind
3	tablespoons plus ⅓ cup granulated sugar		10X (confectioners') sugar Strawberry jam

1. Grease and flour 2 cookie sheets. Preheat oven to 300°.

2. Beat egg whites with salt in a small bowl with an electric mixer until foamy. Gradually beat in the 3 tablespoons sugar until meringue forms soft peaks.

3. With same beaters, beat egg yolks in a large bowl with electric mixer on high speed until thick, about 5 minutes. Gradually beat in the ⅓ cup sugar until yolks are pale and very thick, about 3 minutes.

4. Sprinkle ⅓ of the sifted flour over the egg yolk mixture. Fold in gently, using a rubber spatula. Repeat with remaining flour just until blended.

5. Stir ¼ of the meringue into the batter to loosen it a little. Gently fold in lemon rind and remaining meringue until no streaks of white remain.

6. Fit a pastry bag with a ½-inch plain round tip; fill bag with batter. Press batter out onto prepared cookie sheets to form strips about 3 inches long and spaced 1 inch apart. Sprinkle lightly with 10X sugar.

7. Bake in upper third of a preheated slow oven (300°) for 20 minutes or until a delicate brown. Remove to wire racks with spatula; cool. Store in container with tight-fitting cover. Before serving, sandwich in pairs with strawberry jam and sprinkle generously with 10X sugar. May also be served singly.

LUSCIOUS ORANGE SPONGE CAKE

A delightful combination of tender fresh orange cake, cream, and crunchy walnuts to make a very special dessert.

Bake at 375° for 15 minutes.
Makes 8 servings.

Cake:
1	cup *sifted* cake flour
1	teaspoon baking powder
¼	teaspoon salt
½	cup finely ground walnuts
3	eggs
¾	cup granulated sugar
⅓	cup orange juice
½	teaspoon orange extract
	10X (confectioner') sugar

Filling and Frosting:
1	cup granulated sugar

⅓	cup all-purpose flour
3	egg yolks
¼	teaspoon grated orange rind
½	cup orange juice
1	tablespoon lemon juice
	Dash salt
1	tablespoons orange-flavored liqueur or orange juice
2	cups heavy cream, whipped
1	cup coarsely chopped walnuts
	Orange slices (optional)
	Fresh mint (optional)

1. For Cake: Grease a 15½ x 10½ x 1-inch jelly roll pan. Line bottom with wax paper, grease paper. Sift flour, baking powder, and salt onto wax paper; stir in nuts. Preheat oven to 357°.

2. Beat eggs in a medium-size bowl with an electric mixer on high speed until thick and light, about 5 minutes. Gradually beat in sugar and continue to beat 2 minutes longer. Blend in orange juice and orange extract with mixer on low speed. Fold in flour mixture gradually. Turn mixture into prepared pan, spreading evenly.

3. Bake in a preheated moderate oven (375°) for 15 minutes or until center springs back when lightly pressed with fingertip. Turn out onto a towel that has been lightly sprinkled with 10X sugar. Lift towel with cake to a wire rack; cool completely.

4. For Filling: Combine sugar, flour, and egg yolks in the top of a double boiler; beat until well blended. Stir in orange rind and juice, lemon juice, and salt. Place over simmering water. Cook, stirring constantly until thickened, about 20 minutes. Cool quickly by emptying the bottom of the double boiler, filling it with ice and cold water, and replacing the top. Stir mixture occasionally as it cools.

5. Cut cake crosswise into 3 equal size recctangles, each 5 x 10 inches. Sprinkle layers with orange liqueur.

6. Fold orange mixture into whipped cream. Use about ⅓ of the mixture to spread on two of the layers. Sandwich the layers with the plain one on top. Spread remaining orange filling-frosting on top and sides of cake. Sprinkle sides with nuts; chill. Garnish with fresh orange slices and mint, if you wish.

NECTARINE-ALMOND MERINGUE TORTE

Chunks of fresh nectarines and whipped cream nestle between almond-studded meringue torte cake layers.

Bake at 350° for 30 minutes.
Makes 8 servings.

2 cups *sifted* cake flour	¾ cup sliced almonds
2 teaspoons baking powder	1½ pounds firm-ripe nectarines
½ teaspoon salt	(4 to 5) plus 1 more for
5 eggs, separated	garnish (optional)
1¾ cups sugar	1 tablespoon sugar
⅓ cup vegetable shortening or	2 teaspoons lemon juice
butter-flavored shortening	1 cup heavy cream
1½ teaspoons vanilla	Fresh mint (optional)
½ cup milk	

1. Grease two 8 x 8 x 2-inch baking pans; dust with flour; tap out excess. Preheat oven to 350°.

2. Sift cake flour, baking powder, and salt onto wax paper.

3. Beat egg whites in a small bowl with an electric mixer until foamy-white and double in volume. Gradually beat in ¾ cup of the sugar until meringue forms firm peaks.

4. With same beater (don't wash), beat remaining 1 cup sugar, shortening, egg yolks, and vanilla in a large bowl with an electric mixer on high speed until light yellow and thick, about 3 minutes.
5. Stir in flour mixture, alternating with milk, beating until smooth after each addition. Spread batter into prepared pans, dividing evenly; smooth tops. Carefully spread meringue over batter, dividing evenly. Sprinkle with almonds.
6. Bake in a preheated moderate oven (350°) for 30 minutes or until meringue is golden brown and cake begins to pull away from pan. (Meringue may rise and crack, but will settle while cooling.)
7. Cool cake layers in pans on wire racks for 30 minutes or until cool enough to handle. Loosen around edges with a knife; turn out onto your hand, then gently place meringue side up on wire racks; cool.
8. About ½ hour before serving, halve, pit, and coarsely chop nectarines; place in a large bowl; sprinkle with sugar and lemon juice; toss lightly. Beat cream in another bowl until stiff; fold into nectarines.
9. Place one cake layer on platter; top with half the nectarine cream; top with remaining cake layer and nectarine cream. Garnish with additional nectarine slices and fresh mint leaves, if you wish.

APRICOT CREAM TORTE

A grand dessert—layers of puff pastry and cream filling, all topped with apricots, whipped cream, and chopped pistachio nuts.

Bake at 350° for 25 minutes.
Makes 8 servings.

½	of a 17¼-ounce package frozen pre-rolled puff pastry, thawed (1 sheet)	½	cup cottage cheese
		½	cup milk
1	package (3¾ ounces) lemon instant pudding and pie filling mix	1	can (17 ounces) apricot halves, drained
		¼	cup heavy cream
½	cup dairy sour cream	⅓	cup chopped pistachio nuts

1. Preheat oven to 350°.
2. Unwrap thawed pastry. Roll out on a lightly floured board with a lightly floured rolling pin to a 15 x 10-inch rectangle. Cut into three 10 x 5-inch rectangles. Prick pastry all over with a fork. Place on an ungreased cookie sheet.

3. Bake in a preheated moderate oven (350°) for 25 minutes or until golden brown. Remove to wire racks; cool thoroughly.

4. Combine pudding mix, sour cream, cottage cheese, and milk in the container of an electric blender. Cover; whirl until smooth and creamy.

5. To assemble torte: Place one pastry layer on serving platter spread with cream filling. Repeat with remaining pastry layers and cream filling, ending with a small amount of cream filling on top layer.

6. Cut apricot halves in half; arrange over top of torte. Beat heavy cream in a small bowl until stiff. Spoon into pastry bag fitted with decorative tip; pipe rosettes of whipped cream around outer edge of torte. Sprinkle apricots with chopped pistachios. Chill until serving time.

JAM CAKE

Bake at 350° for 35 minutes.
Makes 12 servings.

2½	cups *sifted* all-purpose flour	3	eggs
¼	teaspoon ground nutmeg	1	cup raspberry preserves or
¼	teaspoon ground allspice		strawberry jam
1	teaspoon ground cinnamon	¾	cup buttermilk
1	teaspoon baking soda	2	tablespoons bourbon
¾	cup (1½ sticks) butter, softened		Rich Butter Cream Frosting (page 278)
1	cup sugar		

1. Sift flour, nutmeg, allspice, cinnamon, and baking soda onto wax paper. Grease and flour two 8 x 1½-inch layer-cake pans. Preheat oven to 350°

2. Beat butter, sugar, and eggs in a large bowl with an electric mixer until light and fluffy. Stir in preserves.

3. By hand, stir in the flour mixture alternately with buttermilk and bourbon until batter is smooth. Spoon into prepared pans.

4. Bake in a preheated moderate oven (350°) for 35 minutes or until centers spring back when lightly pressed with fingertip.

5. Cool layers in pans on wire racks for 10 minutes. Loosen around edges with a knife; turn out on racks; cool completely.

6. Put layers together with Rich Butter Cream Frosting. Frost top and side. Decorate with additional jam, if you wish.

CARROT-NUT CAKE

Bake at 350° for 1 hour.
Makes 8 servings.

1	cup *sifted* all-purpose flour	½	cup finely chopped walnuts
2	teaspoons baking powder	2	tablespoons rum, brandy, or
⅛	teaspoon salt		orange juice
½	cup vegetable shortening	1	teaspoon lemon juice
1	cup sugar	⅓	cup apricot preserves
3	eggs, separated		Walnut halves
1	cup shredded carrots		

1. Grease a 2-quart fancy tube pan (or you can use a 9-inch tube pan but cake will not be as high). Dust lightly with flour; tap out excess. Preheat oven to 350°

2. Sift four, baking powder, and salt onto wax paper.

3. Beat shortening, sugar, and egg yolks in a large bowl with an electric mixer on high speed for 3 minutes, scraping down side of bowl and beaters occasionally. (Finish mixing cake by hand.)

4. Stir in carrots, walnuts, rum, and lemon juice. Stir in flour mixture a little at a time until batter is smooth.

5. Beat egg whites in a small bowl with an electric mixer until soft peaks form; fold into cake batter. Spoon into prepared pan, spreading top evenly.

6. Bake in a preheated moderate oven (350°) for 1 hour or until top springs back when lightly pressed with fingertip. Cool in pan on a wire rack for 10 minutes. Loosen cake around edge with a metal spatula; turn out onto a wire rack; cool completely.

7. Heat apricot preserves in a small skillet; press through a sieve into a small bowl. Brush glaze over top and side of cake. Garnish with walnut halves.

OLD-FASHIONED WALNUT CAKE

Bake at 350° for 1 hour, 5 minutes.
Makes 16 servings.

2¾ cups *sifted* cake flour	4 eggs
2 teaspoons baking powder	⅔ cup milk
1 teaspoons salt	2 teaspoons vanilla
1 cup (2 sticks) butter, softened	2 cups finely chopped walnuts
1¾ cups sugar	Brown Butter Frosting (page 278)

1. Grease and flour a 9-inch tube pan. Sift flour, baking powder, and salt onto wax paper. Preheat oven to 350°.

2. Beat butter, sugar, and eggs in a large bowl with an electric mixer until light and fluffy, about 3 minutes.

3. By hand, stir in dry ingredients alternately with milk, beating after each addition until batter is smooth. Stir in vanilla and 1 cup of the nuts. Pour batter into prepared pan.

4. Bake in a preheated moderate oven (350°) for 1 hour and 5 minutes or until center springs back when lightly pressed with fingertip.

5. Cool in pan on a wire rack for 10 minutes. Loosen cake around tube and outside edge with a knife; turn out onto wire rack; cool completely.

6. Frost top and side with Brown Butter Frosting; sprinkle with remaining nuts.

CHOCOLATE ROLL

Bake at 375° for 12 minutes.
Makes one 10-inch roll.

¾ cup *sifted* cake flour	¾ cup granulated sugar
¼ cup unsweetened cocoa powder	3 tablespoons water
1 teaspoon baking powder	1 teaspoon vanilla
3 eggs	10X (confectioner') sugar

1. Grease a 15½ x 10½ x 1-inch jelly roll pan; line bottom with wax paper; grease paper. Sift flour, cocoa, and baking powder onto wax paper.

2. Preheat oven to 375°. Beat eggs in a medium-size bowl with an electric mixer until thick and creamy. Gradually add granulated sugar, beating constantly, until mixture is *very* thick. Stir in water and vanilla. Fold in flour mixture. Spread batter in prepared pan.

3. Bake in a preheated moderate oven (375°) for 12 minutes or until center springs back when lightly pressed with fingertip.

4. Loosen cake around edges with a small spatula; invert pan onto clean towel lightly dusted with 10X sugar; peel off wax paper. Starting at one of the short sides, roll cake and towel up together. Place, seam side down, on a wire rack; cool completely.

WALNUT YULE LOG

This chocolate roll is filled with a coffee and walnut-cream mixture, glazed with chocolate, and decorated with marzipan "mushrooms."

Makes 12 servings.

Chocolate Roll (page 191)	**1 teaspoon vanilla**
2 egg yolks	**1 cup very finely chopped walnuts**
2 tablespoons granulated sugar	**¾ cup semisweet chocolate pieces**
1 teaspoon cornstarch	**3 tablespoons unsalted butter or margaine (for glaze)**
½ cup light cream or half and half	**1 tablespoon milk or cream**
¾ cup (1½ stick) unsalted butter	**Chopped pistachio nuts (optional)**
1 cup 10X (confectioners') sugar	**Marzipan "Mushrooms" (recipe below), optional**
1 teaspoon instant coffee powder	

1. Prepare Chocolate Roll.

2. Combine egg yolks, 2 tablespoons sugar, and cornstarch in a small saucepan; blend in cream. Cook, stirring constantly, over medium heat until mixture comes to a boil. Remove from heat; cool; chill.

3. Beat ¾ cup butter in a medium-size bowl with an electric mixer until soft and smooth. Beat in 10X sugar until smooth. Dissolve coffee in vanilla; add to butter mixture. Gradually add chilled egg yolk mixture, 1 tablespoon at at time, while beating constantly. Beat until light and fluffy; fold in nuts.

4. Unroll cake carefully; spread with about ⅔ of walnut mixture. Roll, lifting cake with the end of the towel. Place, seam-side down, on a small cookie sheet. Spread remaining walnut mixture over roll. Chill overnight.

5. Melt chocolate pieces with 3 tablespoons butter and milk in a double boiler over hot, not boiling, water, stirring occasionally until smooth. Let stand 5 minutes, then quickly spread over roll. Sprinkle top with chopped pistachio nuts, if you wish. Keep chilled until serving time. Garnish with Marzipan "Mushrooms," if you wish.

Marzipan "Mushrooms": Shape packaged marzipan into different size "mushrooms." Brush or spread red frosting from a decorating tube over tops, then dip in coarse sugar. Add green food coloring to 1 or 2 tablespoons marzipan to tint a leaf green; flatten small pieces into leaf shapes.

WHIPPED CREAM CAKE WITH MARZIPAN FRUITS

The colorful marzipan fruits serve as delicious garnish for the tender cake.

Bake at 350° for 30 minutes.
Makes 12 servings.

2⅔ cups *sifted* cake flour	1 jar (12 ounces) apricot
1⅓ cups sugar	preserves
2 teaspoons baking powder	2 tablespoons light corn syrup
1⅓ cups heavy cream	Royal Frosting (page 277)
4 eggs	Marzipan Fruits
2 teaspoons grated lemon rind	(recipe below)

1. Grease and flour one 9 x 1½-inch and one 8 x 1½-inch layer-cake pan. Preheat oven to 350°.

2. Measure flour, sugar, and baking powder into a sifter; reserve.

3. Beat cream in a medium-size bowl until stiff; reserve.

4. Beat eggs in a large bowl with an electric mixer on high speed until very thick and light colored. Beat in lemon rind; fold in whipped cream. Sift dry ingredients over egg mixture while folding gently until smooth; pour batter into prepared pans, adding about ⅔ to larger pan and ⅓ to smaller pan.

5. Bake in a preheated moderate oven (350°) for 30 minutes or until centers spring back when lightly pressed with fingertip. Cool layers in pans on wire racks for 10 minutes. Loosen around edges with a small knife; turn out onto wire racks; cool completely. Layers can be wrapped and frozen for up to 2 weeks.

6. Even off layers with a sharp knife if necessary. Heat apricot preserves and corn syrup to a boil in a small saucepan. Lower heat; simmer 3 to 4 minutes. Press through a strainer; cool slighty. Brush generously over cake layers. Place larger layer on cake plate.

7. Prepare Royal Frosting. Fit cake decorator with a plain round writing tip. Fill with frosting. Pipe frosting onto side of cake in a lattice pattern; pipe border around top and bottom edges. Arrange Marzipan Fruits over half of cake. Place smaller layer on top, leaning it a little to the back so fruits will show and top layer will sit at an angle. Pipe lattice pattern on top and a border around top edge.

8. Keep loosely covered until serving time.

Marzipan Fruits:

2 rolls (7 ounces each) marzipan; Assorted food coloring; Red decorating sugar; and Whole cloves.

Pears: To make 3 "pears," measure a scant ¼ cup marzipan; tint pale yellow-green. Cut into 3 equal-size pieces. Mold each piece to form a "pear." Insert a clove head in blossom and a whole clove for the stem. Using a small artist's brush, paint a red blush on "pears." Place on tray lined with wax paper.

Green apples: To make 3 "apples," measure a scant ¼ cup marzipan; tint pale apple-green. Cut into 3 equal-size pieces. Mold each piece to form an "apple." Insert a clove head in blossom end and a whole clove in end for stem. Paint on a red blush.

Oranges: To make 3 "oranges," measure 2 tablespoons marzipan; Mold each piece into a round orange shape; roll "oranges" over a fine toothed grater to make "pores." Paint entire surface orange color. Insert a whole clove in one end.

Peaches: To make 3 "peaches," measure 2 tablespoons marzipan; tint yellow-peach. Cut into 3-equal-size pieces; mold into peach shapes. With the blunt side of a knife, make indentation down center of each. Paint on red blush.

Plums: To make 2 "plums," measure 4 teaspoons marzipan. Tint purple (red and blue). Cut into 2 pieces; mold to form oval-shaped "plums." With the blunt side of a knife, make indentation down center of each. Paint on a red blush.

Lemons: To make 3 "lemons," measure 1 tablespoon marzipan. Tint yellow. Cut into 3 equal-size pieces. Mold each piece to form a "lemon," slightly tapered at both ends.

Strawberries: To make 4 "strawberries," measure 2 tablespoons marzipan. Cut into 4 equal pieces. Mold each to form a "strawberry." Brush with red food coloring; roll in red sugar while still moist. *Cherries:* To make 6 double-stemmed "cherries" measure 1 tablespoon marzipan. Tint bright cherry-red. Cut into 12 equal-size pieces roll each piece into a round ball. For each pair of "cherries," bend a tie-twist (from plastic bags) in half; push a "cherry" onto each end.

Grapes: To make 1 bunch "grapes," measure 2 tablespoons marzipan. Tint green and purple. Cut into about 18 pieces. Roll each piece to make round "grapes"; press gently together to form a cluster.

Bananas: To make 4 or 5 "bananas," measure 2 tablespoons marzipan. Tint yellow. Cut into 4 or 5 equal-size pieces. Roll each piece into a roll about 2 inches long; taper ends slightly and pinch one side to form rib of "banana." For a fully "ripe" look, touch a few places with plain cocoa.

Let marzipan fruits dry on tray.

Note: Marzipan will keep several weeks in freezer if wrapped tightly in aluminum foil or plastic wrap.

PUMPKIN-WALNUT CHEESECAKE

Bake at 325° for 1 hour, 45 minutes.
Makes 16 servings.

1	package (6 ounces) zwieback crackers, crushed (1½ cups)	5	eggs
1	cup granulated sugar	1	can (16 ounces) pumpkin
6	tablespoons butter, melted	1¾	teaspoons pumpkin pie spice
3	packages (8 ounces each) cream cheese, softened	¼	cup heavy cream
			Walnut Topping (recipe below)
¾	cup firmly packed light brown sugar		Whipped cream (optional)
			Walnut halves (optional)

1. Lightly butter a 9-inch springform pan. Blend zwieback crumbs, ¼ cup of the granulated sugar, and the butter in a medium-size bowl. Press firmly over bottom and up side of prepared springform pan. Chill.

2. Preheat oven to 325°. Beat cream cheese in a large bowl with an electric mixer on medium speed until smooth. Add remaining ¾ cup granulated sugar and brown sugar gradually, beating until well mixed. Beat in eggs, 1 at a time, until mixture is light and fluffy. Beat in pumpkin, pumpkin pie spice, and heavy cream on low speed. Pour into prepared pan.

3. Bake in a preheated slow oven (325°) for 1 hour and 35 minutes. While cake is baking, prepare Walnut Topping. Remove cake from oven; sprinkle with Walnut Topping; bake an additional 10 minutes. Cool cake on a wire rack. Refrigerate several hours or overnight. Garnish with whipped cream and walnut halves, if you wish.

Walnut Topping: Combine 6 tablespoons softened butter with 1 cup firmly packed light brown sugar in a small bowl; mix well until crumbly. Blend in 1 cup chopped walnuts.

CLEAN-CUT CHEESECAKE

If you have problems cutting a cheesecake with a knife, try using a long strand of waxed or unwaxed dental floss. Hold the floss tightly and press gently into the cheesecake. To remove the floss, just pull out from the bottom. Do not try to pull it up through the slice. If the crust is too firm for the floss to cut, finish cutting with a thin knife.

PINEAPPLE-COCONUT CHEESECAKE

A delicious no-bake dessert.

Makes 16 servings.

2	packages (8 ounces each) cream cheese	1	can (15½ ounces) cream of coconut
2	cans (8 ounces each) crushed pineapple in pineapple juice	1	cup zwieback cracker crumbs
3	teaspoons unflavored gelatin (1½ envelopes)	½	cup flaked coconut
3	eggs, separated	¼	cup (½ stick) butter or margarine, melted
		2	tablespoons sugar

1. Let the cream cheese soften to room temperature in a large bowl. Lightly butter a 9-inch springform pan.

2. Drain juice from pineapple into a glass measure; reserve ¾ cup drained pineapple juice and the crushed pineapple.

3. Sprinkle gelatin over pineapple juice in a medium-size saucepan; let stand 5 minutes to soften. Beat egg yolks slightly in a small bowl; stir in cream of coconut; then add mixture to gelatin. Cook over medium heat, stirring constantly, just until mixture starts to boil, but do not allow to boil. Cool

4. Combine zwieback crumbs, flaked coconut, and butter in a medium-size bowl. Sprinkle ¼ cup mixture around sides of prepared springform pan; press remaining mixture onto bottom. Chill briefly before filling.

5. Beat cream cheese just until smooth with an electric mixer on medium speed. Beat in the cooled gelatin mixture.

6. Place pan in a bowl of ice and cold water to speed setting; chill, stirring often, until mixture mounds slightly when dropped from a spoon.

7. While gelatin mixture chills, beat egg whites in a small bowl with an electric mixer until foamy; slowly beat in sugar until meringue stands in firm peaks.

8. Fold meringue and crushed pineapple into chilled gelatin mixture. Turn into prepared pan. Chill several hours, preferably overnight, until firm. Loosen cake around side with a spatula, then release and remove side.

STAWBERRY CHEESECAKE DELUXE

Bake crust at 400° for 6 minutes; then bake cake first at 475° for 12 minutes, then at 250° for 1½ hours.
Makes 16 to 20 servings.

5 packages (8 ounces each) cream cheese
Sweet Pastry (recipe below)
1¾ cups sugar
3 tablespoons flour
5 whole eggs

2 egg yolks
1 tablespoon grated lemon rind
¼ cup heavy cream
Strawberry Topping (recipe below)

1. Let the cream cheese soften to room temperature in a large bowl; while preparing the Sweet Pastry. Preheat oven to 400°.
2. Roll ⅓ of chilled Sweet Pastry between 2 pieces of wax paper to a circle 9 inches in diameter. Remove top sheet of wax paper. Invert dough onto bottom of a 9-inch springform pan. Carefully remove remaining wax paper. Press dough to fit inside rim. Place on a cookie sheet.
3. Bake in a preheated hot oven (400°) for 6 minutes or until lightly browned; cool. Butter side of springform pan; fit over cooled bottom. Roll remaining dough into a rectangle, 4 inches wide and 15 inches long, between 2 pieces of wax paper; remove top sheet of wax paper and cut dough in half lengthwise through bottom paper; press on side of pan; remove remaining wax paper; press firmly to bottom. Refrigerate. Raise oven temperature to 475°
4. Beat cream cheese with an electric mixer on medium speed just until smooth. Add sugar gradually, beating just until light and fluffy; sprinkle flour over mixture; blend thoroughly. Add whole eggs and egg yolks, 1 at a time, beating well after each addition. Beat in lemon rind and heavy cream on *low* speed. Pour into prepared pan.
5. Bake in a preheated very hot oven (475°) for 12 minutes; lower temperature to 250° and bake 1½ hours. Turn off oven heat and let cake remain in oven, with door ajar, 30 minutes longer.
6. Remove cake from oven; let cake cool completely on a wire rack.
7. Decorate top with Strawberry Topping. Refrigerate several hours or overnight.
8. To serve: Loosen cake around edge with metal spatula; then remove side of springform pan. Serve at room temperature. Keep leftover cake in refrigerator.

Sweet Pastry: Combine 1 cup *sifted* all-purpose flour with ¼ cup sugar in a medium-size bowl; cut in 6 tablespoons butter with knife or pastry blender until mixture is crumbly. Add 1 egg yolk, slightly beaten, and ½ teaspoon vanilla; mix lightly with fork just until pastrty is moistened; shape into ball with fingers. Wrap in wax paper; chill 1 hour.

Strawberry Topping: Wash, pat dry, and hull 4 cups (2 pints) strawberries. Combine ½ cup red currant jelly and 1 tablespoon sugar in a small saucepan; bring to a boil over low heat, stirring constantly; boil 1 minute; remove from heat; cool slightly. Dip strawberries into jelly to coat. Transfer to wax paper-lined wire rack with stem-side down; let set. When glaze has set, arrange strawberries on top of cheesecake.

GIVING AWAY CHEESECAKE WITHOUT LOSING THE PAN

If you plan to give a cheesecake away as a gift, you always face the problem of losing the bottom of your springform pan. But if you remove the cheesecake from the metal bottom before you give it away, you may mess up your cake. To avoid this problem, buy an aluminum foil 8- or 9-inch cake pan. Cut out the bottom of the cake pan and insert into the springform pan over the metal bottom. Once the cheesecake is firm and cold, transfer to a doily-lined piece of cardboard or plate, lifting the cake on the foil pan bottom with a broad spatula.

ORANGE CHARLOTTE

Makes 8 servings.

1	package (3 ounces) ladyfingers	4	eggs, separated
3	tablespoons orange-flavored liqueur	1	can (6 ounces) frozen orange juice concentrate, thawed, undiluted
2	envelopes unflavored gelatin	1¼	cups water
½	cup sugar	1	cup heavy cream

1. Separate ladyfingers; place on a cookie sheet; drizzle part of the liqueur over; let stand while making the orange filling.

2. Combine gelatin and ¼ cup of the sugar in a heavy saucepan; beat in egg yolks, juice concentrate, and water.

3. Cook over medium heat, stirring constantly, until mixture thickens and just coats a spoon. Pour mixture into a large bowl; stir in the remaining liqueur. Chill 30 minutes in refrigerator or until mixture is slightly thickened.

4. While gelatin chills, stand ladyfingers around edge of an 8-inch springform pan; arrange remaining ladyfingers in the bottom.

5. Beat egg whites until foamy-white and double in volume in a medium size bowl; beat in remaining ¼ cup sugar, 1 tablespoon at a time, until meringue forms soft peaks. Beat heavy cream until stiff in a small bowl.

6. Fold whipped cream, then meringue, into thickened gelatin mixture until no streaks of white remain. Spoon mixture into prepared pan. Chill 4 hours in refrigerator or until firm.

7. To serve: Remove side of pan; slide dessert, on its metal base, onto a plate.

QUICK SET

Chill gelatin base fast by placing the bowl in a pan of ice and cold water. Gelatin sets first at the bottom and the sides, so stir it often for even thickening.

BOMBE GLACÉ

Prepare this French ice cream dessert up to 2 months ahead.

Makes 8 to 10 servings.

½ cup chopped mixed candied fruits

2 tablespoons apricot liqueur or brandy

1 quart chocolate ice cream, slightly softened

1 pint stawberry ice cream, slightly softened

1 cup heavy cream

¼ cup superfine sugar

Whipped cream

1. Combine candied fruits and liqueur; let stand while preparing remainder of recipe.

2. Rinse a 6-cup fluted mold with cold water. Spread chocolate ice cream evenly around bottom and side of mold with a large spoon; freeze 30 minutes. Spread strawberry ice cream evenly over chocolate; freeze 30 minutes.

3. Beat cream in a small bowl until stiff; fold in sugar and fruits with any liqueur not absorbed. Spoon into center of mold; level off with a spatula.

4. Cover mold with a piece of wax paper, then cover tightly with lid of mold or heavy-duty aluminum foil. Freeze until solid, about 3 hours.

5. Remove mold from freezer 30 minutes before serving. Run a spatula around top edge; hold a hot wet towel around mold for 3 to 4 seconds; turn out onto chilled serving dish. Return to freezer until softened outside has refrozen.

6. Just before serving, garnish outside of bombe with whipped cream. Cut into wedges.

Note: Bombe can be frosted with whipped cream and garnished with candied red cherries.

SNOWBALL ICE CREAM CAKE

Listen for the oohs and ahs when you set this spectacular dessert on the table. No one will ever guess just how easy it was to make!

Makes 16 servings.

½ cup slivered almonds
⅔ cup granulated sugar
1 package (10¾ ounces) frozen chocolate pound cake, partially thawed
2 quarts vanilla ice cream

2 cups heavy cream
¼ cup 10X (confectioners') sugar
Candied lilacs or violets or candied fruits

1. Spread almonds in a small skillet; heat over medium heat, stirring or shaking pan often, until lightly toasted, about 10 minutes. Remove almonds from skillet; reserve. Lightly butter a cookie sheet.

2. Add sugar to skillet; heat slowly until sugar melts and starts to turn golden in color. Stir in almonds; cook and stir over medium heat, 1 minute. Pour mixture onto prepared cookie sheet. Cool completely. Chop coarsely with a large knife.

3. Cut cake lengthwise into about 12 very thin slices; cut each long slice in half crosswise. Line two identical 5-or 6-cup rounded-bottomed mixing bowls with cake slices, overlapping slices to fit. Place in freezer.

4. Remove 1 quart ice cream from freezer; soften slightly in a large bowl. Fold in half of almond mixture. Spoon into one cake-lined bowl. Place in freezer. Repeat with remaining ice cream, almond mixture, and second bowl. (If you have only one bowl, make and freeze one half; remove from bowl; keep frozen; repeat with other half.)

5. When both halves are almost frozen, trim cake to same level as ice cream. Unmold one cake from one bowl and set it on top of the other in second bowl to form a ball. Wrap and freeze several days or weeks until ready to frost and serve.

6. Loosen cake from bowl and unmold ball onto a serving plate. Whip the cream with 10X sugar until stiff. Spread a very thin coating over entire ball, then pipe small rosettes of remaining cream close together to cover completely. Decorate with candied flowers or candied fruits. Return to freezer until serving time.

7. When ready to serve, hold cake with a fork while slicing into wedges with a large knife.

CRANBERRY SHERBET

Makes about 2 cups.

4	cups fresh or frozen cranberries (1⅓ packages)	¾	cup sugar
1	cup water	¼	cup orange juice
		2	tablespoons lemon juice

1. Puree cranberries in container of an electric blender or food processor. Press puree through a fine sieve or coarse sieve lined with several layers of cheesecloth.

2. Bring water and sugar to a boil in a nonaluminum saucepan. Stir in cranberry puree, orange juice, and lemon juice. Simmer until puree is very soft and has turned bright and shiny, about 5 minutes. Cool to room temperature, stirring occasionally.

3. Pour mixture into shallow pan; freeze until mixture is frozen 1 inch from the edge. Turn cranberry mixture into a chilled large bowl; beat with chilled beaters. Return to pan; return to freezer until solidly frozen. Store in tightly covered container.

Note: Sherbet can also be frozen in a manual or electric ice cream freezer following manufacturer's directions.

PUMPKIN-MINCE PIE

Bake at 425° for 15 minutes; then at 350° for 35 minutes.
Makes 8 servings.

1⅓	cups ready-to-use-mincemeat	1	teaspoon ground cinnamon
2	teaspoons grated orange rind	½	teaspoon ground nutmeg
1	unbaked 9-inch pastry shell with a high fluted edge	½	teaspoon ground ginger
		¼	teaspoon salt
2	eggs	1	can (16 ounces) pumpkin
1	can (14 ounces) sweetened condensed milk	½	cup heavy cream, whipped
			Slivers of orange rind

1. Preheat oven to 425°. Combine mincemeat and grated orange rind in a 2-cup measure; spoon into pastry shell, spreading evenly.

2. Beat eggs in a large bowl until frothy. Stir in milk, cinnamon, nutmeg, ginger, salt, and pumpkin. Mix well until smooth. Pour over mincemeat layer in pastry shell.

3. Bake pie in a preheated hot oven (425°) for 15 minutes; lower heat to moderate (350°) and continue baking for 35 minutes or until the tip of a knife, when inserted into filling 1 inch from edge, comes out clean. Cool pie on a wire rack. Garnish with whipped cream and orange rind slivers.

FRUIT IN WINE JELLY

Glistening summer fruits suspended in a Riesling wine jelly.

Makes 8 servings.

2 envelopes unflavored gelatin	½ cup seedless green grapes,
1 cup water	halved
2½ cups Riesling wine	1 cup cantaloupe balls (1
½ cup sugar	medium-size cantaloupe)
½ pint strawberries (1 cup),	Strawberries (optional)
washed, hulled, and patted	Grapes (optional)
dry on paper toweling	Banana slices (optional)
1 medium-size banana, sliced	Cantaloupe slices (optional)
(½ cup)	

1. Sprinkle gelatin over water in a medium-size saucepan; let stand 5 minutes to soften. Place over low heat, stirring constantly until gelatin is dissolved. Cool.

2. Combine wine and sugar in a large bowl; stir to dissolve sugar completely. Stir in cooled gelatin. Place bowl in pan partly filled with ice and cold water to speed setting; chill, stirring often, until mixture is thickened.

3. Place ¾ cup wine jelly in a 6-cup glass bowl; add a layer of strawberries; add more wine jelly. Add layers of grape, banana, and cantaloupe alternating with remaining wine jelly. Chill 4 hours or until set. Garnish with additional strawberries, grapes, bananas (dipped in lemon juice to prevent from discoloring), and cantaloupe slices, if you wish.

FLOATING FRUIT

To keep fruit from floating to the top when making a clear gelatin mold, make sure the gelatin is the consistency of unbeaten egg whites. This way, pieces of fruit will stay in suspension rather than rise to the top.

KRANSEKAGE

A marvelous crunchy almond cookie "tree" from Scandinavia
made for festive occasions.

Bake at 400° for 10 minutes.
Makes 24 servings.

3 cans (8 ounces each) almond   1½ cups 10X (confectioners')
   paste   sugar
3 egg whites   Royal Frosting (page 277)

1. Crumble almond paste into a large saucepan; gradually work in egg whites and 10X sugar with a wooden spoon.

2. Heat, stirring and turning mixture constantly, just until mixture is a little too hot to touch. Do not overheat. Remove from heat. Cool completely. Wrap and refrigerate.

3. When ready to shape and bake, grease and flour 2 large cookie sheets. Starting with about ½ cup mixture for the largest ring, roll into an 18-inch long rope. Shape into a ring measuring 6 inches in diameter, on prepared cookie sheet. Pull up top of ring dough to make a cone shape.

4. Repeat with remaining dough to make 8 more cone-shaped rings, each rope 1½ inches shorter than the previous, each ring ½ inch smaller, with smallest 2 inches. Make a small round ball for top. Referigerate on cookie sheets until ready to bake. Preheat oven to 400°.

5. Bake in a preheated hot oven (400°) for 10 minutes or until golden. Cool on cookie sheet on a wire rack for 10 minutes. Carefully loosen rings with spatula; remove to rack; cool completely.

6. To assemble: Place largest ring on serving plate. Pipe Royal Frosting through a wax paper cone to decorate and "cement" ring together. Continue with remaining rings and frosting, ending with the round cookie on top. Decorate with holly, if you wish.

ORANGE-RUM SAVARIN

Bake at 375° for 50 minutes.
Makes 12 servings.

1 envelope active dry yeast
3 tablespoons sugar
⅓ cup very warm water
4 eggs, at room temperature
3 cups *sifted* all-purpose flour
⅔ cup butter, softened

⅓ cup chopped candied orange peel
Rum Syrup (recipe below)
½ cup apricot preserves, melted
Fresh fruit (optional)
Candied fruit (optional)

1. Sprinkle yeast and a pinch of the sugar over very warm water in a large bowl; stir to dissolve. Let stand until bubbly, about 10 minutes.
2. Add remaining sugar, eggs, and 2 cups of the flour; beat with an electric mixer for 2 minutes. Beat in butter, 1 tablespoon at a time. Stir in remaining flour and orange peel. Cover; let rise in a warm place until double in volume.
3. Butter an 8-cup brioche pan or ovenproof bowl. Stir dough down; turn into prepared pan. Let rise in a warm place until double in volume. Preheat oven to 375°.
4. Bake in a preheated moderate oven (375°) for 50 minutes or until loaf sounds hollow when tapped. Remove to a wire rack; cool.
5. Place cake on a deep platter; baste with hot Rum Syrup until all is absorbed. Brush with preserves. Garnish with fresh and candied fruits, if you wish.

Rum Syrup: Combine 2 cups orange juice and 1½ cups sugar in a large saucepan. Simmer for 15 minutes. Remove from heat; stir in ¾ cup light or dark rum.

DRIED FRUIT STRUDEL

Bake at 400° for 30 minutes.
Makes 16 servings.

1 package (8 ounces) dried apricots
2 cups (8 ounces) pitted prunes
1 cup (6 ounces) pitted dates, snipped
1 medium-size apple, pared, cored, and chopped (1 cup)
2 teaspoons grated lemon rind

3 tablespoons lemon juice
½ cup finely chopped walnuts
⅔ cup granulated sugar
8 strudel or phyllo leaves (from a 1-pound package)
¾ cup (1½ sticks) butter or margarine, melted
10X (confectioners') sugar

1. Soak apricots and prunes in warm water to cover for 15 minutes; drain well. Chop fruits or snip them with scissors.

2. Combine apricots, prunes, dates, apples, lemon rind, lemon juice, walnuts, and granulated sugar in a large bowl; mix well.

3. Preheat oven to 400°. Place a clean kitchen towel on a flat working surface; sprinkle lightly with water. Carefully place one strudel or phyllo leaf on towel; brush with butter. Repeat with 3 more strudel leaves and butter. (Keep remaining leaves covered with a moist towel to prevent drying.)

4. Leaving 2-inch margins on sides, spoon half of the fruit mixture in an even row along one long edge; fold in margins.

5. Using the towel to lift dough, roll dough over filling like a jelly roll, using towel to lift and aid rolling. Repeat with remaining strudel leaves and filling for second strudel.

6. Line a large cookie sheet with heavy-duty aluminum foil. Ease filled rolls onto cookie sheet, placing about 3 inches apart; brush each with some of the melted butter. Turn up edges of foil 1 inch all around in case of spills.

7. Bake in a preheated hot oven (400°) for 30 minutes, brushing several times with remaining butter until pastry is golden.

8. Allow pastry to cool 15 minutes and then slide onto serving board. Sprinkle with 10X sugar. Cut each strudel into 8 slices with a sharp knife. Serve warm.

FLAMED SPICY-NUT CRÊPES

Makes 6 servings.

Sweet Crêpes (page 208)

Filling:
½ cup firmly packed light brown sugar
6 tablespoons butter or margarine
1 teaspoon ground cinnamon
¼ teaspoon ground nutmeg
2 tablespoons apple brandy or applejack
½ cup chopped walnuts

Sauce:
2 tablespoons butter or margarine
2 tablespoons honey
½ cup orange juice
1 red apple, cored and thinly sliced
½ cup apple brandy or applejack

1. Prepare Sweet Crêpes.

2. Prepare Filling: Beat sugar, butter, cinnamon, and nutmeg until light and fluffy in a small bowl; beat in 2 tablespoons apple brandy, 1 at a time. Fold in nuts.

3. Spread each crêpe with butter mixture, dividing evenly. Fold each in half, then in half again. Arrange on plate; cover and refrigerate until ready to serve.

4. Prepare Sauce: Heat shallow chafing dish over an alcohol flame; add butter and honey; heat until bubbly. Add orange juice and sliced apple; bring to a boil and boil for 1 minutes. Arrange the folded crêpes in sauce and heat through.

5. Pour ½ cup apple brandy over crêpes; stand back and ignite with a lighted match; shake chafing dish gently back and forth, spooning the flaming sauce over crêpes until flames die.

SWEET CRÊPES

Makes 12 crêpes (6 to 7 inches in diameter).

3	eggs	2	tablespoons butter or
¾	cup all-purpose flour		margarine, melted
¼	teaspoon salt	2	tablespoons sugar
1	cup milk		Butter

1. Combine eggs, flour, salt, and ¼ cup of the milk in a medium-size bowl; beat with rotary beater until smooth. Beat in melted butter, then remaining milk and sugar. Refrigerate, covered, at least 1 hour.

2. Slowly heat a 7- or 8-inch skillet until a drop of water sizzles when dropped on surface. Butter skillet lightly for the first few crêpes; after that it will be seasoned and crêpes will not stick.

3. Pour 3 tablespoons batter into hot skillet; quickly rotate skillet to spread batter evenly. Cook over medium heat until lightly browned; turn and brown other side. Remove to plate; when cool, stack with wax paper or plastic wrap between each.

SIZING A MOLD

Puzzled about the size of a fancy mold? Figure it out by filling the mold right to the brim with water and then measuring. To save time when you make your next mold, scratch the cup size on the bottom with a nail.

STRAWBERRY-CHEESE MOLD

Two kinds of cheese make this handsome dessert flavored with berries and lime super smooth.

Makes 10 servings.

2	pints strawberries	½	cup milk
1	cup sugar	1	container (16 ounces)
2	envelopes unflavored gelatin		creamed cottage cheese
½	cup cold water	1	package (8 ounces) cream
2	teaspoons grated lime rind		cheese, softened
3	tablespoons lime juice	3	egg whites

1. Wash and hull 1 pint of strawberries; slice into a large bowl; add ½ cup of the sugar; let stand about 30 minutes; then crush or puree in the container of an electric blender. Pour back into large bowl.
2. Sprinkle gelatin over cold water in small saucepan; let stand 5 minutes to soften. Heat, stirring constantly, over low heat just until gelatin is dissolved. Stir in lime rind and juice; add to strawberry mixture.
3. Combine milk and cottage cheese in the container of an electric blender. Cover. Whirl at high speed until smooth. Add cream cheese in several pieces; whirl just until smooth. Add to strawberry mixture, stirring until smooth. Chill, stirring often, until mixture mounds slightly when spooned.
4. Beat egg whites until foamy-white in a small bowl. Gradually beat in ¼ cup of the sugar until meringue stands in soft peaks. Fold meringue into cheese mixture. Spoon into an 8-cup mold. Chill at least 4 hours or until firm.
5. Loosen mold around edge with small knife; dip mold quickly in and out of hot water. Wipe water off mold. Place serving plate over mold; turn upside down; shake mold to release, lift off. Keep refrigerated until serving time.
6. Wash and hull remaining 1 pint strawberries; halve, or slice if large, into a medium-size bowl. Add remaining ¼ cup sugar; toss gently. Let stand 20 to 30 minutes until juices run freely.
7. To serve: Spoon strawberry sauce around base of cheese mold; decorate with additional strawberries and lime slices; sprinkle with grated lime rind, if you wish.

FROZEN GRAND MARNIER MOUSSE

A spectacular centerpiece for the buffet table. Prepare the frozen mousse up to a week ahead, and decorate just before serving.

Makes 12 servings.

⅓	cup sugar	4	egg whites
1	envelope unflavored gelatin	¼	cup sugar
2	teaspoons cornstarch	2	cups heavy cream
6	egg yolks	1	pint strawberries, washed, hulled, and halved
1	cup milk		
⅓	cup Grand Marnier or orange juice	2	kiwi fruit, peeled and sliced

1. Combine ⅓ cup sugar, gelatin, and cornstarch in a medium-size saucepan; add egg yolks; beat until well blended. Gradually stir in milk. Cook, stirring constantly, over medium heat, just until mixture is slightly thickened. Remove from heat; stir in liqueur.

2. Set pan in a larger pan filled with ice and cold water. Chill, stirring often, until mixture mounds when spooned.

3. While mixture is chilling, beat egg whites in a medium-size bowl with an electric mixer until foamy-white and double in volume. Beat in ¼ cup sugar gradually until the meringue forms soft peaks.

4. Beat 1½ cups of the heavy cream in a small bowl until stiff. Fold whipped cream, then meringue into gelatin mixture until no streaks of white remain. Turn into an 8-cup decorative ring mold; smooth top. Wrap mold with aluminum foil or plastic wrap. Freeze overnight or until firm. (The mousse can be frozen for up to 1 week.)

5. To serve: Remove mousse from freezer. Loosen around edges with a small spatula. Unmold onto serving platter. Beat remaining ½ cup cream in a small bowl until stiff. Pipe whipped cream around base and top of mousse. Garnish with strawberries and kiwis.

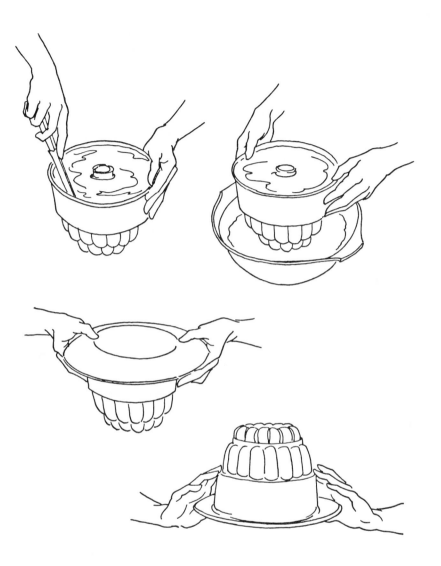

FAIL-SAFE UNMOLDING

To unmold gelatin, follow these steps: First run a small-tip knife around top edge of mold to loosen. Then tip mold from side to side, shaking gently, until gelatin pulls away completely. Cover mold with a serving plate, grasp both firmly, turn upside down, and lift off mold. An alternate method is to loosen with knife as above, dip mold quickly in and out of hot water, and invert onto the plate.

SHERRY BAVARIAN CREAM
WITH SPONGE CAKE

A super-special dessert: A satin smooth sherry bavarian crowning a
tender sponge cake split and layered with raspberry preserves
and whipped cream.

Makes 12 servings.

1	envelope unflavored gelatin	2	cups heavy cream
½	cup granulated sugar	¼	cup 10X (confectioners')
½	cup half and half or light		sugar
	cream	1	jar (12 ounces) raspberry
4	eggs, separated		preserves
⅔	cup cream sherry	1	pint strawberries, washed
	Dash ground nutmeg		and hulled
	Lemony Sponge Cake		Chopped pistachio nuts
	(page 34)		

1. Mix gelatin and ¼ cup of the sugar in a small saucepan; blend in
half and half; let stand 5 minutes. Place egg whites in a large bowl;
add yolks to gelatin mixture. Beat mixture with rotary beater until
blended.

2. Cook over medium heat, stirring constantly, until mixture is
slightly thickened and gelatin is dissolved. Remove from heat; stir in
¼ cup of the sherry and the nutmeg.

3. Place saucepan in a larger pan filled with ice and cold water to
speed thickening. Chill, stirring often, until mixture is thick enough to
mound when spooned.

4. While mixture chills, beat egg whites in a large bowl until foamy-
white and double in volume. Beat in remaining ¼ cup sugar gradually
until meringue stands in soft peaks.

5. Beat about ¼ of the meringue into thickened gelatin mixture; then
fold this mixture into remaining meringue until no streaks of white
remain. Spoon into a 5-cup mold (star-shape if you have it or use any
5-cup mold that will fit over a 9-or 10-inch cake). Chill until firm, about
3 hours.

6. Prepare, bake, and cool Lemony Sponge Cake. Split sponge cake
into 4 layers with a long, thin-bladed knife.

7. Beat cream with the 10X sugar in a medium-size bowl until stiff.

8. Place bottom layer on a serving plate; sprinkle with remaining ¼
cup sherry; spread with ⅓ cup of raspberry preserves; top with second
layer; sprinkle with sherry; spread with 1 cup of the whipped cream.

Top with third layer; sprinkle with sherry; spread with remaining ⅓ cup preserves. Top with fourth layer; sprinkle with remaining sherry. Spread a thin coating of cream on side and top of cake.

9. Loosen gelatin mold around edge with tip of a knife; invert mold over cake. Place a hot damp towel over mold to release. Pipe remaining cream through a pastry bag onto side of cake and on top of mold. Fill in top of star with halved strawberries and garnish with remaining berries.

10. Press remaining preserves through a sieve to remove seeds; brush over berries on top of mold. Garnish with pistachio nuts. Chill until ready to serve.

TWIN ZABAGLIONE SOUFFLÉ

Makes 8 servings.

1	envelope unflavored gelatin	4	egg whites
¼	cup water	¼	cup sugar
7	egg yolks	½	cup heavy cream, whipped
½	cup sugar		Whipped Cream
⅔	cup Marsala or cream sherry		Semisweet chocolate curls
1	tablespoon instant espresso powder		

1. Prepare a 5-cup soufflé dish or straight-sided glass dish with a collar this way: Fold a 24-inch length of 12-inch-wide aluminum foil in thirds lengthwise; wrap around dish to make a 2-inch collar. Fasten with tape or string. To make divider for the two mixtures: Tear off a length of aluminum foil that will just fit vertically inside the dish. Fold in thirds and stand it inside dish. Tape to collar at top.

2. Sprinkle gelatin over water in a 1-cup measure. Let stand 5 minutes to soften. Set cup in a saucepan of simmering water, stirring until gelatin is completely dissolved.

3. Beat egg yolks and ½ cup of the sugar slightly in the top of a double boiler. Beat in all but 1 tablespoon of the Marsala. Place over simmering, not boiling, water.

4. Cook, beating constantly with a rotary hand mixer or portable electric mixer on medium speed, until mixture thickens slightly and is more than double in volume. This will take about 20 minutes. Remove double boiler top from water; add gelatin and continue beating a few minutes longer. Divide mixture evenly between 2 medium-size bowls.

5. Dissolve espresso in reserved tablespoon of Marsala; beat into mixture in one of the bowls. Chill both bowls until mixture mounds slightly when spooned.

6. Beat egg whites until foamy; gradually beat in ¼ cup sugar and continue beating until meringue stands in soft peaks.

7. Fold half the meringue and half the whipped cream into each bowl of gelatin mixture. Spoon both mixtures simultaneously into prepared dish, placing espresso mixture on one side of the divider and plain mixture on the other. When dish is full, gently pull divider out, scraping off each side. Gently smooth soufflés with spatula. Refrigerate 4 hours.

8. To serve: Remove collar carefully; garnish with additional whipped cream and curls or gratings of semisweet chocolate.

CHESTNUT BAVARIAN CREAM

Makes 8 servings.

1 can (16 ounces) chestnuts in light syrup	¼ cup Grand Marnier or orange juice
¾ cup sugar	1½ cups heavy cream
2 envelopes unflavored gelatin	Whipped cream (optional)
¼ teaspoon salt	Orange wedges (optional)
6 egg yolks, slightly beaten	Candied green cherries
3 cups milk	(optional)

1. Whirl chestnuts in their syrup, half at a time, in the container of an electric blender or food processor until finely pureed (or press through a sieve). Reserve.

2. Combine sugar, gelatin, and salt in a medium-size heavy saucepan; add egg yolks; beat until well blended. Stir in milk. Cook, stirring constantly, over medium heat, just until mixture coats a spoon and is slightly thickened (do not let mixture boil). Remove from heat; stir in liqueur and chestnut puree.

3. Pour mixture into a large bowl; place in a larger bowl filled with ice and cold water. Chill, stirring often, until the mixture mounds when spooned.

4. While mixture chills, beat cream until stiff in a medium-size bowl; fold into gelatin mixture. Pour into a 6-cup mold; chill until firm, at least 4 hours or overnight.

5. Just before serving, loosen bavarian around edge with a knife; dip mold very quickly in and out of hot water. Cover mold with serving plate; turn upside down; shake gently; lift off mold. Garnish with extra whipped cream, orange wedges, and candied green cherries, if you wish.

CHERRY-CHOCOLATE MOUSSE MERINGUES

Bake at 275° for 1 hour.
Makes 8 servings.

3	egg whites, at room temperature	1	cup heavy cream
1	teaspoon vanilla	2	tablespoons sugar
½	teaspoon cream of tartar	1	pound sweet cherries, stemmed, halved, and pitted
¾	cup sugar	⅓	cup orange-flavored liqueur or orange juice
¼	cup unsweetened cocoa powder		
6	squares semisweet chocolate	½	cup sugar
4	eggs, separated	1	cup water

1. Preheat oven to 275°. Grease cookie sheets; dust with flour, tapping off excess. Mark eight 3-inch circles with butter or vegetable shortening on cookie sheets.

2. Combine egg whites, vanilla, and cream of tartar in a medium-size bowl. Beat with an electric mixer until foamy. Add ½ cup of the sugar, 1 tablespoon at a time, beating constantly until meringue forms stiff, glossy peaks. Combine the remaining ¼ cup sugar and cocoa, blending well; gradually beat into meringue until blended.

3. Fit a pastry bag with a large star tip; fill bag with meringue; pipe meringue onto circles on cookie sheets.

4. Bake in a preheated very slow oven (275°) for 1 hour. Turn off oven heat. Let meringues stay 2 hours in cooling oven. Remove to wire racks. Carefully remove from cookie sheets with wide spatula.

5. Melt the chocolate in the top of a double boiler over hot, not boiling, water, stirring until completely melted.

6. Beat egg yolks in a medium-size bowl until fluffy. Beat in melted chocolate slowly until well mixed.

7. Whip ½ cup of the heavy cream until stiff; gently fold into chocolate mixture until no streaks of white remain. Refrigerate while preparing cherries.

8. Beat egg whites in a medium-size bowl until foamy; gradually beat in the 2 tablespoons sugar. Continue to beat until meringue forms soft peaks. Gently fold into chocolate mixture. Return mixture to refrigerator.

9. Combine cherries, liqueur, remaining ½ cup sugar, and water in a medium-size saucepan. Bring to a boil; lower heat. Simmer gently for 5 minutes. Remove from heat; let stand 30 minutes. Drain cherries thoroughly. Reserve cooking syrup. Reserve 8 cherries; cool. Fold into mousse mixture. Spoon cherry-chocolate mousse into chocolate meringue shells.

10. Beat remaining ½ cup heavy cream until stiff. Top each meringue with whipped cream, a reserved cherry, and a few spoonfuls of cooking syrup.

8

Fruit Desserts

Juicy fresh fruit is the most natural of desserts. It's light, refreshing, and sweet. In many cuisines, fresh fruit is the *only* dessert.

Fresh fruit is often the object of an artist's brush. Their mouth-watering colors mean they do not take much if any adornment for a beautiful table presentation. Since much of the pleasure of fresh fruit lies in its naturalness, it's foolish not to enjoy it at the height of its season.

Summer is the time for the richest assortment of fruit. Fresh fruit then should possess a sweet smell and each variety should emit its own special fragrance. Some fruit will improve with several days of ripening at room temperature.

Summer is the season for berries. Fragile berries need only be piled in a shallow dish, splashed with cream, and touched with sugar before serving. Most berries, except strawberries, are delicious cooked in cobblers or pies. Berries are also delicious made into "fools" simply by folding a puree into whipped cream.

Sweet succulent melons are as much a part of summer as lemonade. A compote of luscious marinated fruit can fill a watermelon basket. Cool shimmering gelatin desserts let fresh fruits sparkle through. Colorful red, purple, or green plums, rosy peaches, or nectarines are a summer treat in themselves but when turned into pies, sauces, mousses, or other desserts, their tart-sweet flavor improves. Sweet, plump grapes excell with cheese but are also great fillers for baked pastry tarts. Sweet cherries are best eaten fresh rather than cooked for any period of time.

Autumn brings on the crisp apples and pears. Enjoy them as a healthy snack or made into numerous desserts. Cranberries and citrus fruit are synonymous with winter holidays. They can make delicious desserts.

Exotic tropical fruits, such as papaya, mango, kiwi, and pineapple, have become widely and readily available. They're terrific to use in desserts.

As the summer and fall seasons wear on, the variety diminishes, forcing us to rely on canned, frozen, or dried fruit.

Drying changes fruits' characteristics dramatically. Not only does the appearance change but also the texture, flavor, and color. The nutrients and flavor are intensified in canned fruits, providing a storehouse of summer goodness during the bleak winter months. They can be served in compotes, soufflés, whips, and pies. Dried apricots are especially good cooked with honey just until soft, then topped with lightly whipped cream or vanilla yogurt. Apples, figs, pears, grapes, peaches, and plums are all available dried (not candied) and are equally good in countless desserts.

In this chapter you will find lots of fruit ideas but look to other chapters for more delicious fruit tarts, pies, and ice creams.

APRICOT CREAM

Makes 4 servings.

1	cup dried apricots, chopped coarsely	½	teaspoon salt
1	cup water	1	container (16 ounces) dairy sour cream (2 cups)
⅓	cup honey		Toasted slivered almonds

1. Cook apricots in water in a small saucepan until tender, about 10 minutes. Drain well; cool.

2. Combine honey, salt, and sour cream in a bowl; stir in cooled apricots. Chill before serving. Garnish with almonds.

APRICOT-YOGURT WHIP

Makes 6 servings.

1	envelope unflavored gelatin	1	teaspoon lemon juice
½	cup orange juice	½	teaspoon almond extract
1	can (17 ounces) apricot halves, drained	1	container (8 ounces) plain yogurt
2	tablespoons honey		Plain yogurt (optional)
1	teaspoon grated lemon rind		Sliced almonds (optional)

1. Sprinkle gelatin over orange juice in a 1-cup measure; let stand 5 minutes to soften. Place cup in hot, not boiling, water. Heat until gelatin is clear; cool.

2. Place apricots in container of an electric blender; cover; whirl until smooth. Turn into a large bowl. Stir in honey, lemon rind, lemon juice, and almond extract, then cooled gelatin mixture.

3. Place bowl in a pan filled with ice and cold water to speed setting; chill, stirring frequently, until mixture is thickened.

4. Beat with an electric mixer on high speed, 3 minutes, or until mixture triples in volume; add yogurt; beat 1 minute longer. Spoon into six dessert glasses. Chill until set. Garnish with additional yogurt and sliced almonds, if you wish.

AVOCADO WHIP

Especially refreshing. Serve as a party dessert with thin butter cookies.
Makes 4 servings.

1	large avocado	½	pint (1 cup) vanilla ice cream, softened
2	tablespoons lemon juice		
2	tablespoons sugar		Lemon twists (optional)

1. Halve avocado; pit and peel. Cut into small pieces; then mash in a medium-size bowl with a fork until smooth, sprinkling with the lemon juice to prevent darkening. Stir in sugar. (You should have 1 cup of avocado mixture.)

2. Spoon softened ice cream into avocado mixture. Beat with an electric mixer until well mixed, but do not let ice cream melt.

3. Spoon into stemmed glasses and serve at once or spoon into a shallow pan and place in freezer until semi-firm, but not hard-frozen, about 2 hours. If frozen in pan, spoon into serving dishes. Garnish with lemon twists, if you wish.

BANANAS BAKED WITH PINEAPPLE AND HONEY

Bake at 375° for 20 minutes.
Makes 6 servings.

6 small firm-ripe bananas	1 tablespoon lemon juice
1 can (8 ounces) crushed pineapple in pineapple juice	2 teaspoons cornstarch
¼ cup honey	2 tablespoons butter or margarine

1. Peel bananas and place in single layer in baking dish just large enough to hold them. Preheat oven to 375°.
2. Combine pineapple with juice, honey, lemon juice, and cornstarch in a bowl; pour over bananas. Dot with butter.
3. Bake in a preheated moderate oven (375°) for 20 minutes or just until bananas are softened and sauce is bubbly.

BANANA DESSERT CRÊPES

Try this recipe on your family first, then put it on the menu for your next dinner party.

Makes 6 servings.

Crêpes:
½ cup *sifted* all-purpose flour
1   tablespoon sugar
⅛   teaspoon salt
2   eggs
¾   cup milk
1   tablespoon butter, melted

Orange Sauce:
¼   cup (½ stick) butter or margarine
⅓   cup sugar
2   teaspoons grated orange rind
⅓   cup orange juice
3   small bananas
2   tablespoons light or dark rum

1. Make Crêpes: Combine flour, sugar, salt, eggs, and milk in a medium-size bowl; beat with rotary beater until smooth. Beat in the 1 tablespoon butter. Let stand 20 minutes.
2. Slowly heat a 7-inch skillet or crêpe pan until a drop of water sizzles when dropped on surface. Butter skillet lightly for the first few crêpes.
3. Pour batter, 2 tablespoons for each crêpe, into heated skillet; quickly rotate skillet to spread batter evenly. Cook over medium heat

until lightly browned; turn and brown other side. Remove to plate. Cool, then fold in quarters.

4. Make Sauce: Combine butter, sugar, orange rind, and orange juice in a large chafing dish or skillet; bring to a boil. Peel bananas; cut in quarters lengthwise; add to skillet; heat 1 minute. Add crêpes (do not unfold them) and heat, spooning sauce over. Heat rum in a small saucepan; ignite; pour over crêpes. Serve 2 crêpes and 2 pieces of banana per serving.

BLACKBERRY BUCKLE

A coffee cake-style dessert dappled with soft blackberries and covered with a thin crunch of sugar.

Bake at 350° for 45 minutes.
Makes 6 servings.

1⅔ cups *sifted* all-purpose flour
1¾ teaspoons baking powder
½ teaspoon salt
½ teaspoon ground cardamom
¼ cup (½ stick) butter, softened
¾ cup sugar
1 egg

½ teaspoon vanilla
⅔ cup milk
2 cups frozen unsweetened blackberries (from a 1-pound bag), thawed and drained
2 tablespoons sugar
Whipped cream

1. Sift flour, baking powder, salt, and cardamom onto wax paper.

2. Beat butter and the ¾ cup sugar in a medium-size bowl until creamy. Beat in egg and vanilla until smooth and light. Butter a 9 x 1½-inch layer-cake pan. Preheat oven to 350°.

3. Add milk alternately with flour mixture to the butter and sugar, beating just to blend thoroughly.

4. Spread less than half the batter in prepared pan. Sprinkle with half the berries. Spoon remaining batter evenly over the berries; smooth with a spatula. Sprinkle with remaining berries, then top with the 2 tablespoons sugar.

5. Bake in a preheated moderate oven (350°) for 45 minutes or until center springs back when lightly pressed with fingertip. Cool slightly on a wire rack. Serve warm with whipped cream.

BLUEBERRY FOOL

Makes 6 servings.

2 cups (1 pint) fresh blueberries	1 package (3 ounces) cream cheese
¼ cup granulated sugar	¼ cup 10X (confectioners') sugar
1½ teaspoons cornstarch	1 teaspoon vanilla
1 teaspoon grated lemon rind	1 cup heavy cream

1. Cook blueberries, sugar, and cornstarch over medium heat, stirring until mixture thickens and bubbles for 1 minute. Stir in lemon rind. Pour into a 5-cup glass bowl; cover and chill.

2. To serve: Beat cream cheese, 10X sugar, and vanilla until smooth; add cream and beat until fluffy. Fold mixture into blueberries.

CLAFOUTI

Traditionally made with just-picked, unpitted cherries (the seeds contain the perfume, according to the French), clafouti is just as good baked with peach wedges or apricot halves.

Bake at 400° for 45 minutes.
Makes 6 servings.

1 pound fresh sweet cherries Or: 1 can (17 ounces) dark sweet cherries	3 eggs, slightly beaten
	1½ cups milk
	3 tablespoons butter or margarine, melted and cooled
½ cup *sifted* all-purpose flour	
⅔ cup sugar	
Dash salt	

1. Wash and dry fresh cherries or thoroughly drain canned cherries. Preheat oven to 400°.

2. In a large bowl, combine flour, ½ cup of the sugar, and salt. Add eggs, blending thoroughly with a wire whisk or wooden spoon. Add milk and melted butter, stirring until mixture is quite smooth. (Do not beat.)

3. Butter a 9 x 9 x 2-inch baking pan. Sprinkle in 1 tablespoon of the remaining sugar. Spread cherries on bottom; pour in batter.

4. Bake in a preheated hot oven (400°) for 30 minutes. Sprinkle top with remaining sugar. Continue baking for 15 minutes or until the custard is firm and a knife inserted near center comes out clean.

CHERRY COBBLER

Bake at 400° for 30 minutes.
Makes 8 servings.

2	cans (21 ounces each) cherry pie filling	¼	cup (½ stick) butter
1½	cups *sifted* all-purpose flour	½	cup milk
2	teaspoons baking powder	½	cup toasted slivered almonds
¼	cup sugar	2	tablespoons sugar
½	teaspoon salt		Light cream or half and half

1. Preheat oven to 400°.
2. Spoon cherry pie filling into a shallow 3-quart baking dish.
3. Sift flour, baking powder, the ¼ cup sugar, and salt into a bowl; cut in butter with pastry blender until mixture is crumbly. Stir in milk until a stiff dough forms. Drop by tablespoonfuls onto cherries. Sprinkle with toasted almonds and sugar.
4. Bake in a preheated hot oven (400°) for 30 minutes or until topping is golden brown. Serve warm with cream.

COLD CRANBERRY SOUFFLÉ

Makes 8 servings.

1	envelope plus 1 teaspoon unflavored gelatin	5	egg whites
2¼	cups cranberry juice	½	teaspoon salt
1½	cups fresh or frozen cranberries	1½	cups heavy cream
1¼	cups granulated sugar	2	tablespoons 10X (confectioners') sugar

1. Soften the gelatin in ½ cup of the cranberry juice, about 5 minutes. Prepare a high collar of wax paper for a 6-cup soufflé dish. Secure with tape or string.
2. Wash and pick over the berries. Combine berries with ¾ cup of the sugar and the remaining 1¾ cranberry juice in a large saucepan. Bring to a boil; lower heat. Simmer 4 minutes or until sugar is dissolved and cranberry skins have "popped." Remove from heat; stir in softened gelatin. Strain mixture into a large bowl. Reserve 16 cranberries; chop remainder. Cool gelatin mixture; chill until syrupy.
3. Beat egg whites and salt in a large bowl with an electric mixer until frothy. Add remaining ½ cup sugar gradually, beating until meringue

forms soft peaks. Whip ¾ cup of the heavy cream in a small bowl until stiff. Fold meringue and cream together.

4. Pour the meringue-cream mixture over the thickened cranberry mixture and fold together until no trace of white remains. Fold in the chopped berries. Pour into prepared soufflé dish. Chill until firm, about 4 hours.

5. To serve: Whip remaining ¾ cup heavy cream with the 10X sugar in a small bowl until stiff. Pipe 16 rosettes on soufflé with a pastry bag. Place a cranberry in center of each.

FIGS WITH LEMON CREAM

When fresh figs are out of season, use the canned variety.

Makes 6 servings.

1	package (3 ounces) cream cheese, softened	1	teaspoon sugar
2	tablespoons light cream or half and half	1	teaspoon lemon juice
		12	ripe figs
			Grated lemon rind

1. Blend cream cheese, cream, sugar, and lemon juice in a small bowl until thoroughly mixed.

2. Peel and quarter figs; arrange 8 quarters, petal-fashion, on each of 6 dessert dishes. Spoon a generous dollop of the cream cheese mixture on top; garnish with a sprinkling of grated lemon rind.

MAKING CITRUS CUPS

Hollow out lime, lemon, or orange halves to use as pretty dessert containers for sherbet, ices, or berries.

PREVENTION OF FRUIT DISCOLORATION

To keep apple, banana, peach, or avocado slices from darkening, dip the cut surface into an ascorbic acid mixture for fruit or citrus juice. Also, use a stainless steel knife for cutting rather than a carbon steel knife, which discolors the fruit.

DRIED FRUIT COMPOTE

Chilled poached dried fruit is served with a cool spiced yogurt topping.

Makes 4 servings.

1½ cups water	2 whole allspice
¼ cup honey	Or: ½ teaspoon ground
1 package (8 ounces) mixed	allspice
dried fruit	1 tablespoon chopped walnuts
1 1-inch piece stick cinnamon	Cinnamon-Yogurt Topping
	(recipe below)

1. Combine water and honey in a small saucepan. Heat to a boil; lower heat; simmer 5 minutes. Preheat oven to 325°.
2. Remove pits from prunes, if using; cut all fruit into bite-size pieces. Add fruit, cinnamon stick, and allspice to water.
3. Cover and simmer 10 to 15 minutes, just until fruits are tender but not mushy.
4. Remove from heat. Cool to lukewarm. Remove cinnamon and whole allspice. Spoon into serving dishes or bowl. Cover and chill.
5. Place walnuts on a baking sheet in a slow oven (325°) for 15 minutes until golden. Sprinkle over fruit and serve with Cinnamon-Yogurt Topping.

Cinnamon-Yogurt Topping: Combine ½ cup plain yogurt, 1 table-spoon 10X (confectioners') sugar and ¼ teaspoon ground cinnamon in small bowl. Stir until well blended. Cover and chill before serving.

FRESH FRUIT COMPOTE

Makes 6 servings.

2 large navel oranges, peeled	1 pint strawberries, sliced
and sectioned	1 tablespoon sugar
1 large red apple, cored,	¼ teaspoon ground ginger
quartered, and thinly sliced	⅛ teaspoon ground nutmeg
1 cup green grapes, halved and	
seeded	

1. Combine oranges, apple, grapes, and strawberries in a medium-size bowl.
2. Combine sugar, ginger, and nutmeg; sprinkle over fruits and toss. Chill thoroughly; toss again before serving.

EASY-TO-MAKE FRUIT GARNISHES

Fruit offers one of the easiest, quickest ways to decorate just about any dessert, as we show you here. Try these garnish ideas on your next pudding, pie, cake, or ice cream creation.

To Make a Double-Berry Cup: Make cuts lengthwise from tip almost to stem in a large berry; spread "petals." Place whole berry, tip up, in center.

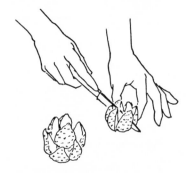

To Make Rosettes: Slice berries lengthwise, then outline a circle in center of dessert with some of the largest slices, points out. Continue with overlapping circles to center; using smallest slices last. Finish with a whole berry.

To Make a Snowdrop: Dip berry into 10X (confectioners') sugar to coat generously, leaving the hull on for a handle. This is the easiest, fastest way to make a pretty garnish for puddings, pies, and cheesecakes.

To Make Lemon, Lime, or Orange Rind Roses: With vegatable parer, pare around and around into a long spiral. Roll rind up, not too tight, shaping into a full-blown "rose."

To Make Lemon, Lime, or Orange Twists: Slice thin; make a cut from edge to center. Twist into a bow or butterfly shape.

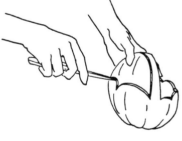

To Make Melon Baskets: Halve melon, scoop out seeds, serrate or scallop the edge. To make "handled" basket, cut as shown at right.

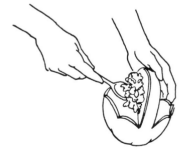

FROSTY CANTALOUPE COMPOTES

Makes 6 servings.

1   container (8 ounces) dairy
    sour cream
⅓   cup firmly packed light
    brown sugar
¼   teaspoon ground cinnamon
1   medium-size ripe cantaloupe

1   pint fresh blueberries, rinsed
    and drained,
½   pound seedless green
    grapes, rinsed, drained, and
    halved

1. Mix sour cream, brown sugar, and cinnamon in a small bowl. Cover; chill until ready to serve.

2. Pare, seed, and cut cantaloupe into 6 wedges; place each wedge in a serving bowl. Divide blueberries and grapes evenly among bowls; cover with plastic wrap; chill.

3. To serve: Spoon sour cream topping over fruit, dividing evenly.

MELON IN SABAYON SAUCE

Makes 6 servings.

½   teaspoon unflavored gelatin
¼   cup sugar
½   cup orange juice

¼   cup white port wine or dry
    sherry
2   eggs, slightly beaten
1   honeydew melon, chilled

1. Sprinkle gelatin and sugar over orange juice and port wine in a large bowl or the top of a double boiler; beat in eggs. Set over barely simmering water.

2. Cook, beating constantly with a whisk or rotary hand beater, until mixture thickens slightly and is double in volume, about 8 to 12 minutes. Remove from hot water and set in ice water. Beat mixture until cool; then remove from ice water.

3. Scoop enough melon balls from melon with melon-ball cutter to fill 6 dessert glasses; keep refrigerated. Just before serving, pour sauce over each serving.

UNWASHED FRUIT KEEPS BETTER

Most fruit should not be washed before being stored. Prewashing fruit will speed up decay. Wash fruit just before you eat it.

WATERMELON BASKET WITH MARINATED FRUIT

Makes 24 servings.

1	small watermelon	1	cup white grape juice
2	cups honeydew melon balls	½	cup orange marmalade
2	cups cantaloupe melon balls	¼	cup orange-flavored liqueur
2	cups strawberries, hulled		or orange juice
1	cup seedless grapes		Fresh mint leaves (optional)
1	cup blueberries		Grape bunches (optional)

1. Draw two 1½-inch wide intersecting diagonal strips lengthwise over top of watermelon to form a handle. Cut down into center of melon along outline of handle. Working from ends of melon, cut horizontally in toward center between ends of handle. Remove pieces from top half of melon. Cut out melon from underside of handle. Scoop out balls with a melon-ball cutter from bottom of melon, to measure 4 cups. Set aside. Scoop out any remaining melon from bottom. Cut edge of watermelon basket into zigzag or scallop pattern, if you wish. Cover all cut surfaces with plastic wrap. Refrigerate.
2. Combine watermelon, honeydew, and cantaloupe balls, strawberries, grapes, and blueberries in a large bowl. Stir together grape juice, orange marmalade, and orange liqueur; pour over fruits; toss gently. Cover; chill 2 hours.
3. To serve: Spoon marinated fruits into watermelon. Garnish with mint leaves and bunches of grapes, if you wish.

POACHED NECTARINES WITH FLUFFY PASTRY CREAM

Summery fresh nectarines are cooked in lemony syrup just until tender and used to garnish the rich pastry cream.

Makes 8 servings.

1	cup sugar		**Fluffy Pastry Cream**
1½	cups ice water		**(page 289)**
8	large ripe nectarines	1	tablespoon chopped
½	cup kirsch or dry white wine		pistachio nuts
1	small lemon, thinly sliced		

1. Bring sugar and water to a boil in a large saucepan; boil 5 minutes.

2. Meanwhile, dip nectarines into boiling water for 30 seconds, then into ice water for 1 minute. Peel, halve, and pit nectarines.

3. Add nectarines, kirsch, and lemon slices to sugar syrup. Cover. Cook over low heat, stirring gently, until nectarines are firm but tender, about 10 minutes. Cool; chill.

4. To serve: Drain nectarines. Arrange in a dish around the rim; spoon pastry cream in center; sprinkle with nuts.

GLACÉED ORANGES

Bright slivers of candied orange peel and a touch of orange-flavored liqueur add zest to this simple dessert.

Makes 6 servings.

6	large navel oranges	2	tablespoons orange-flavored
2	cups sugar		liqueur
1	cup water		Candied violets (optional)

1. Remove thin, bright-colored rind (no white) from each orange with a vegetable parer or sharp knife; cut into thin strips; reserve.

2. Simmer rind in 4 cups boiling water for 8 minutes; drain and reserve the rind.

3. With a sharp knife, cut remaining white membrane from oranges. Remove core from center of orange. Place oranges in a bowl just large enough to hold them.

4. Combine sugar with water in a heavy saucepan; cook over medium heat, stirring constantly, until sugar is dissolved. Continue cooking without stirring until mixture is syrupy, about 10 minutes. Add blanched orange rind; cook about 5 minutes or until rind becomes translucent. Remove from heat; add orange liqueur. Pour hot syrup with rind over oranges. Cool; chill several hours or overnight. Garnish each orange with candied violets, if you wish.

JUICIER FRUIT

Citrus fruits will be juicer if they are warmed or at room temperature. If they are cold, put them in a microwave oven for a few seconds or in a bowl of hot water.

INDIVIDUAL ORANGE SOUFFLÉS

Fragrant and fragile, yet easy to make, these tiny orange dessert soufflés are a pure pleasure to eat.

Bake at 375° for 18 minutes.
Makes 6 to 8 servings.

¼	cup (½ stick) unsalted butter	2	large navel oranges
½	cup all-purpose flour	5	egg yolks
⅓	cup plus 1½ tablespoons granulated sugar	2	tablespoons Grand Marnier
		6	egg whites
1½	cups milk, scalded		10X (confectioners') sugar

1. Butter 8 small individual soufflé dishes or 6 slightly larger ones. Dust lightly with sugar; shake out the excess.

2. Melt the butter in a saucepan. Blend in the flour; cook, stirring constantly, 1 to 2 minutes. Cool slightly.

3. Add the sugar to the milk; stir to dissolve. Whisk milk mixture rapidly into the *roux* until smooth. Cook, stirring constantly, until mixture thickens and comes to a boil. Remove from heat.

4. Grate rind from oranges; then peel and section. Preheat oven to 375°.

5. Whisk egg yolks, grated orange rind, and Grand Marnier into hot mixture. Beat egg whites until stiff but not dry; fold into hot mixture.

6. Fill prepared soufflé dishes ⅓ full with soufflé mixture. Divide the orange sections among the dishes. Add enough soufflé mixture to ¾ fill each dish. Smooth surfaces.

7. Bake in a preheated moderate oven (375°) for 18 minutes or until souffles are puffed and golden brown. Sprinkle tops wiht 10X sugar and *serve at once*, while puffed and perfect. Any extra soufflé mixture can be warmed in a double boiler over hot, not boiling, water, thinned down with orange juice and served as a sauce.

Note: The same mixture can, of course, be baked in a 2-quart soufflé dish (filled ¾ full). Bake at 325° for 20 minutes, increase oven temperature to 350° and bake 10 minutes longer or until soufflé is well-puffed and golden brown.

SUGARLESS FRUIT

Try chopped fresh mint or crystallized ginger to flavor fruit instead of sugar.

PEACH MOUSSE WITH RASPBERRY SAUCE

Makes 8 servings.

1¼ pounds firm-ripe peaches (4 large)
2 tablespoons lemon juice
2 tablespoons sugar
2 tablespoons brandy
2 envelopes unflavored gelatin

½ cup water
2 egg whites
⅛ teaspoon cream of tartar
1 cup heavy cream
Raspberry Sauce (page 290)
Peach slices (optional)

1. Drop peaches into boiling water for 15 seconds. Remove with slotted spoon. When cool enough to handle, peel skins; halve and pit.

2. Slice half the peaches into the container of an electric blender. Add lemon juice; cover. Whirl until smooth, stopping once or twice to press down fruit. (You should have 1 cup puree.) Turn into a large bowl.

3. Coarsley chop remaining peaches. Add with the sugar and brandy to pureed peaches; mix thoroughly.

4. Sprinkle gelatin over the ½ cup water in a small cup to soften, 5 minutes. Set cup in a saucepan of simmering water. Stir mixture often, until gelatin is dissolved. Gradually stir into peach mixture.

5. Place bowl in a pan filled with ice and cold water to speed setting; chill, stirring often, until mixture begins to thicken.

6. Beat egg whites with cream of tartar in a small bowl with an electric mixer until soft peaks form. Beat cream with same beaters in another small bowl until stiff.

7. Fold beaten egg whites, then beaten cream into peach mixture until no streaks of white remain. Pour mixture into a 7-cup mold. Refrigerate 4 hours or until set.

8. Prepare Raspberry Sauce.

9. To serve: Unmold mousse on serving plate. Garnish with Raspberry Sauce and additional peach slices tossed with lemon juice and sugar, if you wish.

PEELING SOFT FRUIT

To peel peaches, apricots, or nectarines, dip fruit in boiling water, let stand a minute; then dip into cold water and slip off skins.

PEACH BROWN BETTY

Bake at 385° for 30 minutes.
Makes 4 servings.

8	slices whole wheat bread	¼	teaspooon ground cinnamon
¼	cup (½ stick) butter or margarine	¼	teaspoon salt
		⅛	teaspoon almond extract
1	can (29 ounces) cling peach slices	½	teaspoon grated lemon rind
		2	tablespoons lemon juice
½	teaspoon vanilla	1	tablespoons sugar

1. Place bread slices on a cookie sheet. Toast in a moderate oven (350°) for 20 minutes to dry out; cool. Crush into crumbs with rolling pin or whirl in blender. Melt butter in a small saucepan; stir in crumbs. Butter a 1-quart baking dish.

2. Drain syrup from peaches into a small saucepan. Simmer until syrup has reduced to about ½ cup.

3. Combine peaches, vanilla, cinnamon, salt, almond extract, lemon rind, and juice with the ½ cup syrup.

4. Spread ⅓ of the buttered crumbs in prepared baking dish. Spoon in half the peach mixture. Repeat with crumbs and remaining peach mixture, topping with remaining crumbs. Sprinkle crumbs with sugar. Cover with aluminum foil.

5. Bake in a preheated moderate oven (375°) for 15 minutes. Uncover; bake 15 minutes longer or until top is browned.

SPICY PEAR COBBLER

Bake at 400° for 20 minutes.
Makes 6 servings.

1	can (29 ounces) pear halves	¼	teaspoon ground cinnamon
1	teaspoon grated lemon rind	¼	teaspoon ground allspice
3	tablespoons lemon juice	¼	teaspoon ground nutmeg
3	tablespoons butter	¼	cup molasses
1	cup *sifted* all-purpose flour	1	container (8 ounces) plain yogurt
1	teaspoon baking powder		
½	teaspoon baking soda	1	tablespoon milk
¼	teaspoon salt	1	teaspoon sugar
½	teaspoon ground ginger	½	cup heavy cream

1. Drain pears, reserving syrup. Measure ½ cup syrup into a medium-size saucepan. Stir in lemon rind, lemon juice, and 1 tablespoon of the butter. Bring to a boil; lower heat; simmer mixture for 5 minutes.

2. While sauce is heating, cut pears into 1-inch pieces. Set aside. Butter a 9-inch pie plate.

3. Sift flour, baking powder, baking soda, salt, ginger, cinnamon, allspice, and nutmeg into a medium-size bowl. Cut in remaining 2 tablespoons butter with pastry blender until flour mixture is crumbly.

4. Combine molasses and ¼ cup of the yogurt in 1-cup measure. Stir into flour mixture just until blended (dough will be very soft).

5. Turn dough out onto a well-floured surface; pat into a 5-inch circle. Cut circle into 6 wedges with floured knife. Preheat oven to 400°.

6. When syrup has cooked, gently stir in pear pieces until heated through. Pour pears into prepared pie plate. Place pie plate on a cookie sheet. Arrange gingerbread wedges evenly over pears. Brush with milk. Sprinkle with sugar.

7. Bake in a preheated hot oven (400°) for 20 minutes or until gingerbread is nicely browned.

8. While the cobbler bakes, whip the heavy cream in a small bowl until soft peaks form. Fold in the remaining yogurt. Serve with hot cobbler.

PEARS IN WHITE WINE

A lovely, make-ahead dessert, pears are cooked in white wine, chilled, and served with fruit sauce.

Makes 8 servings.

8 **firm-ripe pears (Bartlett or Anjou)**	1½ **cups sugar**
	Angelica (optional)
2 **tablespoons lemon juice**	**Sauce Cardinale (page 292)**
3 **cups dry white wine**	

1. Wash pears; pare and core from blossom end but leave stems intact. Brush with lemon juice.

2. Combine wine and sugar in large saucepan; bring to a boil, stirring until sugar dissolves. Lower heat; add pears; cover. Simmer 10 minutes or until tender but still firm. Let pears cool in syrup. Refrigerate several hours or overnight.

3. Drain pears; arrange on serving dish; garnish with angelica, if you wish. Serve with Sauce Cardinale.

FRESH PINEAPPLE COMPOTE

Makes 8 serivngs.

1 ripe large pineapple	½ cup kirsch
¼ cup 10X (confectioners') sugar	2 jars (17 ounces each) pitted dark sweet cherries

1. Cut off leafy top, then cut pineapple lengthwise with a sharp knife. Cut each half into 3 or 4 wedges. Loosen fruit in 1 piece from each wedge; trim core. Cut pineapple into ½-inch chunks.
2. Place pineapple in a large bowl; sprinkle with 10X sugar; add kirsch and toss gently. Cover with plastic wrap; refrigerate several hours for pineapple to absorb flavor of brandy, tossing once or twice. Chill the cherries.
3. Just before serving, drain juice from cherries. Add cherries to pineapple; toss thoroughly.

GLACÉED STRAWBERRIES

Fresh strawberries with a crackling sugar-glaze coating
Do not make glacéed berries more than 2 to 3 hours before serving;
1 hour if very humid.

Makes 24 glacéed strawberries.

24 strawberries	¼ cup water
1 cup sugar	⅛ teaspoon cream of tartar

1. Wash berries carefully, leaving hulls on, and pat dry with paper toweling. Lightly oil a cookie sheet.
2. Heat sugar, water, and cream of tartar in a small saucepan over high heat, stirring constantly, until sugar dissolves. Boil 12 to 15 minutes, without stirring, until a candy thermometer registers 295°F. (hard-crack stage). Remove pan from heat.
3. Working quickly, dip berries into syrup, one at a time, holding each by the stem. Remove from syrup and place on cookie sheet to let coating harden. Do not let glacéed berries touch each other while drying.

NEAT CORER

Use a melon-ball cutter to core apple or pear halves for dessert cups.

FLAMING PLUM SUZETTE

Makes 6 servings.

Crêpes:
1¼ cups milk
3 eggs
1 tablespoon butter or margarine, melted
¾ cup *sifted* all-purpose flour
1 tablespoon sugar
⅛ teaspoon salt

Orange-Rum Plum Sauce:
½ cup (1 stick) butter or margarine
⅔ cup sugar
1 tablespoon thin strips orange rind (no white)
⅔ cup orange juice
1 pound firm-ripe plums (5 to 6 large)
2 tablespoons light or dark rum

1. For Crêpes: Place milk, eggs, butter, flour, the 1 tablespoon sugar, and salt in the container of an electric blender. Cover; whirl until smooth. Pour into 2-cup glass measure. Let stand at room temperature for 30 minutes.

2. Slowly heat a 7-inch skillet or crêpe pan until a drop of water sizzles when dropped on the surface. Butter skillet lightly for the first few crêpes to prevent sticking.

3. Stir crêpe batter. Pour batter, 2 tablespoons at a time for each crêpe, into heated skillet; quickly rotate skillet to evenly coat bottom. Cook until lightly browned, about 1 minute; turn and lightly brown the other side. Remove to a large plate. (You should have 12 to 14 crêpes.) Stack between pieces of wax paper. Fold crêpes into quarters.

4. For Sauce: Combine butter, sugar, orange strips, and orange juice in a large skillet; bring to a boil.

5. Halve, pit, and quarter plums.

6. Add plums; toss to coat. Cook just until plums are soft but not mushy, about 7 minutes. Remove with slotted spoon to bowl; keep warm.

7. Bring sauce, to a boil; boil just until mixture becomes syrupy, about 1 minute. Add crêpes; heat, spooning sauce over. Top with plums.

8. To serve: Transfer crêpes, sauce and plums to a heated chafing dish, if you wish. Gently heat rum in a small, long handled saucepan; remove from heat. Carefully ignite with long kitchen match; pour over crêpes. When flame extinguishes, serve crêpes with sauce and some of the plums for each serving.

STRAWBERRY CHARLOTTE WITH STRAWBERRY SAUCE

Makes 8 servings.

2	pints strawberries, washed and hulled	½	cup heavy cream, whipped
2	envelopes unflavored gelatin	1	package (3 ounces) ladyfingers
¼	cup water		Strawberry Sauce (page 290)
2	egg whites		Whipped cream (optional)
¼	cup sugar		

1. Puree 2 cups of the berries in the container of an electric blender or food processor; pour into a large bowl. Slice remaining berries.
2. Sprinkle gelatin over water in a small saucepan; let stand 5 minutes to soften. Heat over very low heat, stirring constantly, until gelatin dissolves. Stir into pureed berries; chill until mixture is almost set.
3. Beat egg whites with an electric mixer on high speed until soft peaks form. Gradually add sugar, beating constantly until whites are stiff and glossy. Fold whites and whipped cream into strawberry mixture.
4. Lightly oil the bottom of a 2-quart soufflé dish and line the sides with 18 ladyfinger halves. Pour in about ⅓ of the strawberry mixture and sprinkle with ½ of the sliced berries. Repeat layering and top with remaining strawberry mixture. Arrange remaining ladyfinger halves on top; chill 6 hours or until very firm.
5. To serve: Dip soufflé dish in and out of warm water for a few seconds. Invert onto serving plate to unmold. Pour some of the Strawberry Sauce over the top of the Charlotte, letting some drip down the sides and onto the dish. Pipe small rosettes of whipped cream around top edge of Charlotte to garnish, if you wish. Serve with remaining sauce.

FROSTED FRUIT

For a festive touch, frost grape clusters, cranberries, or small fruit by brushing them with egg white then sprinkling with sugar. Let dry before using.

9

Light Desserts

ight desserts are low in calories but high in appeal. Imagine making sinfully delicious desserts that aren't sinful at all. They only *look* that way. Our recipe for Strawberry Cheese Pie will help tempt dieting dessert lovers away from the classic cheesecake. You can even have Chocolate Cream Roll or Low-Cal Vanilla Ice Cream without worrying about your waistline.

Our light desserts are easy to make too because they call for shortcuts that save time as well as calories. Even if you're not on a diet, try our light desserts. They may open up a new, healthy way of eating.

TIPS FOR LIGHT BAKING

These are some of the many ways of cutting calories in desserts without sacrificing taste:

• When baking, substitute 3 tablespoons plain cocoa powder for 1 ounce chocolate. You'll save 100 calories.
• Chocolate extract can be substituted for small amounts of chocolate in cold drinks and some desserts to save calories.

- Use less chocolate; you'll need less sugar.
- Combine chocolate desserts with fruit, particularly cherries, oranges, and bananas.
- Use less chocolate or coffee in artificially sweetened desserts. Keep in mind that the bitter overtones of artificial sweeteners will tend to intensify the taste of chocolate or coffee.
- Use 2 egg whites instead of 1 whole egg; save 50 calories.
- Separate eggs, beat the egg whites until stiff and fold into batter to increase the volume of a dessert.
- Use no-cholesterol egg substitute in place of eggs. You'll save about 45 calories for each egg.
- Use skim milk instead of whole milk; save 65 calories per cup.
- Use evaporated milk instead of cream; save 735 calories per cup.
- Blender-whip low-fat, part-skim ricotta cheese with skim milk to make a cream substitute in sauces and batters.
- Use whipped evaporated skim milk instead of whipped cream. Chill milk, bowl, and beaters very well; beat in 1 tablespoon lemon juice for added firmness; sweeten to taste.
- Use low-calorie whipped topping mix, prepared according to package directions as a substitute for whipped cream.
- Use pressurized aerosol whipped cream or, better yet, "light" pressurized whipped cream instead of regular whipped cream; it has more air, fewer calories.
- Use plain low-fat yogurt instead of sour cream; save 350 calories per cup. Blender-whip cottage cheese thinned with buttermilk to use in place of sour cream.
- Use sour half and half or low-fat sour dressing rather than sour cream.
- Use low-fat ("imitation") cream cheese instead of the regular kind. (It's called "imitation" because it's lower in butterfat.)
- Replace cream cheese with lower-caloried Neufchatel cheese.
- Blender-whip fresh farmers cheese smooth as a substitute for cream cheese in cheesecakes. Omit lemon juice.
- Substitute cottage cheese for cream cheese in cheesecake recipes; whip it in the blender or food processor until all graininess disappears.
- Make flatter cheesecakes and pile them with thick fruit toppings: Less cheesecake and more fruit means more servings, fewer calories.
- Cut down on butter whenever you can. Use butter flavorings or butter-flavored salt or granulated butter substitute.

- Use low-fat ("imitation") cream cheese instead of butter in "butter frosting."
- Instead of buying sweetened fruit-flavored yogurts—which are high in calories—make your own by crushing berries into plain yogurt.
- Another idea for fruit-flavored yogurt, skinny-style, is to stir a tablespoon or two of defrosted fruit juice concentrate into plain low-fat yogurt.
- Make your own fresh fruit-flavored, soft-serve frozen yogurt in the blender by combining equal amounts of plain unsweetened yogurt and still-frozen berries. The resulting blend will be soft and creamy.
- Substitute low-fat frozen ice milk or frozen yogurt for ice cream.
- Use store-brand and bargain-priced ice creams. They usually contain less butterfat, calories, and cholesterol.
- Make pies with a single pie crust; save 800 calories. Put the crust on the botton and cover the filling with foil. Or put the crust on top and serve your "pie" cobbler style.
- Make crusts from crushed graham crackers, cereal, gingersnaps, crisp bisuits, even diet cookies.
- Roll pie pastry very thin.
- For frozen, ready-to-bake pastry, defrost, cover with waxed paper, roll until it is 50 percent wider; trim, and discard extra pastry.
- Defrost frozen unbaked pie shells, transfer to larger pie pans, stretch to fit with fingertips, fill with fruit for more servings.
- Cover pies with a lattice of thin crisscrossed pastry strips instead of a solid layer of pie pastry.
- Cover fruit pie mixtures with layers of phyllo pastry, very lightly brushed with melted butter. It's less fattening than a conventional pie.
- Make you fruit pies deep dish—more fruit, less pie!
- Add raisins, diced prunes, and other dried fruits to fruit pie fillings.
- Serve plain fruit for dessert—sliced, cut, or diced. Always keep a jar of fresh fruit compote in your refrigerator. Combine 4 cups of diced or sliced raw fresh fruit with ¾ cup orange juice (or thawed fruit juice concentrate). Vary fruit according to the season; augment the mixture with dried or canned fruit when the fresh fruit harvest is slim. Use as a topping for cottage cheese, yogurt, or sponge cake.
- Freeze fruits in vitamin C-enriched canned juices instead of syrup; the ascorbic acid (vitamin C) will help prevent browning.
- Line a cake plate with a fancy paper doily; serve a tiny wedge of cake, garnished with a perfect strawberry or other in-season fruit.

The tiny portion and special presentation implies richness, and less will satisfy you.

• Serve sponge cake or angel cake instead of pound cake.

• Make after-school snacks healthy ones. Let your kids make their own "sandwich cookies" by spreading graham crackers with farmer cheese or low-fat cream cheese and filling with sliced strawberries instead of strawberry jam. Instead of peanut butter and jelly, try peanut butter and berries.

• Spoon juicy fruit toppings over cake—a refreshing substitute for frosting. Make layer cakes with fruit in the middle rather than frosting. Try sliced bananas or crushed pineapple.

• Use sweet fruit ingredients in place of sugar. You'll add flavor and nutrition too.

• Cut down on sour and bitter ingredients and reduce the amount of sugar needed. For example, use less lemon juice or flavor with "milk chocolate" instead of dark concentrated chocolate.

• At 65 calories a tablespoon, honey has more calories than sugar (45 per tablespoon), but it's much sweeter, so you can use less. Replace 1 cup sugar with only ½ cup honey and save 200 calories.

• Granulated fructose (fruit sugar) has the same number of calories as ordinary white sugar, but it tastes sweeter when you use it on fruit or with other acid ingredients. Substitute ½ to ¾ cup fructose for a cupful of sugar in fruit desserts and save 180 to 360 calories.

• Most fruits taste sweeter when they're served fresh and uncooked. (No one puts sugar on a fresh apple, but baked apples are routinely sweetened.) Design you desserts to take advantage of fresh raw fruits and berries in season.

• Beware of "sugar-free" products sweetened with Sorbitol. Sorbitol sweeteners are intended for diabetics who can't handle sugar, but they don't save you any calories. The calories are equal to those in sugar, but since Sorbitol is less sweet, you need to use more of it.

• The main objection to saccharin-sweetened foods is the bitter aftertaste, which can be avoided by not oversweetening sugarless desserts. Once a certain level of sweetness is achieved, additional saccharin will add only bitterness, not sweetness.

• Pouring the syrup off canned fruit does not remove the sugar from the fruit. Look for "light" or "juice-packed" fruits with no sugar added. Read the label and check for calorie counts.

• Boil rum, brandy, wine, or liqueurs before using them in dessert recipes to boil away the alcohol.

- Substitute rum, brandy, or wine-flavorings for the higher-caloried liqueurs. Beware of fruit-flavored liqueurs; they carry a double wallop of alcohol and sugar calories. Even cooking or flaming sweet liqueurs will not eliminate the sugar calories.
- Use more vanilla than called for; it increases the sweetness.
- Add or augment sweet spices like ginger, cinnamon, and nutmeg.
- Omit or cut down on nuts (they're high in fat). Use dry-roasted or defatted peanuts in place of nuts. Use nutty or crunchy cereals in place of nuts
- Substitute raisins or other dried fruits for nuts and cut down on sugar as well.
- Use walnut flavoring in batters to increase nutty taste. Put the nuts on top, where you see and taste them first. You'll use fewer that way.
- Use peanut butter in place of part of the shortening and use fewer nuts.
- Use coconut flavoring instead of dried coconut; this will cut down on saturated fat and calories.
- Fold pressurized whipped cream into pudding mixtures; serve small amounts and garnish with lots of fresh fruit.
- Substitute 1 envelope plain gelatin and 2 cups fruit for sugary gelatin mixes. First, soften the gelatin granules in a little cold fruit juice; then warm just enough to dissolve completely.
- Substitute decaffeinated coffee for the regular kind in desserts; it's less bitter, so you'll need less sugar.
- Frozen unsweetened berries added to fresh skim milk in the blender froth up a frosty naturally sweet "milk shake." Good for after school.

GLAZED STRAWBERRY-CHEESE PIE

Makes 12 servings at 175 calories each.

Calorie-Saver Graham Cracker Crust (page 245) Or: 1 packaged 9-inch graham cracker crust
1 envelope unflavored gelatin
1 cup cold water
1 cup skim milk
1 package (8 ounces) low-calorie (imitation) cream cheese

¼ cup sugar
¼ teaspoon grated lemon rind
1 tablespoon lemon juice
1 package (3¾ ounces) vanilla instant pudding and pie filling mix
1½ pints strawberries, washed and hulled (about 3 cups)
Low-Calorie Strawberry Glaze (recipe below)

1. Prepare Calorie-Saver Graham Cracker Crust.

2. Sprinkle gelatin over water in a small saucepan; let stand to soften, 5 minutes. Heat over low heat, stirring constantly, until gelatin is dissolved.

3. Beat skim milk, cream cheese, sugar, lemon rind, and lemon juice in a medium-size bowl with an electric mixer until smooth. Beat in gelatin mixture and pudding mix until smooth. Pour filling into prepared crust. Chill about 4 hours or until set.

4. Arrange strawberries on filling, pointed ends up; brush with Low-Calorie Strawberry Glaze. Refrigerate.

Low-Calorie Strawberry Glaze: Heat 1 jar (8 ounces) low-sugar strawberry jelly or jam in a small saucepan over low heat until melted. (If using jam, press through sieve.) Cool slightly.

CHOCOLATE CREAM ROLL

Bake at 375° for 12 minutes.
Makes 12 servings at 89 calories each.

4 egg whites
¼ teaspoon salt
7 tablespoons granulated sugar
3 egg yolks
2 tablespoons skim milk
3 tablespoons unsweetened cocoa powder

½ cup *sifted* all-purpose flour
¾ teaspoon baking powder
10X (confectioners') sugar
1 envelope low-calorie whipped topping mix
¾ teaspoon instant coffee powder

1. Preheat oven to 375°. Beat egg whites with salt until soft peaks form. Gradually beat in 3 tablespoons of the sugar; beat until stiff.
2. Beat egg yolks in a small bowl until thick and lemon-colored. Gradually beat in remaining 4 tablespoons sugar. Beat in milk. Fold into beaten egg whites.
3. Sift cocoa, cake flour, and baking powder together onto wax paper. Fold into egg mixture ⅓ at a time. Turn batter into a wax paper-lined 15½ x 10½ x 1-inch nonstick jelly roll pan; spread evenly.
4. Bake in a preheated moderate oven (375°) for 12 minutes or until center springs back when lightly pressed with fingertip.
5. Turn cake out onto a clean kitchen towel dusted with 10X sugar; remove paper. Roll cake, together with towel, starting at short end; cool completely on a wire rack.
6. Combine whipped topping mix and instant coffee powder; prepare following directions on package. Unroll cake; spread evenly with topping mixture. Re-roll cake; place on serving plate. Sift a little 10X sugar over top, if you wish. Refrigerate until serving time.

CALORIE-SAVER GRAHAM CRACKER CRUST

Bake at 425° for 5 minutes.
Makes one 9-inch crust for a total of 345 calories.

⅔ cup graham cracker crumbs   ¼   teaspoon unflavored gelatin
2½ tablespoons diet margarine

1. Preheat oven to 425°. Blend crumbs, margarine, and gelatin in a small bowl with a fork.
2. Spray a 9-inch pie plate with nonstick cooking spray. Press crumb mixture against the side and bottom of the plate.
3. Bake crust in a preheated hot oven (425°) for 5 minutes or until lightly browned. Cool on wire rack.

Calorie-Saver Chocolate Cookie Crust: Substitute crushed chocolate wafers for graham crackers. Or: Add 1 tablespoon unsweetened cocoa powder and 1 tablespoon sugar to the graham crackers. Makes one 9-inch crust for a total of 405 calories.

SLIM CHEESECAKE

If you love cheesecake but can't afford the calories, try this stingy-on-the-calories version.

Bake at 250° for 1 hour, 10 minutes.
Makes 12 servings at 224 calories each.

1 tablespoon butter or margarine	1½ tablespoons all-purpose flour
½ cup graham cracker crumbs	¾ teaspoon grated orange rind
3 packages (8 ounces each) Neufchâtel cheese, softened	1 teaspoon vanilla
⅓ cup sugar	3 whole eggs
Granulated sugar substitute to equal 6 tablespoons sugar	1 egg yolk
	2 tablespoons skim milk

1. Butter bottom and side of an 8-inch springform pan with the 1 tablespoon butter. Sprinkle with graham cracker crumbs; press firmly into place. Refrigerate 1 hour.
2. Preheat oven to 250°. Place cheese, sugar, sugar substitute, flour, orange rind, vanilla, eggs, egg yolk, and milk in the container of an electric blender. Cover. Whirl 2 minutes or until mixture is the consistency of heavy cream. Spoon carefully into prepared pan with graham cracker crust.
3. Bake in a preheated very slow oven (250°) for 1 hour and 10 minutes. Turn oven off; open door and allow cheesecake to cool gradually. Refrigerate at least 4 hours before serving.

SKINNY NO-BAKE CHEESECAKE

Makes 12 servings at 103 calories each.

Graham-Cracker Crust (recipe below)	¼ teaspoon salt
1 pound low-fat cottage cheese	2 teaspoons lemon juice
2 envelopes unflavored gelatin	1 teaspoon grated orange rind
1 cup cold water	1 teaspoon vanilla
2 eggs, separated	Liquid or granulated sugar substitute to equal ½ cup sugar
¾ cup liquid skim milk	
2 tablespoons sugar	½ cup nonfat dry milk powder

1. Prepare an 8-inch springform pan with the Graham-Cracker Crust.
2. Press cheese through a sieve or food mill into a large bowl.

3. Sprinkle gelatin over ½ cup of the water in a small bowl. Let stand 5 minutes to soften.

4. Beat egg yolks in the top of a double boiler until fluffy; add skim milk, sugar, and salt. Place over hot, not boiling, water. Cook, stirring constantly, until thickened. Add softened gelatin; stir until dissolved. Remove from heat; stir into cheese in large bowl.

5. Add lemon juice, orange rind, vanilla, and sugar substitute to cheese mixture; chill until as thick as unbeaten egg white.

6. Beat egg whites until stiff but not dry in a small bowl. Beat nonfat dry milk powder with remaining ½ cup water until almost creamy in second small bowl. Fold egg whites, then milk into cheese mixture until no streaks of white remain. Spoon into prepared pan. Chill until set, about 4 hours.

Graham-Cracker Crust: Grease side and bottom of an 8-inch springform pan with 1 tablespoon butter or margarine (or 2 table-spoons diet margarine). Sprinkle with ½ cup graham cracker crumbs; press firmly into place. Chill 1 hour or until firm.

SUGAR-FREE STRAWBERRY SAUCE

Makes 2 cups at 7 calories per tablespoonful.

1	bag (16 ounces) frozen whole unsweetened strawberries	2	teaspoons cornstarch Granulated sugar substitute to taste
¼	cup cold water		

1. Remove frozen strawberries from bag to a saucepan; allow to thaw.

2. Combine cold water and cornstarch in a cup; stir until dissolved. Add to strawberries.

3. Place strawberries over moderate heat; cook, stirring constantly, until sauce bubbles and clears. Remove from heat. Stir in sugar substitute. Cool. Serve over low-fat ice milk or sponge cake. Sauce may be served hot over pancakes, French toast, crêpes, or dessert omelets.

LOW-CAL VANILLA ICE CREAM

Makes 8 servings at 71 calories each.

1	tall can (13 ounces) evaporated skim milk		Granulated sugar substitute to equal 16 teaspoons sugar
1¼	teaspoons unflavored gelatin (½ envelope)	4	teaspoons vanilla
¼	cup sugar	½	teaspoon butter flavoring
⅓	cup cold water	2	egg whites
		¼	teaspoon salt

1. Pour evaporated skim milk into a deep bowl. Place bowl and beaters from an electric mixer in freezer for 1 hour or until milk has begun to freeze.

2. Combine gelatin and sugar in a small saucepan. Add water; let stand 1 minute. Heat slowly, stirring constantly, until gelatin and sugar are dissolved. Stir in sugar substitute, vanilla, and butter flavoring; cool.

3. Beat frozen milk on high speed until the consistency of whipped cream. Beat egg whites and salt until stiff in a small bowl. Fold gelatin mixture and beaten egg whites into whipped milk until well blended.

4. Pour into a 9 x 9 x 2-inch pan. Freeze until almost firm. Beat mixture in a bowl with an electric mixer until smooth. Refreeze, 30 minutes. Beat again.

5. Spoon into a container and freeze firm. Let soften slightly before serving.

CHEESE AND GRAPE COMPOTE

A low-calorie goodie.

Makes 6 servings at 133 calories each.

1	pound seedless green grapes	1	container (12 ounces) low-fat cottage cheese
2	tablespoons honey		
1	tablespoon lemon juice	2	tablespoons light brown sugar

1. Wash and remove stems from grapes. (You should have about 3 cups.) Mix honey and lemon juice; toss with grapes.

2. Puree cottage cheese in an electric blender until smooth; spoon over grapes; sprinkle brown sugar over cheese.

CHOCOLATE-GLAZED ÉCLAIRS

Bake at 375° for 45 minutes.
Makes 9 éclairs at 115 calories each.

½ cup water
2 tablespoons butter or margarine
½ cup *sifted* all-purpose flour
½ teaspoon salt
2 eggs
1 envelope (½ package) low-calorie vanilla pudding mix

2 cups skim milk
⅓ cup 10X (confectioners') sugar
1 tablespoon unsweetened cocoa powder
1 tablespoon hot black coffee or boiling water

1. Preheat oven to 375°. Combine water and butter in a medium-size saucepan. Heat until butter melts and water is boiling. Turn heat very low. Add flour and salt; beat until mixture leaves side of pan. Remove from heat. Beat in eggs 1 at a time.

2. Use a pastry bag fitted with a large plain tip or a spoon to shape nine 3 x 1-inch éclairs on a nonstick cookie sheet. Leave a 2½-inch space between éclairs.

3. Bake in a preheated moderate oven (375°) for 45 minutes or until éclairs are crisp and golden. Cool on wire rack.

4. While éclairs cool, combine low-calorie pudding mix with skim milk in a medium-size saucepan. Cook pudding following directions on package. Chill.

5. Slice tops from cooled éclairs with a sharp knife; remove any uncooked dough inside. Fill with the chilled vanilla pudding; replace tops.

6. Combine 10X sugar, cocoa, and hot black coffee in a small bowl; mix until smooth. Drizzle over éclairs. Chill before serving.

LIGHT SNACKS

For low-calorie fruit snacks, peel and slice ripe bananas and place them on a wax-paper-lined cookie sheet. Freeze solid, then store in a plastic container. Or freeze small clusters of seedless grapes or hulled strawberries on bamboo skewers for low-cal "popsicles."

FUDGE TOP CHEESE PIE

Bake at 350° for 40 minutes.
Makes 8 servings at 170 calories each.

	Calorie-Saver Chocolate Cookie Crust (page 245) Or: 1 packaged 9-inch chocolate crumb crust	6	tablespoons granulated sugar substitute
1	cup part-skim ricotta cheese	3	teaspoons vanilla
¾	cup skim milk	2	eggs
2	teaspoons cornstarch	1	teaspoon instant coffee powder
½	teaspoon salt	4	tablespoons unsweetened cocoa powder
6	tablespoons sugar		Low-calorie whipped topping (optional)

1. Prepare Calorie-Saver Chocolate Cookie Crust, bake, and cool.

2. Combine ricotta, milk, cornstarch, salt, 3 tablespoons of the sugar, 3 tablespoons of the granulated sugar substitute, and 1 teaspoon of the vanilla in the container of an electric blender; whirl until smooth. Add eggs; whirl again until smooth. Pour 1 cup of the ricotta-egg mixture into the cooled piecrust.

3. Bake in a moderate oven (350°) for 20 minutes or until firm.

4. Add remaining 3 tablespoons sugar, 3 tablespoons sugar substitute, 2 teaspoons vanilla, the instant coffee, and cocoa to the remaining ricotta mixture; blend until smooth. Pour chocolate-cheese mixture over vanilla layer.

5. Bake an additional 20 minutes or until set. Turn off oven and leave door slightly ajar. Cool pie in oven 1 hour. Chill several hours before serving. Garnish pie with low-calorie whipped topping, if you wish.

CALORIE-SAVER CHERRIES JUBILEE

Makes 4 servings at 175 calories each.

4	scoops (1 pint) low-fat vanilla ice milk or frozen yogurt	2	cups (1 pound) pitted, unsweetened frozen dark sweet cherries, thawed
¾	cup low-calorie cranberry juice	½	cup brandy
1	teaspoon cornstarch		

1. Scoop ice milk or frozen yogurt into 4 serving dishes; return to freezer.

2. Combine cranberry juice and cornstarch in a chafing dish or large skillet over low heat, stirring constantly, until sauce thickens. Stir in cherries and any juice; simmer until thoroughly heated.

3. Pour brandy over cherry mixture. (Do not stir.) Heat until vapors begin to rise; ignite mixture with a long match. Spoon over ice milk or frozen yogurt.

MOCHA SPONGE CAKE

Makes 16 servings at 155 calories each.

1   package (2½ ounces) containing 2 envelopes low-calorie whipped topping mix
1½ cups cold water
1   package (4½ ounces) instant chocolate pudding and pie filling mix
1   teaspoon vanilla

1   package baked sponge cake layers (two 8-inch layers)
1   teaspoon instant coffee powder
1   teaspoon chocolate extract
2   tablespoons granulated sugar substitute

1. Combine whipped topping mix and cold water in a medium-size bowl. Reserve 2 tablespoons of chocolate pudding mix; add remaining pudding mix and vanilla to topping mix. Beat on high speed with an electric mixer until thick and fluffy. Reserve ½ cup of the chocolate frosting mixture.

2. Split sponge layers in half to form 4 layers. Spread a thin layer of frosting between each layer; stack. Spread remaining frosting on side and top.

3. Blend reserved ½ cup of frosting, instant coffee, chocolate extract, and sugar substitute in a small bowl. Swirl the darker frosting on the top and side of cake, blending with the lighter frosting. Chill.

STRAWBERRIES ROMANOFF

Makes 6 servings at 66 calories each with sugar;
53 calories with sugar substitute.

3   cups fresh strawberries
½   cup orange juice
2   tablespoons orange-flavored liqueur

2   tablespoons sugar or granulated sugar substitute to equal 2 tablespoons sugar
Low-calorie whipped topping

1. Wash and hull the berries. Leave whole. Combine them in a bowl with orange juice, liqueur, and sugar or sugar substitute. Refrigerate.
2. At serving time, spoon the berries and liquid into 6 champagne glasses.
3. Top each with 1 tablespoon of the prepared low-calorie whipped topping.

CREAM PUFFS

These are always a special treat! The filling is made with reduced sugar and low-fat milk, so the calorie count belies its luscious appeal.

Bake at 350° for 40 minutes.
Makes 8 servings at 142 calories each.

¼	cup vegetable shortening	2	tablespoons sugar
½	cup boiling water	1	cup skim milk
½	cup all-purpose flour	1	egg yolk*
2	eggs	½	teaspoon vanilla
1	tablespoon cornstarch		

1. Grease a cookie sheet. Preheat oven to 350°. Heat shortening and water in a medium-size saucepan until shortening is melted. Add flour all at once, beating until mixture is smooth and leaves side of pan clean. Remove from heat. Beat in eggs, 1 at a time, until mixture forms a thick, shiny paste.
2. Drop paste by rounded tablespoonsful 2 inches apart on prepared cookie sheet to make 8 puffs.
3. Bake in a preheated moderate oven (350°) for 40 minutes or until puffed and brown. Cool on a wire rack.
4. Combine cornstarch and sugar in a medium-size saucepan; stir in milk. Cook, stirring constantly, until mixture thickens and bubbles. Beat egg yolk slightly in a small bowl. Stir in ½ of the thickened mixture until smooth; return mixture to saucepan. Cook and stir 2 minutes longer. Remove from heat; stir in vanilla. Cool.
5. Split cooled puffs; fill with vanilla filling.

*If you want to omit the egg yolks for cholesterol's sake, add an extra teaspoon of cornstarch and a few drops of yellow food coloring.

RICOTTA CHEESE PIE

This is unusual, very good, and tastes rich. No sugar is used except what is already in the chocolate pieces and graham crackers.

Bake at 350° for 8 minutes.
Makes 16 servings at 145 calories each.

½	cup graham cracker crumbs (about 8)	½	cup semisweet chocolate pieces
¼	cup (½ stick) margarine, softened	½	cup blanched almonds
		1	pound ricotta cheese
½	teaspoon ground cinnamon	½	teaspoon almond extract
1½	teaspoons unflavored gelatin		Semisweet chocolate pieces (optional)
1	cup skim milk		Blanched almonds (optional)

1. Preheat oven to 350°. Combine crumbs, margarine, and cinnamon in a small bowl; mix well. Press onto bottom and side of a 9-inch pie plate.
2. Bake crust in a preheated moderate oven (350°) for 8 minutes or until firm. Cool on a wire rack.
3. Sprinkle gelatin over milk in a small bowl; let stand 5 minutes to soften. Heat over hot water, stirring constantly, until gelatin is dissolved. Cool; chill until mixture is as thick as unbeaten egg white.
4. Put chocolate pieces and almonds in the container of an electric blender; whirl 1 minute. Add ricotta and almond extract; whirl 1 minute longer. Spoon into a large bowl.
5. Beat thickened gelatin mixture with an electric mixer until fluffy. Fold into ricotta mixture; spoon into cooled shell. Refrigerate 2 hours or until set. Garnish with additional chocolate and almonds, if you wish.

BLUSHING PEAR SQUARE

Bake at 325° for 25 minutes.
Makes 12 servings at 104 calories each.

¾	cup *sifted* cake flour	¼	cup firmly packed light brown sugar
1	teaspoon baking powder		
½	teaspoon pumpkin pie spice	¼	cup boiling water
¼	teaspoon salt		Blushing Pears
2	eggs		(recipe below)
⅓	cup granulated sugar		

1. Sift cake flour, baking powder, pumpkin pie spice, and salt onto wax paper.

2. Separate eggs, placing whites in a medium-size bowl and yolks in a small bowl.

3. Preheat oven to 325°. Beat egg whites until foamy-white and double in volume; beat in granulated sugar, 1 tablespoon at a time, until meringue forms soft peaks.

4. Beat egg yolks until fluffy-thick; beat in brown sugar, 1 tablespoon at a time. Stir in boiling water; beat vigorously for 5 minutes, or until mixture forms soft peaks.

5. Fold egg yolk mixture into egg white mixture until no streaks of yellow remain; fold in flour mixture, ¼ at a time. Pour batter into an ungreased 9 x 9 x 2-inch baking pan.

6. Bake in a preheated low oven (325°) for 25 minutes or until center springs back when lightly pressed with fingertip. Cool completely in pan on a wire rack.

7. While cake cools, prepare Blushing Pears.

8. Loosen cake around edges with a knife; turn out, then turn right side up on a serving plate. Lift pears from syrup and arrange in a pattern on top of cake; spoon syrup evenly over all. Cut into 12 serving pieces.

Blushing Pears: Pare 3 medium-size firm, ripe pears; quarter and core. Place pears and ½ cup low-calorie cranberry-juice cocktail in a medium-size skillet. Bring to a boil; lower heat; simmer, turning pears several times, 10 minutes, or until tender. Blend 1 tablespoon cornstarch and ¼ cup more cranberry-juice cocktail until smooth in a cup; stir into liquid in skillet. Cook, stirring constantly, until mixture thickens and bubbles 1 minute; remove from heat; cool.

GLAZED FRUIT MERINGUES

Bake at 250° for 1 hour.
Makes 8 servings at 58 calories each.

2	egg whites	
1	teaspoon lemon juice	
⅓	cup sugar	
1	teaspoon vanilla	
2	teaspoons cornstarch	

Dash ground cardamom
1 can (16 ounces) calories-reduced fruits for salad
Red food coloring

1. Line a large cookie sheet with brown paper; draw eight 3½-inch rounds, 2 inches apart, on paper. (A regular coffee cup makes a handy pattern.) Preheat oven to 250°.

2. Beat egg whites with lemon juice until foamy-white and double in volume in a small bowl. Sprinkle in sugar, 1 tablespoon at a time, beating all the time until sugar completely dissolves and meringue stands in firm peaks; beat in vanilla.

3. Divide the meringue onto the 8 circles, with spoon, building up edge so meringue will hold the filling when baked.

4. Bake in a preheated slow oven (250°) for 1 hour or until delicately golden. Cool on cookie sheet 5 minutes; loosen carefully from paper with a spatula; place on wire racks to cool.

5. About an hour before serving, mix cornstarch and cardamom in a small saucepan. Drain syrup from fruits and blend into cornstarch mixture until smooth.

6. Cook, stirring constantly, until mixture thickens and comes to a boil, in about 3 minutes; remove from heat. Stir in a drop or two of food coloring to tint rosy red; cool.

7. Halve any large pieces of fruit; arrange pieces in meringue shells. Brush fruits with tinted syrup to glaze lightly.

PEARS IN BURGUNDY

Makes 4 servings at 110 calories each with sugar;
86 calories with sugar substitute.

1 can (16 ounces) diet-pack pear halves	¼ teasoon grated lemon or orange rind
½ cup Burgundy or dry red wine	3 tablespoons sugar
½ cup orange juice	Or: Granulated sugar
½ teaspoon ground cinnamon	substitute to equal 3
¼ teaspoon ground cloves	tablespoons of sugar

1. Drain pear juice into a small saucepan; add wine, orange juice, cinnamon, cloves, lemon or orange rind, and sugar. Bring to a boil; lower heat. Simmer, uncovered, until liquid is reduced to ½ of original volume. Cool a few minutes.

2. Arrange pear halves in 4 stemmed glasses. Pour warm liquid over pears; chill before serving.

PINEAPPLE PUFF

Makes 8 servings at 113 calories each.

4	eggs, separated
1	can (20 ounces) crushed pineapple in pineapple juice
	Granulated, liquid, or tablet no-calorie sweetener to equal 8 tablespoons sugar
2	envelopes unflavored gelatin
¾	cup instant nonfat dry milk powder
¾	cup ice water
	Fresh mint (optional)

1. Prepare a 4-cup soufflé dish: Cut a strip of aluminum foil, 12 inches wide and long enough to go around dish with a 1-inch overlap; fold in half lengthwise. Wrap around dish to make a 2-inch stand-up collar; hold in place with tape.

2. Beat egg yolks in the top of a double boiler; stir in pineapple and juice and your favorite no-calorie sweetener. Sprinkle gelatin over top; let stand several minutes to soften gelatin. Place top of double boiler over simmering water.

3. Cook, stirring constantly, 15 minutes or until gelatin dissolves and mixture coats a spoon; pour into a large bowl.

4. Set bowl in a pan filled with ice and cold water; chill, stirring several times, until as thick as unbeaten egg white.

5. While pineapple mixture chills, beat egg whites just until they form soft peaks in a medium-size bowl; beat with an electric mixer on high speed until stiff.

6. Fold beaten egg whites, then whipped milk into gelatin mixture, keeping bowl over ice, until no streaks of white remain. Pour into prepared soufflé dish. Chill several hours or until firm. Spoon into serving dishes; garnish each with a sprig of mint, if you wish.

HEAVENLY ANGEL CAKE

Bake at 350° for 40 minutes.
Makes 16 servings at 79 calories each.

1	cup *sifted* cake flour
1	cup sugar
10	egg whites (1¼ cups)
¼	teaspoon salt
1	teaspoon cream of tartar
½	teaspoon vanilla
1½	tablespoons liquid sugar substitute

1. Sift flour and ½ cup of the sugar onto wax paper. Preheat oven to 350°.
2. Beat the egg whites with salt and cream of tartar in a large bowl with an electric mixer until very foamy and peaks begin to form. Gradually beat in the remaining ½ cup sugar. Continue beating until stiff peaks form. Beat in vanilla and liquid sugar substitute.
3. Gently fold the flour mixture into the egg whites, a few tablespoons at a time. Turn into an ungreased 9-inch springform pan. Carefully cut through batter with a spatula to avoid air pockets.
4. Bake in a preheated moderate oven (350°) for 40 minutes or until surface of cake is dry and center springs back when lightly pressed with fingertip. Invert cake in pan on a wire rack until cold. Carefully loosen cake from side of pan; remove side.

PUMPKIN-SPICE CAKE

Bake at 325° for 1 hour.
Makes 16 servings at 160 calories each.

2¼ cups *sifted* cake flour	1 cup canned pumpkin
3 teaspoons baking powder	¾ cup firmly packed brown
2 teaspoons pumpkin pie spice	sugar
½ teaspoon ground cinnamon	Granulated sugar substitute
½ teaspoon butter-flavored salt	to equal ⅔ cup sugar
6 eggs, separated	½ teaspoon cream of tartar
⅔ cup diet margarine	

1. Sift flour, baking powder, pumpkin pie spice, cinnamon, and salt onto wax paper. Preheat oven to 325°.
2. Combine egg yolks, diet margarine, pumpkin, brown sugar, and sugar substitute in a large mixing bowl; beat until smooth.
3. Add flour mixture gradually to egg-pumpkin mixture; blend well after each addition.
4. Combine egg whites and cream of tartar in a large bowl. Beat with an electric mixer until stiff peaks form. Gently fold egg-pumpkin mixture into egg whites until just blended. Turn into a 10-inch nonstick tube or Bundt pan.
5. Bake in a preheated slow oven (325°) for 1 hour or until top springs back when lightly pressed with fingertip. Invert cake in pan on a wire rack; cool. Carefully loosen from pan.

21-CALORIE PEANUT BUTTER COOKIES

Bake at 375° for 8 minutes.
Makes 5 dozen cookies at 21 calories each.

⅔ cup *sifted* all-purpose flour
½ teaspoon baking soda
½ teaspoon baking powder
3 tablespoons butter or margarine, softened
4 tablespoons peanut butter

2 tablespoons firmly packed brown sugar
Granulated sugar substitute to equal 4 tablespoons of sugar
1 teaspoon vanilla
2 eggs, beaten

1. Sift flour, baking soda, and baking powder onto wax paper.
2. Beat the butter, peanut butter, brown sugar, and sugar substitute together. Add vanilla and eggs; beat until fluffy.
3. Add dry ingredients to peanut butter mixture; mix well. Preheat oven to 375°.
4. Use a measuring teaspoon to drop level spoonfuls of cookie dough onto nonstick cookie sheets.
5. Bake in a preheated moderate oven (375°) for 8 minutes. Cool on paper toweling.

23-CALORIE APPLESAUCE COOKIES

Bake at 375° for 15 minutes.
Makes 9 dozen cookies at 23 calories each.

1⅔ cups *sifted* all-purpose flour
1 teaspoon baking soda
½ teaspoon salt
2 teaspoons apple pie spice
1 cup (8 ounces) diet margarine
5 tablespoons firmly packed brown sugar

Granulated sugar substitute to equal 6 tablespoons of sugar
1 teaspoon vanilla
1 egg
1 cup unsweetened applesauce
⅔ cup raisins
1 cup whole bran cereal

1. Sift flour, baking soda, salt, and apple pie spice onto wax paper.
2. Beat diet margarine, brown sugar, sugar substitute, vanilla, and egg until blended (mixture will be rough and broken in texture due to composition of the diet margarine).

3. Add sifted dry ingredients alternately with applesauce. Mix well after each addition. Stir in raisin and bran cereal. Preheat oven to 375°.
4. Use a measuring teaspoon to drop level spoonfuls of cookie dough onto nonstick cookie sheets.
5. Bake in a preheated moderate oven (375°) for 15 minutes or until cookies are golden brown. Cool on paper toweling. Store in a covered container.

BAKED APPLE ALASKA

Bake at 425° for 30 minutes; then at 500° for 3 minutes.
Makes 10 servings at 145 calories each.

5	apples, pared, cored, and thinly sliced		Dash salt
3	tablespoons granulated sugar	1	quart vanilla ice milk
2	teaspoons cornstarch	3	egg whites
½	teaspoon ground cinnamon	⅛	teaspoon cream of tartar
		¼	cup 10X (confectioners') sugar

1. Preheat oven to 425°. Arrange sliced apples in a 9-inch pie plate. Combine sugar, cornstarch, cinnamon, and salt; sprinkle evenly over apples. Cover with aluminum foil.
2. Bake in a hot oven (425°) for 30 minutes or until apples are just tender. Remove from oven; cool. Refrigerate. This may be done ahead.
3. At serving time, cover chilled apples with an even layer of ice milk. Place in freezer.
4. Preheat oven to 500°. Beat egg whites and cream of tartar until frothy. Gradually add 10X sugar, a tablespoon at a time. Continue beating until mixture stands in peaks. Spread meringue over ice milk, being sure to bring it to the edge of the pie plate. Place pie plate in a roasting pan; surround with ice cubes to keep cold.
5. Bake in a preheated very hot oven (500°) for 3 minutes or until meringue is lightly browned. Remove from oven and ice; serve immediately.

10

Quick and Easy Desserts

Last-minute desserts *can* be elegant enough to serve to company or simple enough for everyday meals. The desserts in this chapter were planned to fit into the tightest schedule. They rely on convenience or store-bought ingredients and a little imagination. Some are updated classics, while the others are new creations. They are all uncomplicated to prepare yet great to eat. Stock up your cupboards or freeze with the necessary staples so that you will always have the makings for several of these fast and fabulous desserts.

APRICOT CREAM TORTE

A grand dessert—layers of puff pastry and cream filling, all topped with apricots, whipped cream, and chopped pistachio nuts. And it takes no time at all to make, thanks to convenience foods.

Bake at 350° for 25 minutes.
Makes 8 servings.

½ of a 17¼-ounce package frozen pre-rolled puff pastry, thawed (1 sheet)
1 package (3¾ ounces) lemon instant pudding and pie filling mix
½ cup dairy sour cream
½ cup cottage cheese
½ cup milk
1 can (17 ounces) apricot halves, drained
¼ cup heavy cream
⅓ cup chopped pistachio nuts

1. Preheat oven to 350°.

2. Unwrap thawed pastry. Roll out on a lightly floured board with a lightly floured rolling pin to a 15 x 10-inch rectangle. Cut into three 10 x 5-inch rectangles. Prick pastry all over with a fork. Place on an ungreased cookie sheet.

3. Bake in a preheated moderate oven (350°) for 25 minutes or until golden brown. Remove to wire racks; cool thoroughly.

4. Combine pudding, sour cream, cottage cheese, and milk in the container of an electric blender. Cover; whirl until smooth and creamy.

5. To assemble torte: Place one pastry layer on serving platter; spread with cream filling. Repeat with remaining pastry layers and cream filling, ending with a small amount of cream filling on top layer.

6. Cut apricot halves in half; arrange over top of torte. Beat heavy cream in a small bowl until stiff. Spoon into pastry bag fitted with decorative tip; pipe rosettes of whipped cream around outer edge of torte. Sprinkle apricots with chopped pistachios. Chill until serving time.

CHOCOLATE-APRICOT CAKE

Just a few ingredients make this spectacular-looking cake!

Makes 12 servings.

1 package (10¾ ounces) frozen pound cake
⅓ cup apricot preserves
1 tablespoon brandy, rum, or orange juice
1 container (16.5 ounces) milk chocolate ready-to-spread frosting
Whipped cream (optional)
Whole blanched almonds (optional)

1. Cut frozen pound cake lengthwise into 4 thin layers. Combine apricot preserves and brandy in a small bowl.
2. Place top of pound cake, cut side up, on serving plate; spread with ⅓ of the apricot-brandy sauce. On a second piece of pound cake spread a thin layer of frosting; place slice, frosting side down, on top of apricot-glazed slice. Repeat with remaining layers. Frost sides and top of cake with remaining chocolate frosting. Garnish with pressurized whipped cream and whole blanched almonds, if you wish.

CHERRY-CHEESE PARFAITS

Lemony no-bake cheesecake filling layered with graham cracker crumbs and cherry pie filling is simply scrumptious!

Makes 6 servings.

1 package (10½ or 11 ounces) cheesecake mix
2 teaspoons grated lemon rind
1 can (21 ounces) cherry pie filling
Sliced almonds (optional)

1. Prepare graham crumbs from mix in a small bowl following package directions; reserve. Prepare cheesecake filling following package directions; fold in lemon rind.
2. Spoon half the graham crumbs into the bottoms of 6 parfait glasses; layer some cheesecake filling, some cherry pie filling, more crumbs, remaining cheesecake filling, and remaining cherry pie filling. Refrigerate. Garnish with sliced almonds, if you wish.

ORANGE-CHEESE PARFAITS

Makes 8 servings.

1 package (10½ or 11 ounces) cheesecake mix
2 tablespoons sugar

2 tablespoons butter or margarine, melted
1 orange
2 cups milk

1. Mix crumbs from cheesecake mix with sugar and butter. Spoon about half into 8 parfait glasses, dividing evenly. Reserve remaining crumb mixture.

2. Grate 2 teaspoons rind from orange. Remove white membrane from orange with a sharp knife; section orange; halve each section.

3. Prepare cheesecake mix from package with milk. Stir in orange rind and orange. Layer with reserved crumb mixture in glasses.

BLUEBERRY CRISP

Bake at 350° for 10 minutes.
Makes 8 servings.

2 cans (21 ounces each) blueberry pie filling
1½ cups granola-type cereal

½ cup (1 stick) butter or margarine, melted

1. Preheat oven to 350°. Spoon pie filling into shallow baking dish.

2. Combine cereal and melted butter in a medium-size bowl; toss to blend well. Sprinkle over pie filling.

3. Bake in a preheated moderate oven (350°) for 10 minutes. Serve warm or cold.

STRAWBERRY CREAM

Makes 4 servings.

1 cup boiling water
1 package (3 ounces) strawberry-flavor gelatin
1 package (10 ounces) frozen strawberries in syrup, thawed

½ cup dairy sour cream
4 whole strawberries (optional)

1. Pour boiling water over gelatin in a medium-size bowl; stir until thoroughly dissolved.
2. Stir in thawed strawberries. Stir in sour cream until well blended.
3. Pour into 4 individual dessert dishes. Quick-chill in freezer until ready to serve.
4. Garnish top of each dessert with a fresh whole strawberry, if you wish.

BAKED STREUSEL PEARS

Bake at 350° for 10 minutes.
Makes 6 servings.

½ **cup flaked coconut**	3 **tablespoons butter or**
⅓ **cup firmly packed light**	**margarine**
brown sugar	1 **can (29 ounces) pear halves,**
¼ **cup chopped walnuts**	**drained**

1. Preheat oven to 350°. Combine coconut, sugar, walnuts, and butter in a small saucepan. Heat, stirring until well blended.
2. Arrange pear halves in a shallow baking pan. Spoon topping over each.
3. Bake in a preheated moderate oven (350°) for 10 minutes. Serve warm or at room temperature.

HOT APPLE-SPICE SUNDAE

Like pie à la mode without the pastry.

Makes 8 servings.

2 **tablespoons butter or**	1 **can (20 ounces) unsweetened**
margarine	**apple slices, drained**
½ **cup firmly packed brown**	¼ **cup walnut pieces**
sugar	1 **quart vanilla ice cream**
½ **teaspoon ground cinnamon**	

1. Melt butter in a small skillet; add sugar, cinnamon, and apple slices. Heat just until bubbly hot. Remove from heat.
2. Stir in nuts. Serve warm over ice cream.

WAFFLES SUZETTE

A take-off on the popular Crêpes Suzette.

Makes 8 servings.

1	package (11 ounces) frozen round waffles (8 to a package)	¼	cup (½ stick) butter or margarine
2	large oranges	4	teaspoons sugar
		½	cup Grand Marnier

1. Toast waffles following package directions. Cut each into four wedges. Place in a large chafing dish or skillet.
2. Pare the orange rind (no white part) from one orange with a vegetable parer; cut into julienne strips. Cut and squeeze oranges to extract ⅔ cup juice.
3. Melt butter in a small saucepan over low heat. Add sugar, orange juice, and julienne strips. Simmer 3 minutes. Stir in ¼ cup of the Grand Marnier. Pour mixture over waffles.
4. Gently heat remaining ¼ cup Grand Marnier in the same saucepan for 2 minutes. Pour over waffles. Ignite; serve when flames subside.

QUICK APRICOT CREAM

Makes 4 servings.

1	package (3¾ ounces) vanilla instant pudding and pie filling mix	1	can (17 ounces) apricot halves, drained
1	cup milk	½	cup dairy sour cream
1	cup heavy cream	¼	cup firmly packed light brown sugar

1. Prepare pudding using milk and heavy cream following package directions. Turn into a dessert bowl.
2. Arrange drained apricots over pudding. Spread sour cream over fruit. Sprinkle with brown sugar. Chill.

PEARS MELBA

Makes 6 servings.

1   package (10 ounces) frozen
    raspberries in quick-thaw
    pouch, thawed
2   tablespoons cherry brandy,
    orange-liqueur, or orange
    juice

1   can (29 ounces) pear halves,
    drained
1   quart chocolate ice cream

1. Combine thawed raspberries and brandy. Divide pear halves among 6 dessert dishes.
2. Scoop ice cream into each dish. Top with brandied raspberries.

FRESH FRUIT FLAN

Assemble this spectacular no-bake dessert in just minutes.

Makes 8 servings.

1   ready-to-use sponge cake
    shell (7.1 ounces)
    Or: Homemade Sponge Cake
    Layer (page 268)
1   tablespoon heavy cream
3   tablespoons cream sherry

½   cup apricot preserves
½   cup heavy cream
1   pint strawberries, washed
    and hulled
1   medium-size banana
½   cup blueberries

1. Prepare Homemade Sponge Cake Layer, if using.
2. Place cake shell on a serving plate. Combine the 1 tablespoon heavy cream and 1 tablespoon of the sherry in a small bowl; brush over top surface of cake.
3. Mix apricot preserves and the remaining 2 tablespoons of the sherry in a small bowl until well blended; brush about half the mixture over top and sides of cake.
4. Beat the ½ cup heavy cream in a small bowl until stiff. Pipe whipped cream rosettes through a medium-size decorating tip around the inside edge of the cake. Arrange strawberries hulled end down in a circle just inside the cream rosettes.
5. Peel and slice the banana. Arrange slices, overlapping, in a circle next to the strawberries. Pile the blueberries in the center. Brush remaining apricot glaze over the fruit. Refrigerate for 30 minutes.

BLUEBERRY PETAL SHORTCAKE

A new way to use the bake-and-serve cinnamon rolls found in the refrigerator case of your supermarket.

Bake at 400° for 13 to 17 minutes.
Makes 8 servings.

1 package (9.5 ounces) refrigerated cinnamon rolls with icing	½ teaspoon sugar
	⅛ teaspoon ground cinnamon
	1 pint fresh blueberries
⅔ cup heavy cream	Lemon slices (optional)
⅓ cup dairy sour cream	Fresh mint leaves (optional)

1. Preheat oven to 400°. Grease a cookie sheet.

2. Remove rolls from cylinder and separate. Place 7 of the rolls, cinnamon topping side up, in a tight circle with sides touching on prepared cookie sheet; place remaining roll in center.

3. Bake in a preheated hot oven (400°) for 13 to 17 minutes or until golden brown. Carefully transfer cake in 1 piece to a wire rack to cool. Drizzle hot rolls with enclosed icing, if you wish. Cool to room temperature.

4. Slice cake in half horizontally to make 2 layers. Combine heavy cream and sour cream in a small bowl; beat until stiff; mix in sugar and cinnamon.

5. Place bottom cake layer, cut side up, on serving plate. Spread with two thirds of the cream. Arrange half the blueberries over the cream. Place second cake layer, cut side down, over filling. Top with remaining cream and blueberries. Garnish with lemon slices and mint leaves, if you wish.

HOMEMADE SPONGE CAKE LAYER

Bake at 325° for 30 minutes.
Makes one 10-inch sponge layer.

½ cup *sifted* cake flour	½ cup sugar
½ teaspoon baking powder	½ teaspoon grated lemon rind
¼ teaspoon salt	1 teaspoon lemon juice
3 eggs, separated	

1. Preheat oven to 325°. Grease and flour a 10-inch pie plate.

2. Sift flour, baking powder, and salt onto wax paper.

3. Beat egg whites in a large bowl with an electric mixer on high speed until foamy-white and double in volume. Beat in ¼ cup of the sugar, 1 tablespoon at a time, until meringue forms soft peaks.

4. Beat egg yolks with lemon rind and juice in a small bowl with electric mixer on high speed until thick and lemon-colored. Beat in the remaining ¼ cup sugar, 1 tablespoon at a time, until mixture is very thick and fluffy.

5. Fold flour mixture, ⅓ at a time, into yolk mixture until completely blended. Fold flour-egg yolk mixture into meringue until no streaks remain. Spread evenly in prepared pie plate.

6. Bake in a preheated slow oven (325°) for 30 minutes or until center springs back when lightly pressed with fingertip. Remove to wire rack and cool in pie plate 10 minutes. Remove cake from pie plate; cool to room temperature.

PAPAYA VELVET

Makes 6 servings.

1	medium-size ripe papaya (about 1¼ pounds)	1	teaspoon finely chopped crystallized ginger
2	tablespoons sugar	1	cup heavy cream
2	tablespoons honey	¼	cup toasted chopped almonds
2	tablespoons lemon juice		

1. Halve papaya lengthwise; scoop out and discard seeds. Peel; chop pulp coarsely.

2. Place pulp, sugar, honey, lemon juice, and ginger in the container of an electric blender. Cover; whirl until smooth. Turn into a medium-size bowl.

3. Beat cream in a small bowl until stiff. Fold cream and almonds into papaya mixture. Spoon into six ½-cup custard cups or other dessert dishes. Quick-chill in freezer for 30 minutes or freeze until frozen.

BLUEBERRY-LEMON CHEESE PIE

A quick cheese "cake" in a pie shell. If you like chocolate, try the Cherry Chocolate variation which follows.

Makes 6 servings.

1   package (3¾ ounces) lemon instant pudding and pie filling mix
1¾ cups cold milk
1   package (8 ounces) cream cheese, at room temperature

1   packaged 8-inch graham cracker crust
1   cup fresh blueberries
⅓   cup apple jelly
½   teaspoon lemon juice
2   teaspoons water
½   cup heavy cream

1. Combine instant pudding and milk in a medium-size bowl; beat with an electric mixer until smooth. Beat in cream cheese until blended. Pour into crumb crust. Refrigerate at least 30 minutes or until set.
2. To serve: Sprinkle blueberries over top of pie. Combine apple jelly, lemon juice, and water in a small bowl until smooth; spoon over berries. Beat heavy cream in a small bowl until stiff. Garnish pie with cream.

Cherry-Chocolate Cheese Pie: Substitute chocolate flavor instant pudding and pie filling for the lemon flavor, a packaged chocolate crumb crust for the graham cracker crust, pitted fresh sweet cherries for the blueberries and apricot preserves thinned with a little water for the Apple Glaze. Make the pie following the recipe above.

BAKED BANANAS

Bake at 375° for 15 minutes.
Makes 4 servings.

4   bananas, peeled
¼   cup lemon juice
½   cup dark rum

¼   cup firmly packed light brown sugar

1. Preheat oven to 375°. Slice bananas lengthwise; place in a shallow baking dish. Sprinkle with lemon juice. Pour rum over; sprinkle evenly with brown sugar.
2. Bake in a moderate oven (375°) for 15 minutes or until glazed.

PEACHES HÉLÈNE

Makes 4 servings.

1   can (30 ounces) peach
   halves, drained
1   quart vanilla ice cream

1   jar (12 ounces) hot fudge or
   chocolate sauce

1. Divide peach halves among 4 dessert dishes.
2. Scoop ice cream into center of peaches. Top with sauce.

SPEEDY HOT FUDGE SAUCE

Drizzle this fudge sauce, made in just minutes, over ice cream, fudge
cake, or a Chocolate Chip Banana Split (recipe follows).

Makes about 1 cup.

⅔   cup sweetened condensed
   milk (not evaporated milk)
4   packets (1 ounce each)
   premelted unsweetened
   baking chocolate flavor

¼   cup water
1   tablespoon butter or
   margarine
1   teaspoon vanilla

1. Combine condensed milk, premelted chocolate flavor, water, and
butter in a small saucepan. Cook over low heat, stirring constantly,
until mixture is smooth and heated through.
2. Remove from heat; stir in vanilla. Use warm; refrigerate any
leftover sauce.

Note: To reheat sauce, place over simmering water, stirring
occasionally, until heated through. Add a little hot water, if necessary,
to thin to disired consistency.

Chocolate Chip Banana Split: Halve a banana lengthwise and place
in a banana split dish or other dessert dish. Top with 2 scoops of your
favorite ice cream. Roll a third scoop of ice cream in chocolate chip
cookie crumbs; place in dish. Spoon Speedy Hot Fudge Sauce over all.
Garnish with whipped heavy cream and a maraschino cherry.

ORANGE CREAM

Makes 4 servings.

1 large navel orange	½ teaspoon ground ginger
1 package (8 ounces) cream cheese, softened	2 tablespoons toasted slivered almonds
½ cup dairy sour cream	

1. Grate 2 tablespoons orange rind. Combine with cream cheese, sour cream, and ginger in the container of an electric blender. Whirl until well blended.

2. Pare remaining white pulp from orange. Halve and seed oranges. Add to blender; whirl until well blended. Chill. Top with almonds.

CHERRY-CHEESE JUBILEE

All it takes is 15 minutes to put this spectacular dessert together; chill it while you're having dinner.

Makes 12 servings.

1 baker's 8-inch angel food cake (about 13 ounces)	½ cup half and half or milk
¼ cup apricot preserves	1 can (21 ounces) cherry pie filling
1 teaspoon sugar	Red food coloring (optional)
1 package (8 ounces) cream cheese, softened	1 container (4½ ounces) frozen whipped topping, thawed
1 container (8 ounces) dairy sour cream	Mint sprigs
1 package (3¼ ounces) French vanilla instant pudding and pie filling mix	

1. With a sharp knife, cut down into cake about ¾ inch in from outer edge, cutting about 1½ inches deep. Scoop out cake part in center; fill hole in bottom with a piece cut from removed cake. (Freeze remaining crumbled cake to use with packaged pudding for a quick dessert at another meal.)

2. Heat apricot preserves and sugar in a small saucepan until bubbly; press through a strainer. Brush over side and edge of cake.

3. Beat cream cheese in a large bowl with an electric mixer until smooth, about 1 minute; add sour cream; mix until smooth. Add instant pudding and half and half; beat on low speed just to combine; then on high speed until mixture thickens, about 2 minutes.

4. Measure and reserve ¼ cup cherry pie filling. Fold remaining pie filling into cheese mixture. Add a few drops of red food coloring, if you wish. Spoon into prepared cake shell. Refrigerate.

5. At serving time, pipe whipped topping around top edge and garnish with mint sprigs. Pipe whipped topping on top and around base of cake; garnish with reserved cherry pie filling and mint sprigs.

PEACH COUPES

Makes 6 servings.

1 can (16 ounces) freestone peach slices	1 tablespoon lemon juice
1 tablespoon brandy	1 quart vanilla ice cream
	Sliced almonds

1. Drain syrup from peaches and reserve for another use. Place peaches, brandy, and lemon juice in the container of an electric blender; cover; puree until smooth. Place blender container in refrigerator until ready to use.

2. To serve: Scoop ice cream into 6 individual serving dishes. Pour sauce over. Garnish with almonds.

TRIFLE

The whimsical name for this updated version of the classic Christmas dessert from England will intrigue even the most dessert-resistant guests.

Makes 12 servings.

2 packages (3¾ ounces each) vanilla instant pudding and pie filling mix	¼ cup raspberry preserves
	⅓ cup sweet sherry
2¼ cups milk	3 packages (3 ounces each) ladyfingers (36 double ladyfingers)
2 cups (1 pint) heavy cream	
¼ cup orange-flavored liqueur or orange juice	2 tablespoons 10X (confectioners') sugar
1 package (10 ounces) frozen raspberries, thawed and drained, syrup reserved	2 teaspoons vanilla
	½ cup whole unblanched almonds

1. Prepare instant pudding with milk, 1½ cups of the heavy cream, and the liqueur to make 4 cups liquid, following package directions.
2. Combine 3 tablespoons of the reserved raspberry syrup, the raspberry preserves, and the sherry in a small bowl; mix well. Separate the ladyfingers. Brush mixture over flat side of half the ladyfingers; arrange against the side of a 2-quart glass or crystal bowl, rounded sides out, lining bowl completely.
3. Spoon in half the pudding and top with remaining ladyfingers. Top with drained raspberries and remaining pudding. Cover; refrigerate several hours or overnight until completely chilled.
4. Just before serving, beat remaining ½ cup cream with 10X sugar and vanilla in a small bowl until stiff. Spoon cream into a pastry bag fitted with a star tip. Pipe cream in a lattice pattern on top of custard. Garnish with almonds.

11

Frostings, Fillings, Glazes, and Sauces

The finishing touches to a cake or ice cream make your dessert attractive and add a personal message that you made it. Most cakes need a frosting, though some are better with sauce served over. Pound cake, angel cake, and fruitcakes need no embellishments, but plain or not-so-rich cakes should be filled and frosted.

Frostings can be prepared from butter or shortening plus confectioners' sugar and flavoring or can be made of beaten egg whites and confectioners' sugar. A frosting can be used for a cake filling or you can fill a cake with a custard or other filling. Glazes and icings are thin sugar toppings used to decorate some cakes and cookies.

Sauces such as the fruit sauces or chocolate sauces in this chapter are perfect toppings for homemade or commercial ice cream. They may also be served over plain sponge or angel cake slices. Dessert sauces can enhance a simple rice pudding or fruit mousse.

VANILLA BUTTER CREAM FROSTING

Makes enough to fill and frost two 8- or 9-inch cake layers.

½   cup (1 stick) butter or
    margarine, at room
    temperature
1   package (1 pound) 10X
    (confectioners') sugar

4   tablespoons milk
2   teaspoons vanilla

Beat butter in a medium-size bowl with an electric mixer until soft. Beat in 10X sugar alternately with milk and vanilla, until smooth and spreadable.

Orange Butter Cream Frosting: Follow basic recipe but omit vanilla. Add 1 tablespoon grated orange rind and substitute orange juice for the milk.

Mocha Frosting: Follow basic recipe but omit vanilla; add 1 tablespoon instant coffee powder, 3 tablespoons coffee liqueur, and add only 2 tablespoons of the milk.

Butter Cookie Frosting: Follow basic recipe but use only ¼ cup butter, 2 to 2½ cups 10X sugar, 2 tablespoons milk, and 1 teaspoon vanilla. Spoon into a pastry bag fitted with a plain round writing tip.

LEMON BUTTER CREAM FROSTING

Makes enough to frost Mimosa Cake.

¾   cup (1½ sticks) butter,
    softened
1½ packages (1½ pounds) 10X
    (confectioners') sugar, sifted

1½ teaspoons grated lemon rind
6   tablespoons lemon juice

Beat butter in a medium-size bowl with an electric mixer until fluffy. Gradually beat in 10X sugar and lemon rind alternating with lemon juice until smooth and spreadable.

ENOUGH FROSTING

If a frosting recipe makes enough for two 8- or 9-inch layers, you'll have enough to frost any 13 x 9 x 2-inch cake, or between 24 and 36 cupcakes, depending on their size.

COFFEE BUTTER CREAM FROSTING

Makes enough to frost 2 dozen Coffee-Almond Squares.

¾ cup (1½ sticks) butter or
margarine, softened
5 to 5½ cups 10X
(confectioners') sugar

3 tablespoons instant coffee
dissolved in 6 tablespoons
warm water

Beat butter until light and fluffy in a small bowl with an electric mixer.
Add sugar and coffee alternately to butter until smooth and creamy.

HONEY-CREAM CHEESE FROSTING

Makes enough to frost 24 to 26 cupcakes.

2 packages (3 ounces each)
cream cheese, softened
1 package (1 pound) 10X
(confectioners') sugar

6 tablespoons honey

Beat cream cheese in a medium-size bowl with an electric mixer until
soft. Beat in 10X sugar alternately with honey until smooth and
spreadable.

ROYAL FROSTING

Makes enough to fill and frost two 8- or 9-inch cake layers.

2 egg whites
¼ teaspoon cream of tartar

2½ to 3 cups 10X
(confectioners') sugar

Beat egg whites and cream of tartar in a small bowl until foamy.
Gradually beat in sugar until frosting stands in firm peaks and is stiff
enough to hold its shape when cut through with a knife. (Keep bowl
covered with damp paper toweling while working to keep frosting
from drying out.)

Note: For ½ recipe, use 1 egg white, ⅛ teaspoon cream of tartar, and
1¼ to 1½ cups 10X sugar.

RICH BUTTER CREAM FROSTING

Makes enough to fill and frost two 8- or 9-inch cake layers.

½ cup (1 stick) butter or
margarine
1 egg yolk
1 package (1 pound) 10X
(confectioners') sugar

3 tablespoons milk
1 teaspoon vanilla

Beat butter with egg yolk in a medium-size bowl with an electric mixer until soft. Beat in 10X sugar alternately with milk and vanilla, until smooth and spreadable.

BROWN BUTTER FROSTING

Makes enough to frost one 9-inch tube cake.

½ cup (1 stick) butter or
margarine
1 package (1 pound) 10X
(confectioners') sugar, *sifted*

¼ cup milk

1. Heat butter over low heat in a medium-size saucepan until liquid bubbles up, gets very foamy, then settles and is lightly browned. *Remove from heat at once.* (Watch carefully to prevent over-browning; procedure should take only 3 to 5 minutes.)
2. Pour browned butter over 10X sugar in a large bowl; mix until evenly crumbly.
3. Drizzle milk over; blend until smooth. Add 1 to 2 teaspoonsful more milk, if needed, to make smooth and spreadable.

FREEZING LEFTOVER FROSTING

If you have leftover butter cream frosting or whipped cream, fill a pastry bag with the leftover frosting and pipe decorative puffs or flowers onto a wax-paper lined cookie sheet. Freeze until firm. Store decorations in plastic containers and use them to decorate desserts in a hurry.

CHOCOLATE FUDGE FROSTING

Makes enough to fill and frost two 9-inch layers.

4	squares unsweetened chocolate	1	package (1 pound) 10X (confectioners')sugar
½	cup (1 stick) butter or margarine	½	cup milk
		2	teaspoons vanilla

1. Combine chocolate and butter in a small, heavy saucepan. Cook over low heat just until melted; remove from heat.
2. Combine 10X sugar, milk, and vanilla in a medium-size bowl; stir until smooth; add chocolate mixture.
3. Set bowl in pan of ice and cold water; beat with wooden spoon until frosting is thick enough to spread and hold its shape.

DECORATOR'S FROSTING

Makes enough to decorate a 4-tiered cake.

½	cup (1 stick) butter or margarine, softened	¼	teaspoon salt
½	cup vegetable shortening	3	tablespoons milk
2	packages (1 pound each) 10X (confectioners') sugar, sifted	2	tablespoons apricot brandy
		2	tablespoons light corn syrup
		1	teaspoon vanilla

1. Beat butter and vegetable shortening until smooth in a large bowl. Beat in 10X sugar and the salt until the mixture is crumbly and all of the 10X sugar has been added.
2. Add milk, brandy, corn syrup, and vanilla to bowl. Beat until the mixture is very thick and smooth.

WHITE DECORATING FROSTING

Makes about 1¾ cups.

½	cup vegetable shortening	2	tablespoons milk
2½	cups 10X (confectioners') sugar	½	teaspoon vanilla

Beat shortening, sugar, milk, and vanilla in a small bowl until smooth.

WEDDING CAKE FROSTING

Makes enough to frost a 4-tiered cake.

1 cup (2 sticks) butter or margarine, softened	½ teaspoon salt
¾ cup vegetable shortening	¼ cup milk
3 packages (1 pound each) 10X (confectioners') sugar, sifted	3 tablespoons apricot brandy
	3 tablespoons light corn syrup
	1 tablespoon vanilla

1. Beat butter and shortening until smooth in a large bowl. Beat in 10X sugar and salt until mixture is crumbly and all of the sugar has been added.

2. Add milk, brandy, corn syrup, and vanilla. Beat until the mixture is smooth and spreadable.

Note: Keep bowl of frosting covered with a dampened paper towel.

WHITE MOUNTAIN FROSTING

Makes enough to frost two or three 8-inch cake layers.

½ cup sugar	2 egg whites
¼ cup light corn syrup	⅛ teaspoon cream of tartar
2 tablespoons water	½ teaspoon vanilla

1. Combine sugar, corn syrup, and water in a small saucepan; cover. Bring to a boil; uncover; boil gently, without stirring, until mixture registers 242° on a candy thermometer or until a small amount of the hot syrup falls, threadlike, from a spoon.

2. While syrup cooks, beat egg whites with cream of tartar in a large bowl with an electric mixer until stiff peaks form when beaters are removed. Pour hot syrup into egg whites in a very thin stream, beating all the time on high speed, until frosting is stiff and glossy. Beat in the vanilla.

FROSTING CUPCAKES

For an easy way to frost cupcakes, twirl the top of each in a bowl of fluffy-type frosting (Fluffy 7-Minute or White Mountain). You'll get pretty swirls in only a couple of seconds.

FLUFFY 7-MINUTE FROSTING

Makes enough to fill and frost two 8- or 9-inch cake layers.

1½	cups sugar	2	tablespoons light corn syrup
¼	cup water	¼	teaspoon salt
2	egg whites	1	teaspoon vanilla

1. Combine sugar, water, egg whites, corn syrup, and salt in the top of a double boiler; beat mixture until well blended.

2. Place over simmering water; cook, beating constantly on high speed with an electric hand mixer or rotary beater, about 7 minutes or until mixture triples in volume and holds firm peaks. Remove from heat; beat in vanilla. Spread on cooled cake while still warm.

VANILLA CUSTARD FILLING

Makes about 3½ cups filling (enough for 12 éclairs or cream puffs).

2½	cups milk	2	tablespoons butter or
5	egg yolks		margarine
¾	cup sugar	1	tablespoon vanilla
⅔	cup *sifted* all-purpose flour		

1. Heat milk in a large, heavy saucepan until bubbles appear around edges.

2. Beat egg yolks and sugar in a large bowl with a wire whisk or electric mixer until pale yellow and thick. Beat in flour until well mixed. Gradually beat in hot milk; pour all back into saucepan. Cook, stirring constantly, over moderately high heat until mixture thickens and comes to a boil; lower heat. (Mixture will be lumpy in the beginning, but lumps disappear during cooking and stirring.) Continue cooking 2 to 3 minutes, over low heat, stirring constantly. Mixture will be quite thick. Remove from heat.

3. Stir in butter and vanilla. Place a piece of wax paper directly on surface of filling to prevent a skin from forming. Chill at least 2 hours. If filling becomes too stiff after it's chilled, gradually stir in 2 to 4 tablespoons cream or milk, 1 tablespoon at a time.

Chocolate Custard Filling: Follow the directions for Vanilla Custard Filling, adding 3 squares unsweetened chocolate to milk in step 1, stirring often until melted.

COCONUT CREAM FILLING

Makes 2½ cups.

¼ cup sugar
2 tablespoons cornstarch
⅛ teaspoon salt
2 egg yolks
1¼ cups milk

1 tablespoon butter or margarine
½ cup flaked coconut
½ cup heavy cream

1. Combine sugar, cornstarch, and salt in a small saucepan; beat in egg yolks; then gradually blend in milk.

2. Cook, stirring constantly, until mixture thickens and bubbles for 1 minute. Remove from heat.

3. Stir in butter and coconut. Place a piece of wax paper directly on filling. Cool completely. Beat cream until stiff; fold into filling.

CINNAMON-WHIPPED CREAM FILLING

Makes 4 cups.

2 cups heavy cream
¼ cup 10X (confectioners') sugar

¾ teaspoon ground cinnamon

Combine cream, 10X sugar, and cinnamon in a medium-size deep bowl. Beat with an electric mixer until stiff peaks form. Refrigerate until ready to use.

CREAMY PRALINE FILLING

Makes about 2 cups.

¼ cup sugar
¼ cup toasted slivered almonds

1 cup heavy cream

1. Lightly butter a cookie sheet. Heat sugar in a small heavy skillet over medium heat, stirring constantly, until melted and light brown. Stir in almonds. Turn out onto prepared cookie sheet. Cool completely.

2. Coarsely chop about ¼ of the praline; finely crush remainder. Beat cream in a small bowl until stiff peaks form; fold in all the praline.

FIVE STEPS TO FROSTING A CAKE

1. Place the cake plate on something you can turn—a lazy Susan, if you have one. Or, set plate on a large, inverted bowl or a sugar canister. Then rotate the plates as you frost the cake. Before frosting the cake, brush off all loose crumbs.

2. Place bottom layer on plate, *flat side up,* and frost.

3. Add next layer, *flat side down,* so the cake will be steady and level.

4. Frost the entire outside of the assembled cake with a *very thin layer of frosting;* let it set about 20 minutes. The thin coating holds the crumbs in place and keeps them from mixing with the final coat of frosting.

5. Frost the sides of the cake first from bottom up; then frost the top, swirling frosting into soft peaks.

ROYAL CREAM FILLING

This one is billowing and buttery.
Makes 3 cups.

½ cup sugar
6 tablespoons all-purpose flour
¼ teaspoon salt
3 eggs, slightly beaten

2 cups milk
2 tablespoons butter or margarine
1 teaspoon vanilla

1. Combine sugar, flour, and salt in a heavy, medium-size saucepan; gradually blend in eggs and milk.
2. Cook slowly, stirring constantly, until mixture thickens and bubbles for 3 minutes.
3. Pour into a medium-size bowl; stir in the butter or margarine until melted; stir in vanilla; cover; chill.

WHIPPED CHOCOLATE FILLING

Makes about 4 cups.

4 squares unsweetened chocolate
6 tablespoons butter or margarine
⅓ cup milk

2 eggs, slightly beaten
2 teaspoons vanilla
1 package (1 pound) 10X (confectioners') sugar

1. Melt chocolate and butter in a small, heavy saucepan over low heat.
2. Combine milk, eggs, vanilla, and 10X sugar in a large bowl; beat with an electric mixer until blended. Add chocolate mixture; beat until light and fluffy and of spreading consistency.

ORANGE-DATE FILLING

Makes enough to fill one 10-inch tube cake.

1 package (10 ounces) pitted dates, chopped

1 cup orange juice
2 tablespoons sugar

Combine all ingredients in a medium-size saucepan. Bring to a boil; lower heat and simmer 10 minutes, stirring often, until thickened. Cool before using.

VANILLA ICING

Makes about 1⅓ cups.

3   **egg whites, lightly beaten**   **1**   **teaspoon vanilla**
3¾ cups *sifted* **10X**
       (confectioners') sugar

Combine egg whites, sugar, and vanilla in a medium-size bowl. Beat with an electric mixer until smooth.

Chocolate Icing: Follow basic recipe but reduce 10X sugar to 2¾ cups and add 3 tablespoons unsweetened cocoa powder.

LEBKUCHEN ICING

Makes about ¾ cup.

¾   cup granulated sugar   **¼   cup 10X (confectioners')**
⅓   cup water   **sugar**

Combine granulated sugar and water in a small saucepan. Bring to a boil, stirring constantly. Lower heat, simmer 3 minutes. Remove from heat; stir in 10X sugar.

SUGAR ICING

*Makes about 2 cups (enough to cover about 2 dozen
3- to 4½-inch cookies).*

1   package (1 pound) 10X   **1   teaspoon vanilla**
     (confectioners') sugar   **⅓   to ½ cup water**

Combine 10X sugar, vanilla, and ⅓ cup water in a medium-size bowl; stir until smooth. Add more water, a tablespoon at a time, until icing is spreadable or flows easily from spoon.

SPREADABILITY

Frosting will be much easier if you occasionally dip your spatula or knife in warm water. The water also adds a nice glossy look to the frosting, and swirls are easier to make.

ORANGE-BUTTER GLAZE

Makes about ½ cup.

1¼ cups 10X (confectioners')   1   teaspoon butter, softened
    sugar   1½ to 2 tablespoons orange juice

Blend all ingredients in a small bowl until smooth and spreadable.

APRICOT GLAZE

Makes about 2 cups.

1½ cups apricot preserves   ½   cup water
½   cup sugar   ¼   cup dark rum

Combine preserves, sugar, and water in a medium-size saucepan. Bring to a boil. Simmer over low heat for 5 minutes, stirring frequently. Strain into a bowl. Stir in rum. Cool.

Raspberry Glaze: Substitute red raspberry preserves for apricot preserves. Omit rum.

HONEY GLAZE

Makes about ⅔ cup.

½   cup honey   1   cup 10X (confectioners')
                                          sugar

Combine honey and sugar in a small saucepan. Heat over low heat just until mixture comes to a boil. Use while still warm.

SUPER-QUICK FROSTING

Here's a super-quick way to frost cupcakes: Place a piece of milk chocolate or semisweet chocolate, on the top of each warm cupcake; spread with a knife or spatula as the chocolate melts.

CHOCOLATE GLAZE

Makes about 1 cup.

3   tablespoons butter or margarine
2   squares unsweetened chocolate

2   cups *sifted* 10X (confectioners') sugar
¼   cup boiling water

1. Melt butter and chocolate over low heat in a small saucepan. Cool.
2. Combine chocolate mixture with 10X sugar and boiling water in a medium-size bowl. Beat with wire whisk or rotary beater until smooth. (Mixture will be thin, but will thicken upon standing.) Spread on cake while the cake is still warm. For cookies, cool until thickened.

VANILLA SUGAR GLAZE

Makes ½ cup (enough to drizzle over a 10-inch tube cake, or over 3 dozen bar cookies, or over 8-dozen 1-inch cookies).

1   cup 10X (confectioners') sugar, sifted

1   to 2 tablespoons milk
½   teaspoon vanilla

Blend 10X sugar, 1 tablespoon milk, and vanilla in a small bowl until very smooth. Stir in more milk until glaze is thin enough to drizzle from a spoon.

COFFEE WHIPPED CREAM

Makes 2 cups.

1   cup heavy cream
2   tablespoons 10X (confectioners') sugar

1   teaspoon instant coffee powder

Combine all ingredients in a medium-size bowl. Beat with an electric mixer on high speed until stiff peaks form. Refrigerate until ready to use.

Honey Whipped Cream: Omit sugar and coffee. Beat cream until soft peaks form. Fold in 2 tablespoons honey.

COFFEE BUTTER CREAM

Makes about 3 tablespoons.

¼ teaspoon instant coffee
    powder
½ teaspoon water

1   tablespoon butter, softened
¼ cup 10X (confectioners')
    sugar

Dissolve coffee in water in a small bowl. Stir in butter and sugar until smooth. Spoon into a small pastry bag fitted with a small star tip. Press out into rosettes.

RUM CREAM

Makes 1 cup.

½ cup heavy cream
1   tablespoon sugar

2   teaspoons light or dark rum

Combine all ingredients in a small bowl. Beat with an electric mixer on high speed until soft peaks form.

PASTRY CREAM

Makes 1⅓ cups.

1   cup milk
4   egg yolks
⅓ cup sugar

¼ cup *sifted* all-purpose flour
⅛ teaspoon salt
1   teaspoon vanilla

1. Heat milk to scalding in a medium-size saucepan.
2. Beat egg yolks with sugar in a medium-size bowl with a wire whisk or electric mixer until thick and creamy. Beat in flour and salt; gradually beat in scalded milk until smooth.
3. Pour mixture back into saucepan; cook, stirring constantly, until mixture thickens. (Mixture may become lumpy; if this occurs, beat with either a wire whisk or electric mixer until it becomes smooth.)
4. Lower heat and continue to cook for 2 to 3 minutes, stirring constantly until mixture is very thick. Remove from heat; add vanilla; pour into a small bowl. Cover with plastic wrap to keep skin from forming; chill.

FLUFFY PASTRY CREAM

Makes about 2¾ cups.

⅓   cup sugar
2   tablespoons cornstarch
1½ teaspoons unflavored gelatin
2   egg yolks
1½ cups milk

1   tablespoon butter or
    margarine
1   teaspoon vanilla
½   cup heavy cream

1. Combine sugar, cornstarch, and gelatin in a small saucepan. Beat in egg yolks until well mixed. Stir in milk. Cook mixture over low heat, stirring constantly, until thickened, about 10 minutes. Remove from heat.
2. Stir in butter and vanilla. Cover surface with wax paper to prevent skin from forming. Chill until cold.
3. Beat cream in a small bowl with an electric mixer until soft peaks form. Stir chilled custard mixture to soften; then fold in whipped cream until no streaks of white remain.

INSTANT PASTRY CREAM

Makes 2 cups.

1   package (3¾ ounces) French
    vanilla instant pudding and
    pie filling mix

1   cup milk
½   cup heavy cream

Prepare pudding mix with milk following package directions. Whip cream until stiff; fold into pudding. Cover surface with plastic wrap. Chill.

SWEET CHERRY SAUCE

Makes about 1¾ cups.

1   can (17 ounces) dark sweet
    cherries

1   tablespoon cornstarch
1   tablespoon port wine

Drain syrup from cherries into a small saucepan; blend in cornstarch. Bring to a boil, stirring constantly; boil 1 minute. Stir in cherries and port wine. Cool.

RASPBERRY SAUCE

Makes 1¼ cups.

1	package (10 ounces) frozen red raspberries, thawed	¼	cup sugar
		2	tablespoons kirsch or light rum

Put raspberries into the container of an electric blender; add sugar; cover; blend on high speed until smooth. Strain through a sieve over a bowl to remove seeds. Cover with plastic wrap; chill. Stir in kirsch just before serving.

STRAWBERRY-WINE SAUCE

Makes about 3 cups.

2	tablespoons quick-cooking tapioca	¾	cup water
¼	cup sugar	1	pint strawberries
		½	cup ruby port wine

1. Combine tapioca, sugar, and water in a small saucepan. Let stand 5 minutes. Cook until thickened, stirring constantly. Remove from heat. Cool.
2. Wash, hull, and pat berries dry on paper toweling. Halve or slice, if large, into tapioca mixture. Stir in wine. Cover and chill until cold.

STRAWBERRY SAUCE

Makes 1¾ cups.

1	pint strawberries	1	tablespoon brandy
3	tablespoons sugar		

Wash and hull strawberries. Puree in the container of an electric blender or food processor with sugar and brandy.

BRANDY HARD SAUCE

Makes about 1¼ cups.

½ cup (1 stick) butter or   1 tablespoon brandy
   margarine, softened
2½ cups *sifted* 10X
   (confectioners') sugar

Beat all ingredients until creamy in a small bowl with an electric mixer.

CREAMY CUSTARD SAUCE

Makes 1½ cups.

3 egg yolks   1 teaspoon vanilla
3 tablespoons sugar   ½ cup heavy cream, whipped
¾ cup milk, scalded

1. Beat egg yolks and sugar until light and fluffy in a small bowl with an electric mixer. Gradually beat in scalded milk. Pour mixture back into saucepan; cook, stirring constantly, over moderate heat until custard thickens slightly. Remove from heat. Pour into small bowl; stir in vanilla; cover. Chill.
2. Just before serving, fold in whipped cream.

CUSTARD SAUCE

Makes 2½ cups.

4 egg yolks   2 cups milk, scalded
¼ cup sugar   1 teaspoon vanilla
2 teaspoons cornstarch

1. Beat egg yolks with sugar and cornstarch in a medium-size bowl; gradually stir in milk. Pour into a medium-size saucepan; cook over moderate heat, stirring constantly, until custard thickens slightly and coats a spoon.
2. Remove from heat. Pour into a small bowl; stir in vanilla; cover. Chill.

LEMON SAUCE

Makes 1⅓ cups.

½ cup sugar
1 tablespoon cornstarch
1 cup water
1 tablespoon butter or
   margarine

2 tablespoons lemon juice
½ teaspoon grated lemon rind

Combine sugar and cornstarch in a medium-size saucepan. Stir in water. Cook over moderate heat for 5 minutes, stirring constantly with a wire whisk, until smooth and bubbly. Add butter, lemon juice, and rind. Stir until butter is melted. This can be made ahead of time and then reheated just before serving.

SAUCE CARDINALE

Makes 1½ cups.

1 package (10 ounces) frozen
   raspberries, thawed
1 teaspoon cornstarch

1 cup strawberries, fresh or
   frozen
¼ cup red currant jelly

Drain raspberries, reserving juice. Dissolve cornstarch in a little raspberry juice in a small saucepan; add remaining juice and strawberries, raspberries, and jelly. Cook, stirring constantly, until mixture thickens slightly and clears. Force mixture through a sieve to remove seeds. Chill.

APRICOT-BRANDY SAUCE

Makes about 2 cups.

1½ cups apricot preserves
⅓ cup water

2 tablespoons sugar
2 tablespoons brandy

Combine apricot preserves, water, and sugar in a medium-size saucepan. Bring to a boil; boil for 15 minutes or until slightly thickened. Puree in a blender or food processor; add brandy. Serve warm.

BRANDIED FRUIT SAUCE

Delicious served over ice cream, plain cakes, or puddings.

Makes 3½ cups.

½ cup golden raisins
1 package (6 ounces) dried apricots
1 cup water
1 can (8¼ ounces) pineapple chunks in syrup

1 3-inch piece stick cinnamon
½ cup brandy
¼ cup grenadine syrup
2 tablespoons maraschino cherries (optional)

1. Combine raisins and apricots with water in a medium-size saucepan. Let stand 10 minutes to soften fruits.
2. Drain pineapple; add syrup to pan with cinnamon stick. Bring to a boil; lower heat; simmer 5 minutes until apricots are soft, but not mushy. Stir in brandy, grenadine, pineapple chunks, and cherries. Pour into a container. Cover and store in refrigerator for at least a week. Mixture will thicken slightly on standing.

HOT FUDGE SAUCE

The real fudgy kind that stiffens when it's poured on cold ice cream.

Makes about 2 cups.

4 squares unsweetened chocolate
2 tablespoons butter or margarine

¾ cup boiling water
2 cups sugar
3 tablespoons corn syrup
2 teaspoons vanilla

1. Coarsely chop chocolate; heat with butter and boiling water in a large, heavy saucepan over low heat, stirring constantly, until chocolate is melted. Add sugar and corn syrup.
2. Bring mixture slowly to a boil; lower heat; simmer gently for 7 to 8 minutes. Watch carefully, but do not stir. Test on ice cream or an ice cube, until it firms up as you like it. Add vanilla. Remove from heat. Serve while warm. Refrigerate any leftover sauce in canning jar; cover.
3. To reheat: Remove cover from jar. Place jar in saucepan of water; cover. Heat, stirring occasionally, until sauce is softened enough to pour. This sauce is great on ice cream, pound cake, ice cream-filled meringue shells, and banana splits.

HOT CAROB-BUTTER FUDGE SAUCE

Health food addicts claim many virtues for the fruit of the carob tree; at any rate, it makes a fine substitute for chocolate.

Makes about 2¼ cups.

1	cup (2 sticks) butter or margarine, melted	½	cup carob powder
¾	cup honey	1	teaspoon instant coffee powder
¼	cup milk		

Combine butter, honey, and milk in the container of an electric blender. Add carob powder and coffee slowly; whirl until smooth. Pour mixture into the top of a double boiler or a heavy medium-size saucepan. Place top over boiling water, or if using saucepan, simmer; lower heat. Cook, stirring constantly for 10 minutes. (Sauce burns easily, so watch carefully.) Serve over ice cream.

CHOCOLATE FUDGE SAUCE

Serve over ice cream or cake.

Makes 2 cups.

1	package (6 ounces) semisweet chocolate pieces	1	teaspoon vanilla
1	can (14 ounces) sweetened condensed milk (not evaporated milk)		Dash salt
		⅓	cup hot water

1. Melt chocolate pieces in top of double boiler over simmering water. Add condensed milk, vanilla, and salt, stirring constantly until mixture is slightly thickened. Stir in water.
2. Let cool; cover and refrigerate. If too thick, stir in hot water, 1 tablespoon at a time.

12

Cake and Cookie Decorating

Artfully decorated cakes and cookies have a way of conveying a message for a very special day or occasion. You don't have to be a master baker to create lovely cakes or cookies. It's your imagination that can transform simple packaged cake and frosting mixes into delightful creations. Our techniques and shortcuts give you perfect results. Although a pastry bag or cake decorator with different tips or tubes is all that you will need in the way of special equipment, some of the cakes and cookies can be decorated without one.

Cakes must be baked before they can be decorated. After baking, you can cut and rearrange the pieces into numerous shapes. Cakes have been associated with celebrations since early Roman times. However, the style of decorated cakes done today evolved over the last three centuries.

Cookies may be decorated either before or after baking. To decorate cookies before they go into the oven, you can sprinkle them with colored sugars or press on nuts or chopped hard candies. To decorate cookies after baking, use a butter cream frosting or an egg white-based frosting called royal frosting. Then you can sprinkle them with colored sugars, coconut, chopped nuts, or whatever decorations you wish. You can also paint baked or unbaked cookies using food coloring.

There are no magic ways to decorate cakes or cookies. All you need is patience and determination!

FATHER'S DAY WORD GAME CAKE

Spell out a greeting to Dad with chocolate mint letters.

Makes 16 servings.

1	package chocolate or yellow cake mix	1	package (8 ounces) round chocolate-covered mints
1	container (16½ ounces) chocolate ready-to-spread frosting		Yellow food coloring
1	container (16½ ounces) vanilla ready-to-spread frosting		

1. Prepare, bake, and cool cake mix following package directions for a 13 x 9 x 2-inch cake. Level top of cake with a serrated knife. Frost cake with all but ½ cup of the chocolate frosting.

2. Fit a pastry bag with a small plain tip; fill with ½ the container of vanilla frosting. Pipe lines on the cake dividing evenly into squares: 7 squares across the long side, 5 squares across the short side. Pipe HAPPY FATHER'S DAY on the chocolate mints, one letter to each mint.

3. Tint remaining vanilla frosting yellow with food coloring. Carefully spread yellow frosting randomly to simulate a word game board.

4. Place mint "tiles" on cake "board."

5. Fit a pastry bag with a small star tip; pipe a wavy border around top and bottom edges of cake with remaining chocolate frosting.

DECORATING INSERTS

To press on decorations, such as candied cherries, nuts, chocolate pieces, or raisins, brush unbaked cookies with lightly beaten egg white before inserting decorations.

FOURTH OF JULY STAR CAKE

Makes 12 servings.

1 package yellow cake mix	Red decorating sugar
2 containers (16½ ounces each) vanilla ready-to-spread frosting	Blue food coloring

1. Prepare, bake and cool cake mix following package directions for two 9 x 1½-inch layers. Level cake layers with a serrated knife. Assemble and frost cake with 1 container of the frosting.
2. Place a large star-shaped cookie cutter in the center of the frosted cake. Sprinkle red sugar evenly inside cutter. Press sugar lightly into frosting with fingertip. Gently remove cookie cutter.
3. Fit a pastry bag with a very small star tip. Fill bag with half of the remaining container of frosting. Pipe a rosette border outlining the star. Transfer remaining frosting to another pastry bag fitted with a small star tip. Pipe a rosette border around bottom of cake.
4. Tint remaining vanilla frosting blue with food coloring. Fit pastry bag with washed and dried small star tip. Pipe a zigzag border around top of cake.

PREPARE THE PLATE

Tear 4 strips of wax paper, each about 12 x 3-inches. Arrange the strips in a square pattern around a plate or doily-lined plate. Place cake layer on plate. After the cake is frosted, remove the wax paper by pulling the strips out toward a narrow end.

DISPOSABLE DECORATING BAG

To make a disposable wax paper decorating bag, tear off a 12-inch square of wax paper. Fold in half to form a triangle. Pull opposite points around to form a tight cone. (Cone should come to a point at the bottom.) Secure with tape; fill cone with frosting; snip off point to whatever size opening you wish.

NOTE: Try making a leaf tip by cutting an inverted "V" at the bottom of the unsnipped cone, or a notched tip by cutting the letter "M". The tips won't be as well-defined as those in a cake-decorating set, but they will offer you some variation—and with only the snip of a scissors!

APPLIQUE ANNIVERSARY CAKE

You can't make a mistake when decorating this cake. All the decorations are easy to shape on paper, then peel off and place on the cake just where you want them.

Makes 18 servings.

2 packages yellow cake mix	2 containers (16½ ounces
Royal Frosting (page 297)	each) vanilla ready-to-spread
Red food coloring	frosting
Silver dragees	

1. Prepare, bake, and cool one cake mix for a 13 x 9 x 2-inch cake. Prepare, bake and cool remaining cake mix for two 9 x 1½-inch layers. (Reserve one layer for another meal.) Level tops of the cakes with a serrated knife.

2. Cut a 5-inch round and a 7-inch round from the 13 x 9 x 2-inch cake, using a saucer or bowl.

3. Write or trace HAPPY ANNIVERSARY on a sheet of white paper, allowing a ½-inch space between letters. Tape paper to a cookie sheet. Tape a sheet of wax paper on top of taped sheet.

4. Prepare Royal Frosting; tint light pink with red food coloring. Keep bowl covered with a damp towel to keep frosting from caking.

5. Fit a pastry bag with a small- to medium-size open star tip. Trace letters with either a straight line or a series of connecting rosettes. Make sure all rosettes in the letter touch each other. If you make a mistake, it's easy to scrape off the frosting and start again. Pipe out about 50 teardrops onto paper. Pipe out 40 spirals, placing a silver dragee in center of each. Pipe out as many spirals, just a bit larger, to match the years you are celebrating. These will be candle holders; put a birthday candle in center of each. Allow decorations to dry for at least 2 hours.

6. Place the 9-inch layer on a serving plate. Frost side and top with part of the vanilla frosting. Center 7-inch layer; frost. Top with 5-inch layer; frost.

7. Gently loosen decorations with a thin metal spatula or knife. Arrange letters for HAPPY on middle tier. Arrange ANNIVERSARY on lower tier. Place remaining decorations, except candle holders in bow tie patterns, one spiral between two teardrops, around the vertical sides of the tiers. Space candles and holders on top.

CALICO CAT CAKE

Makes 12 servings.

1 package yellow cake mix
2 containers (16.5 ounces each) vanilla ready-to-spread frosting
2 tablespoons unsweetened cocoa powder

1 package small chocolate-covered mints
Red and yellow food colorings

1. Prepare, bake, and cool cake mix following package directions for two 9 x 1½-inch layers. Level cooled cake layers with a serrated knife.
2. Place a 5½-inch bowl or saucer in the center of one layer. Cut out the circle to make the cat's head (B). Cut out ⅓ of the outer ring to form a curved cat's tail (C). Cut four 1½-inch triangles from the remaining ring to form ears (D) and the bow tie (E).
3. Assemble cat on a tray, placing small circle (B) above the 9-inch layer (A). Position the ears (D), then the tail (C). The bow tie will be frosted and placed on top of cake where the two circles meet. Extra piece of cake may be used as treat for the children.
4. Combine ½ cup of the vanilla frosting with cocoa in a small bowl. Stir in a little water, if needed, to thin.
5. Spread a small amount of vanilla frosting from the neck halfway down the large layer, or body area to form a bib. Spread wide horizontal lines of white frosting across the body, tail, and head with a small metal spatula, leaving space to spread alternating orange lines.
6. Tint remaining container of frosting a light orange with a few drops of red and yellow food coloring. Spread orange stripes in the spaces left between the white lines. Gently swirl stripes to blend and soften lines. Frost side of cake with the remaining orange frosting.
7. Frost bow tie with cocolate frosting; put in place. Put two chocolate mints in place for eyes. Pipe whiskers and a mouth with remaining chocolate frosting.
8. Fit a pastry bag with a small plain tube; fill with remaining vanilla frosting. Pipe a pair of glasses around eyes, and decorate bow tie.

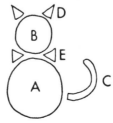

HOW TO DECORATE A CAKE

THERE ARE THREE BASIC METHODS OF CAKE DECORATING:

Pastry Bag: Fit required tip into pastry bag. Fill bag with frosting, pressing the frosting all the way to the end of the tip. Twist or fold the open end of the pastry bag to keep a slight amount of pressure on the frosting. Hold the bag at the twist or fold, between the thumb and forefinger of the right hand (or left hand, if left-handed). Guide the bag with the opposite hand.

Cake Decorator: Fit required tip on the cake decorating cylinder; fill cylinder with frosting. Gently press plunger to remove any air bubbles. Press plunger with an even steady pressure, guiding the tip with the opposite hand.

Wax-Paper Cone: Measure off a perfect 12-inch square of wax paper; fold diagonally (see illustration). Using center of diagonal line as center point of cone, bring corners up and wrap around, closing tip of cone tightly; fasten cone with tape. Cut off just enough of the point of the cone to hold decorating tip snugly. Or, you can use the cone by itself for the simple plain designs.

DECORATING DESIGNS

The decorative designs that most bakers favor fall into these six categories:

Wavy: Hold pastry bag with tip at a 45° angle to and almost touching cake. Squeeze with an even pressure, working from far edge to near edge in a push (up and away) and pull (down and toward) motion. At the completion of the border, release pressure; lift tip away.

Rosette: Hold the pastry bag with the tip at a 90° angle to and almost touching the cake. Squeeze with an even pressure forming the size rosettes you wish. Release pressure; lift tip away.

Zigzag: Hold pastry bag with tip at a 45° angle to and almost touching the cake. Squeeze with an even pressure back and forth (left to right) in a tight "S" pattern flat on the cake. At the completion of the border, release pressure; lift tip away.

Teardrop: Hold pastry bag with the tip at a 45° angle to and slightly above cake. Squeeze with an even pressure until frosting fans out. Ease up slightly on pressure and pull toward you, tapering off flow of frosting. Release pressure; lift tip away.

Ball: Hold pastry bag with the tip at a 90° angle to and almost touching cake. Squeeze with an even pressure to form the size ball you wish. Release pressure; lift tip away.

Spiral: Hold pastry bag with the tip at a 90° angle to and slightly above cake. Squeeze with even pressure in a circular motion and, at the same time, moving upward. Ease pressure as circle is completed. Release pressure; lift tip away.

ADVANCED DESIGNS

After you've mastered the basics, try some of these decorative touches:

Feather Top: Drizzle melted chocolate (2 squares melted with ½ teaspoon shortening) across frosting, in thick lines about 1 inch apart. Draw edge of thin spatula at right angles to chocolate lines, to connect.

Shadow Design: Drizzle glaze or melted chocolate (prepared as for feather pattern) around edge of cake, with the tip of a teaspoon; let glaze or chocolate drip down side.

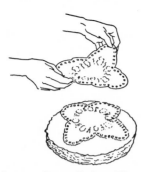

Sugar Snowflake: Place paper doily on top of cake. Sift 10X (confectioners') sugar over doily. Lift doily off, leaving snowflake design on cake. Important: Be sure cake is completely cooled before sprinkling with sugar; otherwise sugar may turn gray.

Plaid Design: Pull a fork across the top of the cake at equally-spaced intervals. Turn cake one-quarter turn; repeat.

Candle Highlight: Pipe tinted frosting in "spokes" from center of cake. (You may wish to vary the lengths of the spokes, particularly if there are many candles going on the cake.) Place candle holders with candles at ends of spokes.

PASTRY BAG SUPPORT

The easiest way to fill a pastry bag with frosting is to support the bag by placing it in a large cup or glass.

SELECT THE RIGHT DECORATING TOOLS

For easy and precise spreading of frostings on cakes, use a flexible metal spatula available in houseware or kitchen supply stores or a painter's pallette knife, sold at art supply stores. Keep a supply of tiny paint brushes for decorating cookies.

DAISY CHAIN GRADUATION CAKE

A garland of snowy daisies tops this two-tiered, orange-flavored frosted cake. The many layers are sandwiched together with a fluffy chocolate filling and look like the pages of a book when cut.

Bake at 325° for 45 to 50 minutes.
Makes about 30 servings.

1 tablespoon grated orange rind
2 packages (18¾ ounces each) yellow cake with pudding mix
6 eggs
2 cups water
⅔ cup vegetable oil
Whipped Chocolate filling (page 284)

2 recipes Orange Butter Cream Frosting (page 276)
White Decorating Frosting (page 279)
Yellow and green food colorings

1. Grease one 13 x 9 x 2-inch and one 8 x 8-inch baking pan and line with wax paper; grease paper. Preheat oven to 325°.

2. Add the orange rind to the cake mix and prepare the 2 packages of mix with eggs, water, and oil following package directions.

3. Measure ⅓ of batter into the 8-inch pan and remaining ⅔ into the 13 x 9 x 2-inch pan.

4. Bake in a preheated slow oven (325°) for 45 minutes or until centers spring back when lightly pressed with fingertip. Cool in pans on wire racks for 10 minutes. Loosen around edges with a small spatula; turn out onto racks; cool completely. Wrap cakes and refrigerate or freeze until ready to fill and frost. Cakes can be refrigerated up to 3 days or frozen for up to 2 weeks.

5. Prepare Whipped Chocolate Filling.

6. Split large cake with a long, thin-bladed knife into 6 thin layers. Stack cake layers, spreading about ½ cup filling between each layer.

7. Trim about 1 inch from one side of square cake. Stack layers with remaining filling between each layer. Trim edges even on both sides.

8. Prepare Orange Butter Frosting. Reserve 2 tablespoons in a small cup; tint deep yellow for daisy centers. Reserve ¼ cup in another cup; tint green for leaves and lettering. Place larger cake on a serving tray; frost sides and top with Orange Frosting. Arrange smaller cake on top; frost.

9. To make daisies: Prepare White Decorating Frosting. Reserve 2 tablespoons in a small cup; tint deep yellow for daisy centers. Reserve ¼ cup in another cup; tint green for leaves and lettering. Fit pastry bag or tube of cake decorating set with a small round tip. Pipe a dot of White Decorating Frosting onto wax paper to mark the center of each daisy. (It's easier if a small square of wax paper is cut for each daisy.) Holding tip almost parallel to paper, squeeze out petals from center to edge. Pipe a dot of deep yellow in center of each daisy. Chill or freeze until firm.

10. Fit pastry bag with a star tip. Pipe edges of cake with remaining White Frosting.

11. Scoop daisies off wax paper with a flexible spatula; arrange on frosted cake. Pipe green leaves around daisies with green frosting using a leaf tip. Pipe "Class of '00" or special message with green.

12. Roll a small piece of white paper into a cylinder; tie with green yarn. Place "diploma" on top of cake.

ENCHANTED COTTAGE CAKE

This tiny pink cottage is surrounded by a shredded coconut "lawn" and fantasy "shrubs."

Bake at 350° for 25 minutes.
Makes 10 servings.

2	packages pound cake mix	Red, yellow, and green food
⅓	cup apple jelly, melted	colorings
3	packages creamy vanilla	Flaked coconut
	frosting mix	

1. Grease two 15½ x 10½ x 1-inch jelly roll pans; line bottoms with wax paper. Grease wax paper. (Or; bake one cake at a time, re-using pan.)

2. Preheat oven to 350°. Prepare cake mixes following package directions. Turn batter into prepared pans.

3. Bake in a preheated moderate oven (350°) for 25 minutes or until centers spring back when lightly pressed with fingertip.

4. Cool cakes in pans a few minutes; turn out onto wire racks. Remove wax paper. Cool completely.

5. Cut each into six squares (A). Put four cake squares together with melted jelly for base of house (B). Place on a 10 x 10-inch foil-covered cardboard square.

6. Put three cake squares together with melted jelly for "eaves" or roof support (C). Trim to wedge shape. Reserve cake trimmings. Spread top of house with remaining jelly; press "eaves" into position.

7. Prepare one package of frosting mix following package directions. Spread assembled cake with a very thin coat of frosting to hold crumbs in place. Allow to dry slightly.
8. Tint remaining frosting a deep pink. Frost entire cake except roof area. Reserve remaining frosting for Step 10.
9. Prepare second package of frosting mix; tint bright green. Spread one side of each of two cake squares with frosting. Position on "eaves"; hold in place with wooden picks. If roof does not quite meet at top, insert a strip of cake to fill the space. Spread roof with thin coat of frosting. Allow to dry slightly. Frost roof generously with overlapping strokes for "shingled" look.
10. Prepare third package of frosting mix. Divide into thirds: Tint ⅓ green, ⅓ yellow, and leave remaining third white. Cut "chimney" from "eave" trimmings so it fits roof angle. Top with a small piece of cake for height (D). Frost thinly with white frosting, then reserved pink frosting. Position on roof with wooden picks.
11. Tint coconut green. Spread cardboard with white frosting; sprinkle with green-tinted coconut. Pipe "windows," "shutters," and "door" with green frosting, using a small round tip fitted on cake decorator. With yellow frosting and small notched tip, pipe the "doorknob" and "chimney" decoration.
12. Cut small triangle shapes from remaining cake. Frost with green frosting; pipe on yellow "flowers." Place around cake for "landscaping."

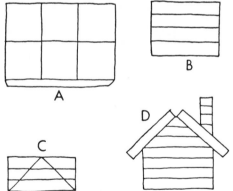

A

B

C

D

HOW TO TINT COCONUT

In a medium-size bowl, dilute a few drops of food coloring with 1 teaspoon water. Add 1 cup flaked coconut and toss until evenly colored. Spread coconut out on wax paper to dry.

ROSE WEDDING CAKE

This 4-tier wedding cake is a masterpiece of cake-decorating art. We include is here not only with the happy thought that there may be a wedding coming up in your family, but also to demonstrate the techniques of cake decorating. Your cake may be made on 3 days, following our easy-does-it plan. 1st day: Bake Groom's Cake (top tier); wrap. 2nd day: Bake the 3 Pound Cake Layers. Brush all cakes with Apricot Glaze (page 286). Cut and wrap the take-home pieces of Groom's Cake. Day 3: Assemble and decorate cake.

This wedding cake makes enough for 100 servings.

Special items you will need:

- 1 three-tier cake pan set (7 x 2¼; 10 x 2¾; 13 x 2½ inches)
- 2 loaf pans, 9 x 5 x 3 inches each
- 1 5-cup mold (6 inches wide, by 3 inches deep)
- 1 cake decorating set: Pastry bag, coupling, and 7 tips (Rose tips: #61, #124; Shell tip: #98; Writing tip: #2; Drop-flower tip: #96; Star tip: #27; Leaf tip: #67).

GROOM'S CAKE

The top tier of our wedding cake is made of fruitcake batter. This is the cake that traditionally is saved for the first anniversary. The loaves are each cut into 25 thin slices and each slice cut in half. These pieces may be packed in wedding-cake boxes or wrapped in plastic wrap, then silver paper and tied with silver cord as momentos for the guests.

Bake at 275° for 2 hours.
Makes one 6-inch cake and 2 loaf cakes.

2	jars (1 pound each) mixed candied fruits	2	cups chopped walnuts
1	package (15 ounces) golden raisins	2	packages pound cake mix
		4	eggs
		1	cup liquid, as package directs
2	cans (3½ ounces each) flaked coconut	2	tablespoons apricot brandy
			Apricot Glaze (page 286)

1. Grease generously and flour a round 5-cup, 6 x 3-inch mold. Also grease two 9 x 5 x 3-inch loaf pans; line with wax paper and grease paper. Preheat oven to 275°.

2. Combine mixed fruits, raisins, coconut, and chopped nuts in a very large bowl or kettle. Add 1½ cups dry pound cake mix and toss to coat fruits and nuts evenly.
3. Prepare pound cake mix with eggs, liquid called for on package, and apricot brandy, following package directions.
4. Pour batter over prepared fruits and nuts, and stir gently until evenly mixed.
5. Divide batter among prepared mold and loaf pans. Place one oven rack in center of oven and arrange all 3 pans on same rack of oven.
6. Bake in a preheated very slow oven (275°) for 2 hours, then begin to test cakes. The cakes are done when a cake tester or long wooden skewer is inserted into center of cake and comes out clean. (The cake may be done in another 15 minutes or may take up to 45 minutes longer. The time varies with the brand of cake mix you use and the size and shape of your oven.)
7. Remove cakes from oven and cool on wire racks for 30 minutes. Loosen cakes around edges with a thin-bladed sharp knife and turn out onto racks; remove wax paper; cool cakes completely. Brush with Apricot Glaze.

Note: If not assembling cakes at once, you may wrap cooled cakes in aluminum foil or plastic wrap; refrigerate or freeze. The cake will stay fresh and moist for 1 month in the refrigerator and up to 3 months in the freezer.

POUND CAKE LAYERS

Bake at 325° for 1 hour.
Makes 3 tiers: 7, 10, and 13 inches.

6	packages pound cake mix	3	tablespoons apricot brandy
12	eggs		Apricot Glaze (page 286)
	Liquid, as package directs		

1. Grease 3 tiered cake pans; line with wax paper; grease paper and then dust with flour, tapping out excess. (An extra step, but very helpful to ensure smooth sides on larger cake layers.) Preheat oven to 325°.
2. Prepare 2 packages pound cake mix with 4 eggs, liquid called for on package, and 1 tablespoon apricot brandy, following package directions.

3. Pour batter into middle tier pan to half-fill the pan. If there is additional batter, pour into the largest pan.

4. Repeat Step 2 twice. Pour batter into largest pan to half-fill the pan, then half-fill the smallest pan. (Any extra batter may be baked as cupcakes for a family treat.)

5. Arrange 1 oven rack in top third of oven and the second rack in the bottom third of the oven. Place largest cake pan on bottom rack in center of oven. Place middle-size pan at back left of top rack and smallest pan at front right of top rack. (Be sure pans do not touch each other, the door, sides, or back of oven.)

6. Bake in a preheated slow oven (325°) for 1 hour. Then begin to test layers. The cakes are done when a cake tester or long wooden skewer inserted into the center of each cake layer comes out clean. (Baking times will vary with the width and depth of individual cake pans and also the size and shape of your oven.) All layers should be baked in 1 hour and 30 minutes. If layers on the top rack get too brown but do not test done, cover lightly with aluminum foil until baked.

7. Remove layers from oven and cool on wire racks for 20 minutes. Then line wire racks with towels. Loosen each cake around edge with a thin-blade sharp knife. Turn cake pan on side and shake layer gently to be sure cake has loosened from pan. Turn out onto a towel-lined rack; peel off paper. Cool cake completely. (Towel-lined wire racks make it much easier to handle the larger cakes.)

8. Brush tops and sides of layers with Apricot Glaze.

Note: If not assembling the cake at once, you may wrap cooled layers in aluminum foil or plastic wrap and freeze unfrosted for up to 3 months.

QUICK CLEAN PASTRY BAG

If you hate to clean cloth or plastic pastry bags, you can, of course, make and use wax paper or parchment cones, but sometimes they aren't large enough for the job. The next time you have to use a large pastry bag, take a regular medium-size plastic bag and put the decorating tip in one corner of the plastic bag. Insert the plastic bag into the pastry bag as a liner. Pull the plastic-covered tip through the opening of the pastry bag. Fill the pastry bag; cut the plastic off the tip end and pipe as usual. After use, pull out the plastic liner and discard.

To Assemble and Decorate Wedding Cake

1. Prepare Decorator's Frosting (page 279). Using half the amount, divide frosting between 2 small bowls. With a few drops of red food coloring, tint 1 bowl a pale pink, and the second bowl a deeper pink. Cut sixty-six 2-inch squares of wax paper.

2. Make 36 Rosebuds: For each rosebud, use a very small amount of untinted frosting to secure a square of wax paper to the top of a small jar. Fill a pastry bag with pale pink frosting. Fit #61 tip into pastry bag. Hold tip so larger end touches center of wax paper. Gently press the frosting out of tip while turning the jar to form the tight center of a bud (Fig. 1). Press out 3 small petals, overlapping around center. Continue to shape 3 to 6 more petals to form a tight, unopened bud. Transfer each finished rose on the wax paper square to cookie sheets.

3. Make 30 Full-Blown Roses: As with the rosebuds, secure a square of wax paper with some untinted frosting to the top of a small jar. Fill pastry bag with deep pink frosting. Fit #124 tip into pastry bag. For each full-blown rose hold the tip with wider end touching center of the wax paper. Gently press frosting out of tip. (Center formed with this tip will be slightly open.) Press out 3 petals around the slightly open center (Fig. 2). They should partially overlap one another around the center. Then tilt top to tip (narrow end) outward as you continue (Fig. 3). Shape each additional petal slightly larger than the last. As you continue, you will create the effect of a rose as it would naturally unfold. To finish: Press several more petals around those already formed. Tilt the pastry tip so that these petals slant in a more outward

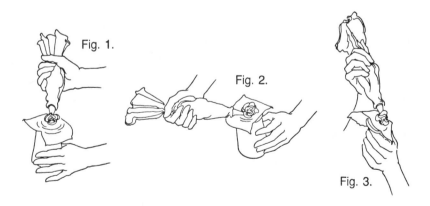

Fig. 1.

Fig. 2.

Fig. 3.

position than any of the others. Use all of the tinted frosting that remains for making roses; then rinse bowls and set aside for use in Step 8.

4. Allow roses to dry on cookie sheets for 2 hours, or until firm enough to peel off wax paper and place on cake.

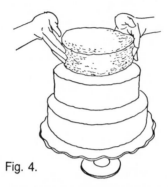

Fig. 4.

5. Meanwhile, cut 3 circles from cardboard: one 14-inch in diameter, one 10-inch in diameter, and one 7-inch in diameter. Place the 14-inch cardboard round on a cake turntable. (Cardboard between each layer makes cutting much easier.) Center largest Pound Cake Layer on cardboard. Frost top and side thinly with Wedding Cake Frosting (page 280).

6. Center the 10-inch cardboard round on cake layer and top with middle Pound Cake Layer; frost. Center a 7-inch cardboard round on cake and top with smallest Pound Cake Layer; frost. Center 6-inch Groom's Cake on top; frost (Fig. 4). This thin basic coat of frosting keeps any stray crumbs in place, and provides a smooth base for final frosting. Allow frosting to dry at least 1 hour.

7. Frost the cake all over with a small, thick layer of the remaining Wedding Cake Frosting.

8. Divide half the remaining Decorator's Frosting into the two small bowls used for the rosebuds; then tint one a pale pink and the other a pale green with red and green food colorings.

9. Make the decorative edgings of your choice. Here are some options (work out the designs on the frosting with a wooden pick, then follow designs with pastry bag): Shell Border: Fit the #98 Shell tip into the pastry bag. Press out pink frosting in overlapping shell design around entire top edge of each tier (Fig. 5). String Scallops: Fit the #2 Writing tip into the pastry bag. Mark out a double scallop pattern on the side of the middle and bottom tiers (Fig. 6). Press out pink frosting,

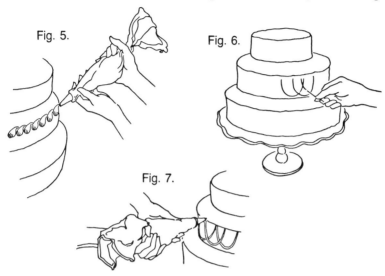

Fig. 5.

Fig. 6.

Fig. 7.

following design, making a single scallop all the way around. Follow with second scallop row to make double scalloping (Fig. 7). Diamond Pattern: Using the same #2 Writing tip, mark out a diamond pattern on the third tier with a wooden pick. Press out all lines in pink or green frosting in one direction first, then follow with crisscross lines to complete pattern. Set remaining tinted frosting aside.

10. Fit the #98 Shell tip in pastry bag; fill bag with part of remaining untinted Decorator's Frosting. Pipe a mound of frosting onto the center of the top tier of cake. Peel full-blown roses off wax paper and arrange on frosting mound.

11. Press several small mounds of untinted frosting onto middle cake tier; arrange more of the roses. Building up from these roses, press out mounds of frosting and place roses on cake side going up from this tier level to meet roses on top. (Should roses start to slide, press a new mound of frosting, arrange roses into frosting, and hold in place for several minutes until frosting begins to set.)

12. Then arrange roses on bottom tier and build up to meet middle tier of roses. Peel rosebuds off wax paper. Pipe a dot of untinted frosting at intervals, following cake design, on the bottom and middle tiers, and press in the rosebuds.

13. Fit the #27 Star tip into pastry bag; fill bag with pink frosting. Press out tiny flowers at intervals: Hold the tip about 1/16 inch away from cake, squeeze, relax pressure and then pull tip away.
14. Fit the #67 Leaf tip into pastry bag; fill bag with green frosting. Pipe leaves onto cake: Press out frosting with a backward and foreword motion, then break off pressure with a quick motion to make pointed tip of leaf (Fig. 8).

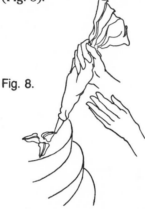

Fig. 8.

15. If the cake is to be served in a day or two, cover loosely with plastic wrap and keep in as cool a place as possible. If the cake is to be frozen, place in freezer just as it is, and allow to freeze until frosting is very firm; then cover cake completely with aluminum foil or plastic wrap. Remove cake from freezer the day before the wedding and remove wrappings. When cake has thawed completely, it may be lightly covered with plastic wrap.

To Cut Wedding Cake

1. Start at bottom tier and remove the roses. Cut a 3-inch-wide strip all the way around the cake. (The bottom and second tier will now be even.)
2. Slice the strip into 1-inch-wide pieces; place on a serving plate. Cut roses into pieces and add some to each cake slice.
3. Next, cut strip from second tier in the same way and slice.
4. Remove the Groom's Cake and save for the first anniversary. Cut the tier under fruitcake tier into small wedges, then remove cardboard and slice second pound cake tier into small wedges. Remove cardboard and cut the last layer into small pieces.

PAINTED COOKIES

Go homemade cookies one better—paint them! It's easy and fun and even the kids can do it. You can try all kinds of designs, from simple free-form squiggles to colorful flowers. A peek through some seed catalogs or children's picture books will give you ideas. Begin by baking and icing the cookies, then paint.

Bake at 375° for 8 minutes.
Makes about 2 dozen 3- to 4½-inch cookies.

1¾ cups *sifted* all-purpose flour	¾ cup sugar
1¼ teaspoons baking powder	1 egg
¼ teaspoon salt	1½ teaspoons vanilla
½ cup (1 stick) butter or margarine	Sugar Icing (page 285)
	Assorted food coloring

1. Sift flour, baking powder, and salt onto wax paper.
2. Beat butter, sugar, egg, and vanilla in a medium-size bowl with an electric mixer until fluffy. Gradually stir in flour mixture on low speed or with wooden spoon until dough is very stiff. If needed, stir in more flour. Wrap dough in plastic wrap; chill overnight.
3. Preheat oven to 375°. Roll out dough, ½ at a time, between a lightly floured sheet of aluminum foil and a sheet of wax paper, to a ⅛-inch thickness, lifting paper frequently to dust with flour and turning dough over for even rolling.
4. Remove wax paper. Cut dough with floured 3-inch scalloped or plain edge round cutter or 4½-inch oval cutter, leaving ½-inch between cookies. Remove dough trimmings from aluminum foil; re-roll together at the end. Place foil with cut-out dough on a cookie sheet.
5. Bake in a preheated moderate oven (375°) for 8 minutes or until lightly browned. Remove foil to wire racks; cool cookies completely. Remove cookies from aluminum foil; store in airtight container until ready to ice and paint.
6. Make Sugar Icing. Place cookies in a single layer on a wire rack set over wax paper to catch drippings. Spoon icing over each cookie to cover top and edges completely. Let stand until icing hardens. Scrape and reuse icing from paper; stir in water if too stiff.
7. Remove cookies from rack; trim off icing drippings around bottom edge of cookies.
8. To paint cookies, pour several drops of different food colorings onto small plates, muffin pans, or even a palette from the five-and-ten.

Do this while the cookies are baking so you have time to practice designs on paper plates. Moisten a paintbrush with water, wipe excess off; dip into coloring and wipe excess again. To make things easier, paint lighter shades first and do all of one color at a time. Use different-sized brushes for your designs—tiny ones for details, larger ones for big colored-in areas. You can mix colors together to get different shades or dilute with water for paler tints. Let designs dry, then cover cookies with plastic wrap to retain freshness.

VALENTINE COOKIE CARDS AND HEARTS

Bake at 375° for 7 to 9 minutes.
Makes six 5 x 7-inch cookie cards and
about twelve 1- to 4-inch cookie hearts.

3	cups *sifted* all-purpose flour	2	eggs
1	teaspoon baking powder	1	teaspoon vanilla
½	teaspoon salt		Red or orange sour ball
⅔	cup (1½ sticks) butter or		candies, crushed
	margarine		Royal Frosting (page 277)
¾	cup sugar		Red and green food coloring

1. Sift flour, baking powder, and salt onto wax paper.
2. Beat butter with sugar in a large bowl with an electric mixer until light and fluffy. Beat in egg and vanilla.
3. Gradually stir in flour mixture on low speed or with wooden spoon until dough is very stiff. If needed, stir in more all-purpose flour. Wrap dough in plastic wrap; chill overnight.
4. Preheat oven to 375°. Roll out dough, one quarter at a time, between a lightly floured sheet of aluminum foil and a sheet of wax paper, to ⅛-inch-thick rectangle, lifting paper frequently to dust with flour and turning dough over for even rolling.
5. Remove wax paper. Cut dough with a pastry wheel or knife into a 5 x 7-inch rectangle. Cut rectangle crosswise in half if small folding card is desired. Cut out heart shapes with floured cutters in various sizes within the rectangle or in dough trimmings from aluminum foil; re-roll together at the end.
6. Place foil with cut-out dough on a cookie sheet. Sprinkle cut-out heart shapes with candies. For a cookie heart within a candy heart, cut a large heart, then a smaller heart in the center of that heart. Remove dough around small heart; sprinkle with candies.

7. If an imprinted or pressed design is desired, use a fork or a mallet and press into dough to obtain a textured or waffled effect. If you want to tie cookie cards together, make 2 small holes in each cookie with plastic drinking straw along edges.

8. Bake in a preheated moderate oven (375°) for 7 to 9 minutes, longer for larger cookies, or until cookies are light brown and candy has melted. Remove cookies on aluminum foil to a wire rack; cool completely. Gently loosen cookies from foil; store in airtight container until ready to decorate.

9. Prepare Royal Frosting. Remove some frosting into 2 small custard cups; tint one pink and the other green with food coloring. Spoon frosting into wax paper cone fitted with a plain writing or small star tip. Pipe decorative borders with white or colored frosting or write a special message on outside and inside of cards or hearts. Or, set smaller cookie hearts on top of larger ones with frosting in between to hold in place before decorating. When frosting is dry, tie cards with ribbon or wrap in plastic wrap for giving.

TO DECORATE UNBAKED COOKIES

The best types of cookies to decorate are rolled cookies, flat drop cookies, and molded or pressed cookies.

PAINTING COOKIES

To paint unbaked cookies, make the paint by mixing 1 egg yolk with ¼ teaspoon cold water and several drops of food coloring. Using tiny paint brushes, paint designs onto cookies and bake.

FROSTY CHRISTMAS TREE COOKIES

Crispy molasses cookie trees sparkle with sugar frosting.

Bake at 350° for 8 minutes.
Makes 3 dozen cookies.

3¾	cups *sifted* all-purpose flour	1	cup (2 sticks) butter,
1	teaspoon baking soda		softened
½	teaspoon salt	1	cup sugar
2	tablespoons unsweetened	1	egg
	cocoa powder	½	cup molasses
2	teaspoons ground ginger		Sugar Icing (page 285)
3	teaspoons ground cinnamon		Colored decorating sugar
2	teaspoons ground cloves		

1. Sift flour, baking soda, salt, cocoa, ginger, cinnamon, and cloves onto wax paper.

2. Beat butter, sugar, egg, and molasses in a large bowl with an electric mixer until fluffy-light. Stir in flour mixture until well blended. Wrap dough in plastic wrap or aluminum foil; refrigerate several hours or overnight.

3. Lightly grease cookie sheets. Preheat oven to 350°. Roll out dough, ⅓ at a time, on a lightly floured surface to a ¼-inch thickness. Cut out with floured large Christmas tree cutter. Brush off excess flour; place cookies on prepared cookie sheets. Repeat with remaining dough. Gather up scraps for second rolling.

4. Bake in a preheated moderate oven (350°) for 8 minutes or until edges are browned. Let cookies cool a few minutes on cookie sheets. Remove to wire racks with a spatula; cool completely. Dip small clean brush into Sugar Icing and "paint" cookies. Sprinkle with colored sugars.

SPRINKLING ON DECORATIONS

To use sprinkled-on decorations, such as colored sugar, chocolate jimmies, coconut or candied fruit, brush the unbaked cookie with milk, cream, or lightly beaten egg white. For a special touch, you can make paper designs and use them like a stencil and sprinkle decorations over or around the cookies.

INDEX

Blueberries *(cont'd)*
  petal shortcake, 268
  and strawberry-topped sponge flan, 35
Bombes, 160
  baked Alaska, 173
  chocolate-raspberry, 134-135
  glacé, 201
Brandy sauces
  -apricot, 292
  fruit, 293
  hard, 291
Bread puddings
  apple-, 144
  cinnamon-raisin, 145-146
Brown betty, peach, 233
Brownies
  carrot, 89
  cream cheese, 133
  double chocolate-walnut, 134
  peanut butter, 90-91
  rocky road, 111
  Southern-style butterscotch, 90
Brown sugar
  emergency, 24
  softening hard, 97
Buckle, blackberry, 221
Burgundy, pears in, 255
Butter, clarified, 99
Butter cake, golden, 7
Butter cookie frosting, 276
Butter cookie stars, 100
Butter cream, coffee, 288
Butter cream frosting, 276-278
  coffee, 277
  lemon, 276
  orange, 276
  rich, 278
  vanilla, 276
Butter frosting, brown, 278
Butter fudge-carob sauce, hot, 294
Butter-orange glaze, 286
Butterscotch brownies, Southern-style, 90

Cacao beans, 113
Cake ingredients, 6
  baking, at high altitudes, 26
  baking powder, checking freshness of, 35
  egg volume in, 29
  flour alternative in, 18
  proper temperature for, 12
Cake pans
  grease mitt for, 11
  oven placement of, 32
  preparing, 10
  substituting, 26
Cakes, 5-39
  angel food, 28-29
  apricot-glazed peach, 11
  bananas Foster-ice cream, 171-172
  carrot-nut, 190
  carrot-pineapple, 13
  carrot-pineapple upside-down, 19
  chocolate-apricot, 263
  chocolate fudge, 116
  chocolate-rum icebox, 119

coconut cream, 27
coconut marmalade, 16-17
colonial seed, 10
deep dark devil's food, 117
filled orange chiffon, 30
fresh orange, 8
fruit, *see* fruitcakes
golden butter, 7
Greek walnut, 18
heavenly angel, 256-257
holiday ice cream, 176
Italian rum, 39
jam, 189
mimosa, 31
mocha velvet, 38
old-fashioned walnut, 191
pound, *see* pound cakes
pumpkin-spice, 257
quick banana, 12
raspberry cream chocolate, 121-122
roll, apricot, 37
roll, piña colada ice cream, 174
snowball ice cream, 202
sour cream, with coconut topping, 9
sponge, *see* sponge cakes
tortoni ice cream, 179
triple chocolate delight, 120-121
walnut-spice, 28
whipped cream, with marzipan fruits,
  193-195
whiskey, 24
  see also cupcakes; tortes
Cakes, decorated, 296-312
  applique anniversary, 298
  calico cat, 299
  daisy chain graduation, 303-304
  enchanted cottage, 304-305
  Father's Day word game, 296
  Fourth of July star, 297
  groom's, 306-307
  rose wedding, 306
  see also wedding cakes
Cakes, decorating tips for
  clean pastry bags, 308
  decorating, 296, 300-302
  disposable decorating bag, 297
  pastry bag support, 302
  preparing plate, 297
  selecting decorating tools, 302
  tinting coconut, 305
  wedding, assembling and decorating,
  309-312
Cakes, tips for
  avoiding failure, 7
  cooling, 32
  cooling foam, 29
  cutting, 36
  dividing batter for even layers, 9
  following recipes exactly, 27
  frosting, 283
  making flat tops, 8
  splitting layers, 36
  storing testers or skewers, 13
  sugar dusting, 37
  testing for doneness, 19
  using stale, 34

Coconut *(cont'd)*
cream filling, 282
dried, freshening, 95
macaroons, 95
marmalade cake, 16-17
-pineapple cheesecake, 197
tart shells, toasted, 68
tinting, 305
toasting, 175
topping, 9, 90
Coffee, 184, 277, 287, 288
Compotes
cheese and grape, 248
dried fruit, 225
fresh fruit, 225
fresh pineapple, 235
frosty cantaloupe, 228
Cookie crust, calorie-saver chocolate, 245
Cookie frostings
butter, 276
cream cheese, 89
Cookie ingredients, tips for
cracking walnuts, 89
freshening dried coconut, 95
making cinnamon sugar, 95
microwaving butter or cream cheese, 93
softening hard brown sugar, 97
Cookies, 87-111
almond crescents, 110
almond spritz, 104
amaretti, 96
apple squares, 94-95
apricot pinwheels, 108
bear paws, 105
chocolate chip, 132
cinnamon cards, 100-101
coconut macaroons, 95
Danish spice, 94
gingerbread, 102
ginger snappy turtles, 109
golden fig nuggets, 110-111
honey date-nut bars, 92
lebkuchen, 103
lemon tuiles, 99
linzer tarts, 91
London fruit bars, 92-93
nutmeg leaves, 101
pretzels, 106-107
prune-oatmeal bars, 93
shortbread, 106
stars, butter, 100
sugar and spice jumbo, 98
sunflower-oatmeal, 97
Swedish rosettes, 107
21-calorie peanut butter, 258
23-calorie applesauce, 258-259
Cookies, decorated, 295-296, 313-316
cards and hearts, Valentine, 314-315
frosty Christmas tree, 316
painted, 313-314
Cookies, decorating tips for
decorating unbaked, 315
painting, 315
sprinkling decorations, 316
Cookies, tips for
cooling, 99

making even-size cookies, 105
making variations, 104
molds, refrigerator, 109
scooping dough, 105
storing, 24, 96
Cookie sheets
choosing, 98
preparing, 102
Cranberries
ice, 166-167
-pecan turnovers, 70
-pineapple mousse, 152
sherbet, 203
soufflé, cold, 223-224
Cream, whipped, 27, 193-195, 282, 287
Cream cheese, 61, 71, 89, 92, 133, 277
Cream puff paste, 73
Cream puffs, 252
Creams, 287-289
coffee butter, 288
fluffy pastry, 289
instant pastry, 289
pastry, 288
rum, 288
Crème brûlée, 147
Crêpes
banana dessert, 220-221
flamed spicy-nut, 207-208
sweet, 208
Crullers, French, 72-73
Cupcakes
frosting, 280
making, 17
spicy oatmeal, 17
Custard fillings, 281
Custard pies
banana cream, 57
crisp crusts for, 52
set test for, 57
Custards, 139-140
caramel-coconut flan, 147-148
cranberry-pineapple mousse, 152
crème brûlée, 147
eggs in snow, 148-149
maple Bavarian, 153
rice imperatrice, 149
Custards, tips for
storing, 141
testing doneness, 143, 152
Custard sauces, 291

Danish almond rice, 146
Danish spice cookies, 94
Dates
-apple pudding, steamed, 150
-nut honey bars, 92
-orange filling, 284
Decorating frosting, white, 279
Decorator's frosting, 279
Devil's food cake, deep dark, 117
Dumplings, apple, in cheese-walnut
pastry, 69

Éclairs, chocolate-glazed, 249
Eggs, 6
in snow, 148-149